Cities and
City Planning

ENVIRONMENT, DEVELOPMENT, AND PUBLIC POLICY

A series of volumes under the general editorship of
Lawrence Susskind, *Massachusetts Institute of Technology,*
Cambridge, Massachusetts

CITIES AND DEVELOPMENT

Series Editor: Lloyd Rodwin, *Massachusetts Institute of Technology,*
Cambridge, Massachusetts

CITIES AND CITY PLANNING
Lloyd Rodwin

THINKING ABOUT DEVELOPMENT
Lisa Peattie

CONSERVING AMERICA'S NEIGHBORHOODS
Robert K. Yin

Other subseries:

ENVIRONMENTAL POLICY AND PLANNING
Series Editor: Lawrence Susskind, *Massachusetts Institute of Technology,*
Cambridge, Massachusetts

PUBLIC POLICY AND SOCIAL SERVICES
Series Editor: Gary Marx, *Massachusetts Institute of Technology,*
Cambridge, Massachusetts

Cities and City Planning

Lloyd Rodwin

Massachusetts Institute of Technology
Cambridge, Massachusetts

With
Hugh Evans, Robert Hollister, Kevin Lynch,
Michael Southworth, and Lawrence Susskind

Plenum Press · New York and London

Library of Congress Cataloging in Publication Data

Rodwin, Lloyd.
　　Cities and city planning.

　　(Environment, development, and public policy. Cities and development.
　　Bibliography: p.
　　Includes index.
　　1. New towns — Addresses, essays, lectures. 2. Metropolitan areas — Addresses,
essays, lectures. 3. Underdeveloped areas — Regional planning — Addresses, essays,
lectures. 4. City planning — Addresses, essays, lectures. 5. Cities and towns — Addresses, essays, lectures. I. Title. II. Series.
HT169.55.R62　　　　　　　　　307.7′6　　　　　　　　　81-13956
ISBN 0-306-40666-7　　　　　　　　　　　　　　　　　　AACR2

© 1981 Plenum Press, New York
A Division of Plenum Publishing Corporation
233 Spring Street, New York, N.Y. 10013

Printed in the United States of America

To Vic, Marc, and Julie

Contents

PART ONE

Images of the City

CHAPTER ONE

The Future Metropolis

Can It Be Made More Humane?

INTRODUCTION

Some 20 years ago, a group of colleagues and I, under the auspices of the American Academy of Arts and Sciences, jointly contemplated the future metropolis. We assumed that within as short a time as 50 years, most people would live in vast metropolitan areas, loosely linked together by facilities for communication and services, but increasingly interdependent for supplies, information, and transportation to and from work.

Given that prospect, we sought ways to enhance the positive features of metropolitan life. We were on the whole cautiously optimistic. We agreed that the metropolis created opportunities for higher income and varied modes of living—in general, a way of life potentially healthier, more stimulating, better informed, more creative. Our papers (published in *Daedalus* and then as a book under the title *The Future Metropolis*) indicated that the present city had not achieved "anything near an optimum variety of styles of living, including an adequate range of environments with varying physical settings, activities and social groups."[1] But very few of us expressed serious doubts that we could move steadily in that direction. We were persuaded that the metropolis, combined with the national government, had the resources to confront problems, and would eventually develop the policies to cope with them. We agreed with the physical planners and urbanists of the last generation, who felt that we should be concerned with the socioeconomic environment as well as the physical, with what happens within cities as well as to them. We

3

looked toward a significantly improved quality of life for city dwellers.

We were no more than temporarily discouraged by the problems that stumped us. One of the most unsavory of these problems was the fate of the "gray areas": the broad swaths of low-standard housing. We predicted that as income rose with demand, residents would move from these areas, and an influx of new families seemed unlikely. We doubted such housing could be rehabilitated at costs low enough to permit attractively low rents; on the other hand, demolition for new use of the land seemed prohibitively expensive. We considered a few quasi-utopian possibilities, such as converting some of these areas into "rural retreats in town, for there is a dearth of nearby inexpensive resorts where individuals or families may go for play or relaxation."[2] But no one saw any easy solutions.

We speculated on how technology might help the course of metropolitan development. If we could specify what was required, as had been done for defense and space programs, could not technology play a similarly successful role for cities? We noted several possibilities, among them substitution of messages for personal journeys, self-contained houses free of utility connections, and a car the size of a bus seat easily attachable to larger vehicles.

But these ideas seemed better suited to long-range plans; we sought remedies that would make significant inroads into urban problems within a generation or less. We therefore focused on a recommendation—advanced, to be sure, with restrained optimism—to improve public transportation so as to make it competitive with the private car. We also proposed that investments in communications and transportation be treated not just as costs to be minimized, but as a means of controlling urban density, form, and growth, and as a way of giving all groups in the community the greatest variety of choices for living and working.

We anticipated worldwide expansion in the physical plant and population of cities, in both the poorer and richer economies. Although the poorer countries have less capital, fewer qualified specialists, and a less mature system of cities, in some ways they have greater governmental control over development, with fewer ideological restraints in applying control. We felt strongly then that large centers away from the primate cities should be developed through a combination of incentives to attract population and investments in community equipment and services, opening of new regions, even the decentralization of political power. Today we might also stress the need for smaller centers, in regions significant for development, to provide rural-urban linkages.

We anticipated a world of cities—we also looked forward to it. We felt that people were attracted to the metropolis by real values: greater opportunities for choice, freedom, privacy, innovation, culture, entertainment. We expected that, given time and good planning, and with rising income and rising standards of demand, the metropolis would also become a more efficient, more socially desirable, more gracious place to live.

Two decades have passed since my colleagues and I expressed our hopeful views in *The Future Metropolis*. In the interim there may have been some progress in making many of our cities more humane, but there have also been some serious setbacks, especially for the poor and disadvantaged.

Until the worst stages of the post-Vietnam inflationary spiral and soaring interest rates gutted the financing of housing in the United States, relatively high income and cleverness in manipulating financial terms enabled many middle-income families to move to more attractive areas, leaving blight in their wake. On the other hand, many middle-income families in the rehabilitated "gray areas," desperate for housing, fell victim to quick-ownership schemes, buying or renting at unmanageable prices. These two trends, coupled with exacerbated central-city problems—unemployment, insufficient revenues, higher costs, poorer services, inadequate schools, and racial conflicts—have led to abandoned housing. At the same time, many hapless people still live trapped within these areas.

We judged correctly that government policy should and would back mass transportation. But nowhere in the United States has mass transportation been developed on a scale to make it competitive with the private car, and even the most com-

prehensive effort—BART (Bay Area Rapid Transit) on the West
Coast—has proven a disappointment to its proponents. Meanwhile, cities almost everywhere find themselves hobbled even
more by inflation than by inefficiency or limited resources. With
retrenchment the order of the day, there is little reason to expect
the situation to change for the better soon.

Although most developing countries have accepted in principle that other urban centers must be encouraged, they lack the
necessary political and administrative support and financial resources. Market forces still lean heavily in favor of a country's
largest cities, often frustrating the desire of other regions to increase urban opportunities, jobs, and income. A solution to this
problem will not come easily.

In *The Future Metropolis*, we observed that

plans and dreams (when applied to cities) have usually been aimed at
solving problems of the present or at inducing a return to some image of
the past: expressways—devised to escape the traffic jams, slum clearance
and housing projects to solve the housing problems, while neighborhood
development looks back to the small community and Broadacre city to
the family farm. Only rarely do we find a contemporary plan that antici-
pates the future with pleasure.[3]

At the time, that statement may have seemed an egregious
exaggeration. Now it appears to be a quite moderate expression
of today's situation.

I am reminded of a cartoon by Max Beerbohm, depicting the
nineteenth century's and the twentieth century's images of the
future. The nineteenth century saw itself as a fat, cheerful man
with a satisfied smile, smoking a big cigar; it imagined the future
to be a fatter man with a more satisfied smile, smoking a bigger
cigar. The twentieth-century man, however, was a thin,
humped-over, cowering being, looking with unease at some
black clouds; the future was a thinner man, more apprehensive,
nervously scanning darker, more threatening clouds. In a way,
present-day pessimism about the city reflects a similar change in
mood from the sixties to the seventies. We have had dishearten-
ing experiences during these years. Political assassinations,

Vietnam, Watergate, inflation, energy crises, and the lack of imaginative leadership all contribute to a general sense of dismay and an erosion of faith in our ability to control the shape of things to come. We resonate more readily today to Brecht's sardonic observation: "The optimists have not yet gotten the news!"

It can hardly be surprising if this book, in unintended and in quite revealing ways, reflects many of the changes in mood and views since *The Future Metropolis* was written. Focusing on city planning as well as cities, it brings together 14 articles written, with one exception, in the 1970s. The subjects vary. They range from the different ways laymen, scholars, and city planners have thought about cities to the new look of the metropolitan problem in the more mature cities of the United States; from the lessons to be derived from the remarkable failure of the New Communities Program to the different and the less reassuring ways of interpreting the meaning and effects of some of the urban policies and development strategies over the past 25 years in Third World countries; and from the varying views on the right approaches for strengthening the capabilities and training of city planners to the various illusions, past and present, which may still hobble the performance of city planners in the field.

In all these discussions there are two underlying and interrelated themes. The first involves the different ways of perceiving the city and its problems over the past two decades. The other concerns the changing ideas about what city planners need to know and to do to cope with the problems and possibilities of the city in the future.

CHAPTER TWO

Great and Terrible Cities

SOME CONTRASTING PERSPECTIVES

Years ago, when traveling in Holland and Provence, I recall admiring the verisimilitude of Vincent van Gogh's paintings of these regions. Still later, I began to wonder whether he had truly captured that reality or had simply imposed his vision on me, had in effect induced—or seduced—me into seeing things his way. Powerful views, of necessity, exclude a lot of reality. This makes them partial; and this partiality, especially if coupled with persuasiveness, is understandably irritating, indeed obnoxious, to those who prize the excluded parts. Only in retrospect do we escape the blinders imposed by our insights; but when we manage to do so, we glimpse the price we pay for our Procrustean views.

By way of example, consider seven different categories of great and terrible cities. The first three I label, respectively, "The Jewel," "The Historic City," and "The World City." Each illustrates some conventional view. The second three challenge or at least qualify or raise questions about these conventional views. The fourth category I call "The Subjective City"; the fifth and sixth, identified as "The Overdeveloped City" and "The Nonexploitative City," respectively, associate the great city with stunted development and exploitation and raise the question whether it is possible to have great cities untainted by these failings. Each view suggests a truth, a partial one to be sure: some overlap, some are reconcilable with each other, others may not be. I shall sum up these views; I will also draw some inferences from this prismatic transformation of the original notion of great and terrible cities. Before I close, I shall suggest still another view, a future-oriented and utopian version of the great city.

The Jewel

My first category is the most obvious one. By "The Jewel" I have in mind such cities as commercial Venice, Renaissance Florence, and eighteenth-century Bath. The selections are arbitrary; the fact that there may be other preferences—Dubrovnik, Katmandu, Bruges, Cordoba, Siena, or Salzburg—does not matter for our purposes. All these cities are great for somewhat the same reasons: they embody a pure, striking, and in many ways superb visual and architectural ambience still relatively unspoiled by subsequent development. The world of affluence and sensibility is in love with them: it is of minor consequence how they came to be; we are aghast if anything should threaten them; if we could, we would try to preserve them; but sooner or later we know they will change or decay in response to new conditions regardless and perhaps even because of this adulation.

The opposite of "The Jewel" is the amorphous city, the blob with hardly any redeeming physical features. Mumford's classic examples were Britain's nineteenth-century coketowns featuring spreading blot: "dark, satanic mills"; poverty and human exploitation; ugly and polluted environments; breeding places of misery and degradation. The range has widened in the twentieth century. Until recently, it has been fashionable to castigate in addition: (a) the omnipresent gas stations, food parlors, and honky-tonk developments around the edges of United States cities, and (b) the mushrooming makeshift settlements, shacks, *favellas*, *bidonvilles*, *gecekondus*, and *ranchitos* around the outer fringes of the big cities in the poorer countries. However, we are changing our views on some of these matters. Venturi's writings[1] have made us reexamine our distaste for the city-limits "vernacular"; we are also developing a grudging appreciation of the various forms of self-help housing in almost all of the major regions of the world. But there is no controversy—at least as yet—about the grim realities of places like, at one extreme, Calcutta, and their sheer absence of services or even shelter for thousands of street dwellers; or about places closer to home like Baltimore, Philadelphia, and the inner fringes of New York (the Bronx and Brownsville, in particular) with their depressing miles of dreary

gray areas, boarded-up, abandoned slums, and messy and currently unutilizable vacant sites.

The Historic City

My second category, which partially overlaps the first, is
"The Historic City." The great ones have played a memorable
role and exercised a formidable leverage in some significant
period of the past. Like O. W. Holmes's great men, they have
been "strategic points in the campaign of history."[2] Their current
greatness consists in their accumulation of arresting artifacts and
residue of this past. The examples are legion: Rome, Cracow,
Fez, Istanbul, Hong Kong, Peking, Berlin, Jerusalem. All have
served creeds or empires, sometimes both. We can hardly mention their names or walk their streets without conjuring up
visions or seeing evidence of their place in history. Their history
softens our judgment of utterly different contemporary
versions—Athens, Cairo, or Kyoto for example—which are un-
distinguished or worse, save for a few spectacular monuments
which have survived from the past.

And once again the opposite is easy to depict: the city minus
history, without significant roots: all foreground, no depth! The
most obvious examples are the new cities. Who can deny their
notorious dullness even when, as in the cases of Chandigarh and
Brazilia, the most flamboyant geniuses have shaped their formal
destiny.

The World City

Great in a quite different sense are "The World Cities." One
of my friends, a knowledgeable, well-traveled European, once
told me that there are today only two or three great "World
Cities": London, Paris, New York (New York, he said, was on the
wane, and perhaps even no longer eligible). Rome did not quite
make it; nor did Tokyo, San Francisco, Stockholm, or Rio de
Janeiro (although he thought the latter might be a possibility for
the future). Pressed to justify his choices, his criteria became
more explicit. His first emphasis was on the liveliness of people

and the range of ideas and activities. In his qualifying cities, there are keen minds and vital new cultural currents as well as great universities and museums. People are diverse, colorful, full of brio. Exciting things are happening at all hours, night and day: theater, music, crafts of all kinds, painting, sculpture, writing, research. There are a marvelous variety of restaurants, shops, and bazaars, delightful streets and varied *quartiers,* attractive spaces, parks, playgrounds, recreational areas, street theater. To the rejoinder that many of these things can be found in Buenos Aires, Tokyo, and other great capitals and metropolises, the reply was: "Yes, most; but not all!" No doubt Rome, Rio de Janeiro, Buenos Aires, Tokyo and the others are no mean cities. But they are not truly cosmopolitan: that is why they are at best runners-up. They do not quite attain the critical threshold produced by the convergence of universities, theater, and galleries, innovative ideas, and most of all an international milieu. Bath, Florence, and Salzburg are very special places, too, but they are not genuine metropolises. "A fact's a fact," my friend insisted. "There are only three great world cities!"

Whether one agrees is not as important for our purposes as the recognition that we are dealing with another conception of greatness—the city with not only an international hinterland but also an international influence and an extraordinary range of qualities.

The opposite is once again easily identified. This is the peripheral city, the desolate towns in declining or stagnating hinterlands, from which people flee as much because of the lack of vital interest as because of the lack of real and meaningful opportunities. What is more, this desolation may acquire an equally powerful and pernicious grip on the decadent areas even within our greatest cities.

So much for my first set of great cities. But before turning to the second set, let us not overlook the fact that all these great cities have their seamy side. What we admire in "The Jewel," in the "Historic City," and especially in the "World City" is—with rare exceptions—only a small part of these cities. The unattractive features—the dreary, the provincial, the callous, the sordid, and the decadent features, are ignored or shrugged away. Even the photographs I use—and those I could not find—to illustrate these ideas provide an oblique commentary on the problem. It is relatively easy to get, from the collections of the libraries of the School of Architecture and Urban Studies at MIT, slides of the highly renowned tourist magnets of cities; and it is a little harder, but not much, to find examples of some of the worst physical features. But it is far more difficult to find slides (and also to represent with slides) the average, the commonplace areas. There is food for thought here on the focus of our ideas, on the way we collect slides, and on the limitations of photography.

The Subjective City

My second set of great cities challenges the basic assumptions of the first set. For example, "The Subjective City," my fourth category, poses the question whether any city is great except in some subjective sense. A personal experience may make this clear.

I visited Fez as a member of an international team to review the plans to conserve and promote this ancient cultural center of Morocco. One of the tantalizing issues was how to preserve this extraordinary medieval environment while fostering the welfare of its inhabitants. A Belgian sociologist working in Meknes, a neighboring city of almost comparable quality, told us that her surveys of the population showed that the people living there have a very limited sense of the city beyond the constrained space and small streets and immediate quartier in which they live. They would not hesitate to transform the streets and housing if they had more income; and indeed they would tear down buildings and walls—including the ancient walls—to create the necessary space. There was no reason to think the people of Fez felt otherwise, she said. This was sacrilege to two members of our team—Professor Lemaire, a world-renowned specialist on the conservation of historic urban areas, and Professor Adan, a French sociologist and scholar who was an admirer of Moroccan culture; but it was not at all shocking or even undesirable to some of the Moroccan sociologists and planners who were hostile to the concept of Fez as a museum for international tourists.

Another example: a colleague of mine, Professor Kevin Lynch, has done a great deal of research on a very simple but, I think, seminal question: What do different kinds of people see in the city? For example, he supervised an international survey of attitudes about play areas for children and their location. What he and his colleagues discovered was that the areas and the types of facilities which adults thought attractive and appropriate were often radically different from the areas and types of facilities preferred by children. But the adults, of course, made the decisions. This difference in attitudes between users and decision makers is true of other types of decisions: in the case of housing for low-income families, in preferences concerning modes of travel, and in decisions concerning housing density as well as urban renewal. Those who value popular decision making and those who value great cities are often at odds with each other. That is one reason why people may respond as an Italian guide once responded to my wife and me when we said that Lucca and Siena and their churches were wonderful. He said, "These things are good—for you" (*"Ces choses sont bonnes—pour vous."*). For what most people see and often want in cities is not what planners, decision makers, and elite groups see and want. It varies for children, for workers, for immigrants, for people of different ages, incomes, occupations, and cultural backgrounds. When we refer to cities as "great" or "terrible," for whom do we mean great or terrible? To the children living there? To workers? To the old and infirm? To the minorities who are harassed and discriminated against? And which parts of the city do we have in mind: the small segments of the city, particularly the inner core, or the rest of the city, including the miles of nondescript housing?

The Overdeveloped City

We can turn matters around even more by suggesting that many of the great cities are terrible cities. On two trips to Portugal and Morocco, my mission was the same: to find out how to deal with the problems of the growth of their great cities—their huge costs, congestion, slums, and social problems—and how to cope with the problem of the lack of development in other major regions of the country—an imbalance exacerbated by the concentration of power, of markets, of income, and of social and cultural facilities in the great capital and commercial cities. In the case of Portugal, Lisbon and Oporto, for example, are great centers, whereas large portions of the north, east, and south of the country are neglected; in the case of Morocco, the growth of Casablanca, Rabat, and possibly Tangier contrasts with the neglect of most of the interior regions.

These are typical problems found in many of the great cities of our time in Asia, the Middle East, Africa, Latin America, Europe, and to a lesser extent even North America. So formidable are the problems that for the first time we have the pressure, almost everywhere—in big countries and small, rich and poor, socialist and nonsocialist—for a national urban policy and national strategies for changing the rates of growth of the different regions of the country. The essence of the new strategies lies in the recognition that cities are necessary for the transformation of resources, of agriculture, and even of lagging hinterlands, and that truly great cities must satisfy these requirements. Indeed, the absence of a "balanced" urban system—the existence, instead, of a few big cities and the absence of thriving medium- and small-size cities and rural centers in other regions—deprives the people and activities within the region of markets and services, and of vital economic and social nourishment and stimuli. Therefore, one of the crucial problems of our time is how to create adequate urban systems: how to combat the distortions and problems created by big cities with the encouragement of regional and rural urban centers and with the development of analytical and development mechanisms which would help lagging regions to offset the impact of the excessively dominant cities, to exploit to the hilt the resources and the development potentials of their regional centers, and to reduce the inequalities of income and influence on public policy and investment.

The Nonexploitative City

Marxists, neo-Marxists, and "leftists" push the exploitation thesis even further. They suggest that the great cities in the more-developed countries are tainted because they owe their greatness to exploitation: to the drawing off of the capital and talent of colonial hinterlands, not only of their own country but of the underdeveloped countries as well. They argue that giant cities of the more-developed countries serve the needs of the exploiting groups, whose power, capital, and greater control of prices of more expensive industrial products give them decisive advantages over their weaker, dependent satellites. In addition, the few giant cities of these underdeveloped countries serve as seats of power for their own local financial, commercial, industrial, and land-owning interests, which also control and exploit for their own advantage the resources and produce of their backward hinterlands, the assembly and final-consumption industries, and the financing of marketing of these activities. What is more, when great empires disintegrate, their urban centers, such as Vienna, Istanbul, and now London also decline, at least until they develop new markets and new functions; and that is why Marxists and neo-Marxists expect that when underdeveloped countries free themselves from the internal exploitation of their own bourgeoisie and land-owning interests, then the big cities based on this exploitation may lose much of their former power and glory.[3] In any case, Marxists are generally loath to predict what the great "Nonexploitative Cities" of the socialist future will be like; but I did once hear an ecstatic Russian architect-planner remind an international conference on "new towns" of the great cities and culture produced by 500 years of feudalism, and the even greater cities and culture produced by 500 years of capitalism, and how it boggled the socialist mind to contemplate the kinds of cities and culture that might emerge from 500 years of socialism.

CONCLUDING OBSERVATIONS

What final observations might we draw from these different ways of viewing cities?

One not-altogether-surprising impression is that our commonsense characterizations of great and terrible cities are essentially arbitrary and even superficial. Define "great" in terms of

architectural distinction, historic significance, or range of intellectual, aesthetic, or economic activities and it is then only a
matter of assigning the right cities to the appropriate classification. Far more intriguing—or disconcerting—are the changes in
thinking about great cities which downgrade aesthetics and place
emphasis on social welfare and significant functions.

Second, sophisticated urban planners—although they are
still moved by Burnham's injunction to "make no small plans"—
no longer suppose they can create great cities. They know that
people will modify and rewrite the script written by planners and
that this is as it should be; and that even a great *physical* city is a
monument to many people who have contributed over several
generations to its character and development.

Third, there may be an increasing consensus that it is misleading to distinguish between great and terrible cities as though
they were either one or the other—for cities are often mixtures of
both elements, and even cities like London, Paris, and New York
are now often symbols not only of the greatest glories but also of
the greatest urban issues and problems of the contemporary
world.

Fourth, the conviction is spreading that the cities deemed
great by intellectuals, artists, and the well-to-do are also flawed
by their profiting from the relative weakness, neglect, and lack of
power of their domestic and foreign hinterlands, by the poverty
and disparities of income and opportunity within these great
cities; and by the cultural and decision-making processes which
have identified the goals of the specific groups who possess
wealth and power with the goals of those who have neither.
These issues may be exaggerated, but they are not without substance; to the extent that they are true or even believed to be
true, they become facts to be reckoned with.

There is some evidence that we are beginning, ever so
slowly, and as yet inadequately, to reckon with these issues. The
attempts to work out more equitable terms of trade between
nations are one example. The persistent effort of nations to
change relative rates of growth of different cities and regions
within and between nations is another. So, too, is the growing

insistence that big cities pay full costs for all urban growth and services, including the costs of dealing with ecological imbalance. Not least is the quest to make it possible for less-developed regions to increase their ability to shape their future development. Powerful corporations are constantly taking on new functions and casting off old ones. Big cities have the resources and "intelligence mechanisms" to do the same. One of the tough problems of the future for smaller cities is how to devise effective ways of offsetting this advantage.

We can speculate on what the trade-offs would be if the situation were changed: that is, if we could systematically offset the advantages of the big cities and the exploiting cities and develop more opportunities elsewhere; and if more people in cities and regions were able to participate effectively in decision making and have their values and preferences respected. It is altogether possible that there might be more medium- and small-size cities; but also that the big as well as the so-called great cities might be less attractive, less large, less varied in facilities, services, and visual experience, yet not necessarily less exciting in the realms of thought, and far more egalitarian and satisfying to the bulk of the population who lives in them. This is not an inescapable consequence; but it is a possible consequence, perhaps even a likely one, and no doubt the grimmest one for some of those who regard cities as jewels fashioned or influenced by persons possessing wealth, power, and taste. And if this should prove to be the case, would it be worth the transformation?

I think it would be, for we might even be led toward the great city in a great urban system. This seventh version of a great city is admittedly utopian—but only modestly so: less glamorous, more commonplace or earthy; less focused on aesthetics or history or international range and more on the ability to serve the needs and aspirations of the bulk of the population. We could judge such a city by a number of relatively simple criteria: for example, a growing and fairly stable economy which provides a variety of well-paid jobs and which interacts constructively with its rural and agricultural hinterlands; an economy that is healthy as measured by conventional indicators of births, deaths, types of illness, and survival rates; a city with housing, neighborhoods, and community facilities and services for households in almost all income ranges and social groups; one with good teachers and well-attended schools, and a wide range of cultural and recreational opportunities; a considerate and tolerant as well as gracious and just city which welcomed variety and individuality and was responsive to change and innovation, a city democratically managed and regarded affectionately by its residents. The final mix of such cities may vary in size, location, and social composition to suit different tastes, technologies, and economic environments. These cities and this urban system of the future would have to come in many forms in order to be responsive to pluralistic values of choice, freedom, security, privacy, individuality, opportunity, culture, and entertainment. What is clear, however, is that, simple and modest as they appear, these cities are harder to achieve in the right balance than the other great cities which we have already built; yet it is my suspicion—or perhaps only a hope—that it is this kind of great city, more than any other, that people of today must yearn to have their cities emulate.

CHAPTER THREE

The Educative City

WITH MICHAEL SOUTHWORTH

Most people are familiar with their own neighborhood and with the customary paths they travel, but the rest of the city is strange and sometimes even dangerous turf. To be sure, with limited time and energy, we can never profit from more than a very small chunk of the world in which we live. Nonetheless, we know far less about that world than we could, and we explore and enjoy it less than we might.

Carr and Lynch have suggested that the "educative city" of tomorrow should take more deliberate advantage of the urban experience. It "would invite exploration and reward it; it would encourage manipulation, renovation and self-initiated changes of many kinds. It would contain surprises and novel experience, challenges to cognition and action."[1] Indeed, if we are really to exploit the educative potentials of the urban environment, the options before us are exciting to contemplate.

How could the city be opened to exploration and discovery? Three past experiments suggest some of the ways in which this might be achieved, perhaps by a new urban service. One of the experiments, which occurred in the summer of 1968, was the Summer in the Parks program, sponsored by the National Park Service. This program was designed to acquaint Washington, D.C., residents with the variety of open space in the region. Through its Surprise Trip program, urban youth who had rarely been outside their own neighborhoods were taken on daily junkets to different areas. Each day more than 1,000 children and teenagers were bussed from recreation centers, block camps, or church centers to new places. At each place, a different program had been developed around unique features of the area. One day, for instance, the youngsters could float a raft to an island with tree houses, where they then took part in crafts and nature activities. On another day they might go to the Chesapeake and Ohio Canal, learning how to fish, and how to clean and cook their catch. The impact of the program did not stop with the trips, for many youngsters returned on other days and brought their parents with them.

Another experiment was undertaken by the Boston Redevelopment Authority. An eye-catching outdoor information center enabled pedestrians to make better use of the wide variety of things to do in the Park Square section of Boston. Films, slides, and sounds conveyed contrasting images of the city; recorded messages reported daily events; large picture maps and directories of local activities aided orientation; teletype printers gave instant news; a computerlike machine printed out answers to a variety of questions on the city. Information described nearby places and Boston's history, culture, and physical organization. But besides imparting information, the center's fanciful form made a lively urban place that gave people a reason to stop and talk. It became a place to meet, to chat, to pass the time of day. Several visitors even remarked that for the first time they had felt at home—welcome—in a strange city.

Still a third effort, Philadelphia's experimental Parkway High School, illustrates what can be done within the public school system using the city as the classroom. The program's philosophy is that people learn best when their education is self-directed and when it involves the world around them. Classes are ungraded, the course requirements are loose, and many teachers are provided by business and industry. Students travel around the city from one source of learning to another, for there is no schoolhouse. Zoology and anthropology, for example, are taught at the Philadelphia Zoo, biology at the Academy of Natural Sciences, statistics and business management at the Insurance Company of North America, law enforcement at the Police Department, and industrial arts at an auto-repair shop.

These ventures (and others elsewhere) have made the city and its surrounding areas more interesting and "educative." Although such efforts are encouraging, numerous other exciting possibilities are still seriously neglected. Lack of funds is one stumbling block. The main obstacle, however, is that we have not recognized the potential for enjoyment and education which cities hold. The country long ago grasped such opportunities in the natural world by creating the National Park Service. Each year the Park Service gives millions of travelers a chance to appreciate some of the finest natural and historic parts of the country. Through its efforts, such diverse places as the Grand Canyon, the Everglades, and Mesa Verde have been preserved unspoiled, while at the same time encouraging tourism and the sharpening of regional identity. Besides protecting such places, the Park Service has pointed up their unique features by means of interpretive trails, wayside exhibits, films, and even revival of colorful ceremonies, music, and crafts. One of the most admirable features of the Park Service has been its staff of applied naturalists, who have become skilled not only in resource management, but in helping visitors appreciate natural and historic phenomena. Partial evidence of the success of the program is that, in the last year alone, the national parks played host to almost 283 million visitors.

This success could be matched in urban regions. Just as the National Park Service offers planned parks to help travelers discover the ecology by firsthand observation, an equivalent urban service could expose people to the intricate functioning of the city by highlighting the many places and ways in which the mind and eye can take an interesting journey. However rich the world of nature, the urban environment provides even greater potentials, for it is a living museum of our culture. Features in the city which are now often hidden or confusing could be highlighted and made more meaningful. Also, following the same high traditions of the park ranger corps, cities could build up over time a professional staff to help interested residents or visitors to learn and to enjoy themselves as they move about the city.

For example, an urban service could greatly increase exposure to the city by making the transportation system more usable. Frequent orientation information is needed to simplify city travel—signs, maps, computerized orientation machines. Besides encouraging travel, the service could exploit a variety of other means, including viewing devices, cutaway sections, pushbutton sonic messages, and film loops to tell about local activities and history. Paths could be planned that would wind through the city, exposing aspects of the environment related to special interests—history, industry, architecture, ecology—and to specific groups—children, teenagers, visitors, and old people. Entire transportation networks, such as railroads, highways, or bicycle paths, could be designed as enjoyable educational networks; factories, parks, or historic places could be included as parts of that system. Private firms throughout the region might participate by providing information along the street about their own activities and by making it possible for passersby to see what is going on inside. They could open their doors to the public, at least on certain days, for demonstrations, lectures, tours, or even work-training courses. The public costs need not be large; indeed, most of the expense might be borne by the participating firms as the best kind of advertising.

There are other ways in which the urban service could promote educative activities for all ages. Large, operable outdoor models of the water, power, and transportation systems could allow participants to learn mathematical principles of flow and capacity. Outdoor replicas of the city and region, like Madurodam, the popular miniature city near The Hague, could help one grasp the region more clearly. Some settings could emphasize the sensual impact of environment; sounds, images, color, and light could be changed in quality, with participants determining the optimal conditions for each impression. Different people's conceptions of the city could be presented and compared in order to encourage people to see the environment in new ways. Other possibilities are outdoor observatories with telescopes for viewing both the stars and city, orientation games that could be played in the city, signs in several languages, and neighborhood gardens and zoos where maintenance is shared by residents.

A city with a port or river might transform it into a living museum with displays and events that are not fixed, but constantly evolving over time. A river could tell its story through boat trips, outdoor dioramas, or special exhibits at landmarks. Underwater television or other sensing devices might communicate what is happening beneath the water. Walk-through models of a harbor and region could show the historical development of the waterfront. A historic ship could be reconstructed and docked at various points to serve as a center for ecology education, as well as for fun, food, and drink. Similarly, bridges, islands, industry, and the people who use the river have stirring sagas to be told about them. From such stories, one could learn about past and present uses of the river or about the many forms of plant and animal life that depend upon the river—their perils, conflicts, and symbiotic relationships.

HOW TO PROMOTE THE EDUCATIVE CITY

The problem in achieving the educative city will be to design a simple mechanism that will encourage these efforts, while allowing maximum local options and initiative in adapting the idea to each area. No completely satisfactory model exists for the type of organization required to make this program work. As we have intimated, the National Park Service in the Department of the Interior comes closest to what we have in mind, but it is too centralized to encourage much local experimentation. It operates chiefly on federal property and works primarily outside urban areas. Nonetheless, its experience is relevant because of its ecological perspective and the high traditions of its service.[2]

With a permanent staff of about 9,000 and yearly expenditures of about $520 million (1978) the National Park Service manages 313 areas, including 93 natural and recreational parks and 220 historical areas—totaling in all about 3 million acres. Established in 1916, its primary functions have been to preserve areas of unique natural beauty or historic significance, to develop public understanding of such areas, and to provide for public enjoyment of them. The service offers assistance to states for public-park and recreational facilities, and it sponsors grant-in-aid programs in preservation planning, acquisition, and development of historic properties. Recently, matching grants-in-aid have become available to historic properties owned by private groups. Thousands of part-time and seasonal jobs have also been created for young people by the service's Youth and Adult Conservation Corps, whose role is to help the service meet increasing demands for recreation facilities, historic preservation, and maintenance of natural areas.

For the urban service that we envisage, however, a decentralized program is needed to ensure expression of regional and local diversity. Although a national agency would be necessary to provide incentives and leadership and to overcome some of the financial and jurisdictional hurdles, the individual programs would be designed and run by local agencies. At the national level, the program might be administered by the Department of Housing and Urban Development, or by other agencies concerned with new development, open space, recreation, and education (for example, the Departments of the Interior and of Health, Education and Welfare). The national agency's main functions would be to set general policies and to provide matching grants-in-aid, loans, training, and technical advice to the local participating agencies.

In addition, state-enabling legislation might be drawn up to authorize city- or regional-governmental agencies or urban-service corporations to develop programs and raise funds. The agencies' or corporations' main functions would be to develop sites and programs of unique interest and educational value, and to encourage and coordinate area-wide participation of local public agencies and private organizations. Agencies which receive public assistance might be encouraged (or required) to reach cooperative agreements with the local urban service agency. As in the case of urban-renewal or economic-development programs, it may also be desirable, at least at the outset, to utilize the device of the public corporation in order to avoid financial, administrative, and jurisdictional restrictions.

Direct incentives to local participation would consist primarily of federal matching grants-in-aid, as well as fully repayable loans at federal rates of interest plus a small amount (say one-fourth of 1%) to cover administrative costs. Several indirect incentives may also be effective. For example, in many areas space could be leased to concessionaires to operate outdoor museums, and to provide guide services, food, or information. Franchise fees could then be used in support of the program. In this way, over 200 concessionaires now operate shops, restaurants, camps, or guide services throughout the park system under terms set by the Park Service.

Another indirect incentive may be to modify city ordinances to require major new construction projects to make educative contributions to the city. The building and zoning ordinances, for instance, may permit special development opportunities, such as zoning variances, for exceptional efforts to create sites and activities of educative value to the city. Perhaps certain construction projects or other environmental programs supported by the federal government could even be required to provide opportunities for visitors to the site to learn about the projects or about the section of town in which they are located.

Railroads, automobile associations, airlines, chambers of commerce, and tourist bureaus have found it to their advantage to cooperate with the Park Service by advertising the National Parks and Monuments, because it helps sell their services while enhancing their public image. Similar cooperation could be anticipated if there were an urban service. In very special cases private organizations could be given assistance to develop the educative or historic quality of their property. Such a method is now used in the oldest area of San Juan, Puerto Rico, where homeowners are given maintenance grants for preserving the historic character of their homes.

At the start, to get things moving on a modest basis, we suggest amending existing legislation to allow supplementary grants for those communities interested in experimenting with educative city environments. During the first few years, the number of interested communities would be limited and political pressures for participation in such grant programs would be minimal, thus providing an opportunity for the programs to prove themselves. To enhance the prospects of success, the federal agency should encourage the assistance of top designers, ecologists, psychologists, as well as other professionals in the formulation of local policies and experiments, especially during the early period.

At this point it is difficult to estimate the costs of such a service. In the fiscal year 1979, we are spending about $520 million on the National Park Serivce. A large portion of these funds is for historic preservation, new acquisitions, and construction of roads, trails, and buildings. The remainder covers management and protection, maintenance and rehabilitation, and general administration expenses. Compared with most other federal expenditures, this program is relatively modest. For instance, expenditures during the same period will be nearly $7.36 billion for highways and about $10.5 billion for manpower training. Nonetheless we suggest that for the first three years, a very modest sum of approximately $100 million for grants on a three-to-one, federal-local matching basis as well as perhaps $200 million for completely repayable loans would suffice to get the program under way and give us a better clue as to the order of magnitude of future costs and benefits.

The Risks and the Benefits

There will be some difficult problems, of course, in trying to make such a program work. The American mania for labeling and packaging everything could seriously betray our aims, as might dull or obtrusive projects. We do not wish to create a city that gives the impression that everything is explainable or that the city is simply a machine for learning. It is important to preserve—perhaps even to heighten—opportunities for discovery and mystery in the environment, while still making many of its complexities and disorders more manageable.

Some might argue that the city is already too stressful and informative—that addition of educative elements would overload our senses or would further invade individual privacy. In some places, such as busy commercial streets, this could be true, but in many more areas, adding information could reduce confusion and monotony. Nevertheless, information-free places should be designed into the system. After all, quiet spaces, especially in the center of the city, are as important to learning as exposure.

Another of our concerns is that the city might become a giant propaganda machine—an environment not unlike the streets of Chinese cities, at least in the recent past, with their street-corner plays, billboards, loudspeakers, and parades, all preaching the Cultural Revolution. A strength, however, of the decentralized organization we have proposed is that it would minimize such dangers by encouraging individual expressions and wide-ranging local experiments.

In short, we concede that an urban service carries risks. But our hopes far exceed our fears. An urban service is hardly a panacea for the problems that plague our cities: clearly, physical and social changes are necessary that would not be directly affected by this program. We would contend, however, that an urban service merits support because it could enable great numbers of people to profit from the educative potentials of the city.

One of the many advantages of such a service is that it would make more available the diversity of experience that is so important to individual development, particularly in the early years. Although television serves this function in some sense, that experience is vicarious; direct exposure or activity is far more vivid and telling. By encouraging encounters with new situations, an urban service might particularly benefit people who come from places that now lack variety or opportunity—suburbs, urban slums, depressed regions, even central cities.

An urban service might also help to compensate for some of the weaknesses of formal education. For many of the young, school is often dull and unrelated to their interests. The rigidity of most schools discourages the involvement of students in a personal way, at their initiative, in discovery of the world. Conventional education is often too specialized, focusing disproportionately on preparing students for jobs and for college rather than for living. An urban service would extend education outside the walls of schools and museums and beyond the years of formal schooling. Learning would be firsthand, personal, and enjoyable. The student would be free to learn what interests him from whatever sources he chooses; he could set his own pace without fear of competition. People would be reached who now have no access to formal education. Moreover, such an emphasis could help offset some of the negative forces of poor schools, homes, or neighborhoods by providing other avenues for learning.

As the workweek shrinks, the urban service may help the already crowded cultural and recreational institutions to accommodate the new leisure interests. This role will be all the more valuable as cities grow—as the need develops for alternative uses of leisure which do not require extensive investments in land or expensive trips to distant places. The Summer in the Parks program previously mentioned provided such alternatives very successfully in outdoor spaces throughout Washington, D.C., by means of a variety of events—children's theaters, art workshops, exhibitions and instruction in sports, concerts featuring both local talent and celebrities, the National Capitol Open bicycle races, and an Indian powwow. For each event talented local designers created settings to give the park a festive mood appropriate to the occasion. These activities might be enhanced in still other ways. For example, the service might have a staff of street people— guides, musicians, storytellers, actors—whose role would be to make the city streets more delightful.

City information systems, such as we have described, could also provide a relatively economical way to brighten the image of a whole region without massive physical changes while achieving other valued ends at the same time. Along with designing elements for learning purposes, such systems could be made to heighten visual order and sensory delight. Use of public transportation systems, for example, which is now usually a stressful and dreary experience, could be made far more enjoyable and educational.

Directly or indirectly, an urban service would nourish critical evaluations of the city and help to bring about constructive changes. By making the interdependence of man and environment more explicit, the consequences of poor management are less apt to be overlooked. Egregious mistakes could even be underscored. Giant air-pollution or noise gauges, visible over large areas, could blacken as pollution or noise reaches danger levels; major polluters could be identified along highways. Similar mechanisms might be devised to show the effects on natural life of pesticides, contaminated water, or the filling of wetlands. Along with exposing the mistakes in environmental management, solutions could be made known by exhibiting places where good environmental decisions have been made.

Future plans—including feasible alternatives—could be demonstrated outdoors through models, pictures, or mock-ups. These could be evaluated by the public and would stimulate lively discussion. The continual decision-making process within the city could also be illustrated, along with the consequences of the decisions on how the city looks and works. Manipulable models and maps might even encourage testing the consequences of alternative public policies that affect the environment.

In sum, the benefits of an urban service could be broad. Almost everyone would be reached—rich and poor, young and old, resident and visitor. Business would be helped. New opportunities would be created, many of which might provide jobs and learning experiences for the disadvantaged. Natural pride in the city, concern with improvement, and outside interest, including tourism, would be fostered. Most importantly, an urban service would satisfy the natural and universal urge to find out about other people, places, and things.

CHAPTER FOUR

The Form of the City

WITH KEVIN LYNCH

The principal concern of the physical planner is to understand the physical environment and to help shape it to serve the community's purposes. Outsiders from other disciplines would ordinarily assume that such a profession had developed some ideas concerning the diverse effects of different forms of the physical environment (not to mention the reverse effects of nonphysical forces on the environment itself). And they might be equally justified in expecting that intellectual leaders in the profession had been assiduously gathering evidence to check and reformulate these ideas so that they might better serve the practitioners in the field. A systematic consideration of the interrelations between urban forms and human objectives would seem to lie at the theoretical heart of city-planning work.

But the expectation would bring a wry smile to the face of anyone familiar with the actual state of the theory of the physical environment. Where has there been any systematic evaluation of the possible range of urban forms in relation to the objectives men might have? Although most attempts at shaping or reshaping cities have been accompanied by protestations of the ends toward which the shapers are striving, yet, in fact, there is usually only the most nebulous connection between act and protestation. Goals are not only put in a confused or even conflicting form, but also the physical forms decided upon have very little to do with these goals. Choice of form is most often based on custom, or intuition, or on the superficial attraction of simplicity. Once constructed, forms are rarely later analyzed for their effectiveness in achieving the objectives originally set.

What does exist are some palliative knowledge and rules of thumb for designing street intersections, neighborhoods, and industrial areas, for separating different land uses, distinguishing different traffic functions, or controlling urban growth. Analysis of urban design is largely at the level of city parts, not of the whole. The prevailing views are static and fragmentary. When ideal models are considered, they take the form of utopias. These serve to free the imagination, but are not substitutes for adequate analysis.

But something better than rule of thumb and shrewd improvisation is required if professional services are to warrant public appreciation. In short, we need better ideas, better theory. Formulated operationally, such theory can be tested, revised, and ultimately verified. Even if inadequate initially, theories can help to develop and extend our ideas, to make them more precise, embracing, and effective. Unless planners can devise more powerful ideas for understanding and controlling the physical environment, they are not likely to be, and perhaps do not deserve to be treated, as more than lackeys for the performance of routine chores.

POSSIBLE ANALYTICAL APPROACHES

It is not easy to create theories "full-blown." Effective theories, as a rule, are products of many men's efforts constantly reworked into a more general and more systematic form. It is also hard to locate the best starting place. In tackling the problems of the physical environment, one can employ a number of approaches ranging from the descriptive to the genetic, from problem solving to process and function analyses. All have certain advantages and disadvantages.

Description is the most obvious approach, and perhaps the weakest, standing alone. To describe the physical environment more accurately is an important aim; but since the descriptive possibilities are endless, it is difficult to be sure what is and what is not crucial or relevant. Description works best when there is enough familiarity with its significance to permit vividness and terse accuracy. Too little is known about the forms of the physical environment, or even about the appropriate analytical categories for analyzing these forms, to provide effective description. Description alone, moreover, yields little insight as to the underlying mechanism of operation.

Another approach might be to study how the physical environment is transformed. The nature of the changes can be recorded, as well as the difficulties and directions in transition, the conditions associated with the changes, and the various social, economic, and political processes by which the changes take place. Often the historical, comparative, and genetic approaches are the best ways of following the dynamics of the physical environment. But those approaches have limitations too; and these lie in the difficulty of disentangling the strategic variables which should be examined and of understanding the mechanism of change.

Another approach, now most popular, is the pragmatic. Each case can be considered more or less unique. The emphasis is on problem solving, or on shaping or reshaping the physical environment to eliminate specific difficulties or to achieve specific effects. Limited generalizations or rules can be formulated; but the tendency is to emphasize the uniqueness of each problem and the inapplicability of "stratospheric generalizations." The advantage here is the "realism"; the weakness is the handicap implicit in the assumption that general ideas and theories are of almost no value as guides for dealing with specific cases or classes of cases.

A more abstract variant of problem solving might be a study of the goal–form relationship. This approach is concerned with how alternative physical arrangements facilitate or inhibit various individual and social objectives. It is an approach directly keyed to action; it would, if perfected, suggest optimum forms or a range of them, once aspirations had been clarified and decided upon. Its weakness is its static nature; its strength lies in the emphasis on the clear formulation of goals and on the probable effects of various forms of physical organization. The more that is learned about these effects, the more light will be shed on the process and perhaps even on the mechanism of change. Similarly, descriptive techniques and genetic and historical approaches might prove more effective if the emphasis were on objectives and if the evidence sought were related to the effectiveness of the environment in serving these ends. Problem solving, too, would be more systematic, less haphazard and subject to rules of thumb, if it were grounded on more solid knowledge of goal–form relationships.

CRITERIA FOR ANALYTICAL CATEGORIES OF URBAN FORM

Since the work on urban form has been negligible, the first task is to decide what it is and to find ways of classifying and describing it that will turn out to be useful both for the analysis of the impact on objectives and for the practical manipulation of form. Without a clear analytical system for examining the physical form of a city, it is hardly possible to assess the effect of form or even to change it in any rational way. The seemingly elementary step of formulating an analytical system is the most crucial. Upon it hangs all the rest; and whereas other questions, such as the statement of objectives or the analysis of effects, may be partly the task of other disciplines, the question of city form cannot be passed off.

There are a number of criteria which a workable system must meet. First, it must apply to cities and metropolitan areas and be significant at that scale. This is simply an arbitrary definition of our particular sphere of interest, but it conceals an important distinction. There are many environmental effects which operate at larger scales (such as the influence of climate or the distribution of settlement on a national level), and even more which are effective at smaller scales (such as the decoration of a room or the siting of a group of houses). Cities are too often regarded simply as collections of smaller environments. Most traditional design ideas (shopping centers, neighborhoods, traffic intersections, and play spaces) reflect this tendency. It is usually assumed that well-designed neighborhoods, with good roads and sufficient shopping and industry, automatically produce an optimum settlement. As another example, many planners are likely to think that a beautiful city is simply the sum of a large series of small areas which are beautiful in themselves.

But this notion may be no more true than the notion that a great building is a random collection of handsome rooms. Every physical whole is affected not only by the quality of its parts but also by their total organization and arrangement. Therefore, the first criterion for form analysis is that it identify form qualities which are significant at the city or metropolitan scale; that is, which can be controlled at that scale and which also have different effects, when arranged in different patterns, that are describable at that scale. This criterion excludes, without in any way denying their importance, such features as intercity spacing (describable only beyond the city level) or the relation of the front door of a house to the street (which is hard to describe on the city scale unless uniform, difficult to control at that level, and whose citywide pattern of distribution would seem to be of no importance).

The second criterion is that categories must deal solely with the physical form of the city or with the distribution of activities within it; and that these two aspects must be clearly and sharply separated. City and regional planners operate primarily on the physical environment, although mindful of its complex social, economic, or psychological effects. They are not experts in all the planning for the future that a society engages in, but only in planning for the future development of the physical and spatial city: streets, buildings, utilities, activity distributions, spaces, and their interrelations. Although cries of dismay may greet such a reactionary and "narrow" view, the currently fashionable, broader definitions lead, in our judgment, only to integrated, comprehensive incompetence.

In this sense planners are aware that the final motive of their work is its human effect, and they should be well-grounded, for example, in the interrelation between density and the development of children in our society. They must understand quite clearly that the physical or locational effects may often be the least important ones, or operate only in conjunction with other circumstances. Above all, they have to understand that the very process of achieving their proposed form—that is, the way in which the group decides and organizes itself to carry it out—may turn out to be the most decisive effect of all. Nevertheless, they take the spatial environment as the focus of their work, and do not pretend to be sociologists, economists, administrators, or some megalomaniacal supercombination of these.

Physical form and the spatial distribution of activities in the city are partly contained in the traditional "land use" categories of the planning field. Unfortunately, these categories are analytically treacherous.

It is true that the very ambiguity of the categories is often useful in field operation, where they can be made to mean what the user wants them to mean. But for theoretical study, these categories thoroughly confound two distinct spatial distributions: that of human activity, or "use" proper, and that of physical shape. The traditional concept of "single-family residential use," for example, unites a certain kind of activity, family residence (and its concomitant features of eating, sleeping, child rearing, etc.), with a type of isolated physical structure, called a "house," which is traditionally allied with this activity. This approach works tolerably well in a homogeneous society, as long as people behave with docility and continue to reside in families in these houses. But if they should choose to sleep in buildings we call "factories," then the whole system would be in danger. Even under present circumstances, "mixed uses," or structures used now for storage, now for selling, now for religious meetings, cause trouble.

The pattern of activities and the physical pattern are often surprisingly independent of each other, and they must be analytically separated if we are to understand the effect of either. In practice, planners operate primarily on the physical pattern, although often aiming to change the activity pattern via the physical change. Only in the negative prohibitions of some parts of the zoning ordinance do planners operate directly on the activity pattern itself. By making a sharp distinction between the two, it is possible to explore how activity pattern and physical pattern interact, and which (if either) has significant effects in achieving any given objective.

This analysis, however, will primarily develop the notion of the urban physical pattern, leaving the question of the activity pattern for another effort. The purpose of this emphasis is not to prejudge the relative importance of the two, but to provide clarity of analysis and to take into account the fact that, at present, most planners operate primarily on the physical rather than the activity patterns. The time may come, of course, when city planners may manipulate the distribution of activities in an equally direct manner. Even should this time not come and should our influence on activities continue to be indirect, it would be important to know the consequences of activity distribution.

Such nonspatial factors as the range of family income, political organization, or the social type of a city are excluded by this second criterion. We will also omit discussion of such factors as the distribution of work place versus sleeping place or the quantity of flow on city streets. These latter points are activity categories, properly considered under their own heading.

A third criterion of our analytical system, which adds to the problems of constructing it, is that it must be applicable to all types of urban settlement used by any human culture. An American city, a Sumerian settlement, or a future Martian metropolis must all be capable of being subsumed under it. The categories must reach a level of generality that might be unnecessary in simply considering present-day cities in the United States. Not only is this generality necessary for complete analysis, but also, by making our categories truly general, we may uncover new form possibilities not now suspected. For example, dwelling-units-per-acre cannot be used as a basic descriptive measure, since some settlements may not have sleeping areas organized into dwelling units. (The fact of having such an organization, of course, may be part of a physical description.)

A fourth criterion is that the categories must eventually be such that they can be discovered or measured in the field, recorded, communicated, and tested. Lastly, the crucial test: all the factors chosen for analysis must have significant effect on whatever goals are important to the group using the facilities and must encompass all physical features significant for such goals.

Our aim is to uncover the important factors that influence the achievement of certain human objectives. Therefore, the categories allowable here will depend on the objectives chosen and on the threshold of effect considered significant. The categories used might shift with each new study. However, it is necessary to set up one system of form categories so that comparisons may be made from one study to another. One must begin, therefore, by considering the familiar human purposes and by guessing what physical features might be significant for those purposes. Subsequent analysis and testing will undoubtedly modify the categories based on these criteria.

In summary, the criteria for an analytic system of city form are that the categories of analysis must: (1) have significance at the citywide scale, that is, be controllable and describable at that level; (2) involve either the physical shape or the activity distribution and not confuse the two; (3) apply to all urban settlements; (4) be capable of being recorded, communicated, and tested; and (5) have significance for their effect on the achievement of human objectives and include all physical features that are significant.

PROPOSED ANALYTICAL SYSTEM

Although several types of analytical systems might be considered, we have attempted to develop a set of abstract descriptions of the quality, quantity, or spatial distribution of various features, of types that are present in some form in all settlements. The abstractness of this system makes it difficult to conceptualize. The system also divides up the total form of city, although not spatially, and therefore raises the problem of keeping in mind the interrelations among categories. But for generality, clarity, and conciseness—and perhaps even for fresh insights—it seems to be the preferable method and will be followed in the rest of this chapter.

A system for activity pattern would probably require a description of two basic aspects: flow of men and of goods, on the one hand, and, on the other, the spatial pattern of more localized activities, such as exchange, recreation, sleeping, or production. Although this side of the analysis will be omitted to concentrate on physical pattern, a similar breakdown is feasible in the physical-form description: (a) the flow *system*, excluding the flow itself; and (b) the distribution of adapted space, primarily sheltered space.

This breakdown is similar to the familiar duet of land use and circulation, with the content of activity removed. It may be remarked that an overtone of activity still remains, since the physical facilities are divided between those primarily used for flow and those accommodating more fixed activities. This is a very convenient division, however, and seems to be a regular feature of all settlements.

There are many cases, of course, in which a given physical space is used both for flow and for other activities. Usually the other activities are alongside the flow, or sometimes intermixed with it, and here the space must be subdivided, or simply counted in both categories. Then, if this is important, a temporal shift of the facility from one category to another can be made. Occasionally there may be a cyclical shift in use, as when a road is shut off for a street dance. It is even conceivable that a city could contain mobile facilities in which both circulation and other activities are performed simultaneously, on the analogy of the ocean liner. But perhaps that possibility can be faced when it happens on a scale that would be significant in a city.

Except for these difficulties, then, the division into flow system and adapted space is a convenient one. The former is usually easy to identify, and includes all the roads, paths, tubes, wires, canals, and rail lines which are designed to facilitate the flow of people, goods, wastes, or information. The latter category, that of adapted spaces, although it seems tremendously broad, has sufficient basic similarity to be treated as an entity. It consists of all spaces that have been adapted in some way to be useful for some one or several significant noncirculatory activities.

In this country's climate, the key spaces of this nature are those which are enclosed and which have a modified climate, that is, the city's "floor space." Elsewhere enclosure may be less important. Almost everywhere, however, the adaptation includes some modification of the ground plane, even to the cultivation of a field; and the key activities are often likely to take place in at least sheltered, if not enclosed, spaces. But in any case, the fundamental function of our physical environment, besides providing means for communication, is to provide spaces for various activities, to adapt the quality of those spaces, and to distribute them in an overall pattern.

Since many of the primary adaptations of a space, such as enclosure or the provision of a smooth, level, hard, dry ground plane, are useful for may different activities, spaces are often used interchangeably. A "storefront" may be used as a store, an office, a church, a warehouse, or even a family residence. This interchangeability argues for the usefulness and necessity of generalizing adapted space into one category. Within it, one may dissect as much as necessary, dividing enclosed floor space from open space, picking out tall structures from the floor-space category, or hard-surfaced lots from total open space. Occasionally, purely for convenience, it may be necessary to use activity-oriented names such as "office structure" or "parking lot." But such names always refer solely to a physical type and not to its use.

Each one of these two general categories, flow system and adapted space, could also be broken down in a parallel way for more exact analysis.

1. *Element types:* The basic types of spaces and of flow facilities can be described qualitatively in their most significant aspects, including the extent to which the different types are differentiated in character, or to which they grade into each other (Figure 1).

Figure 1

Figure 2

2. *Quantity:* The quantities of houses or streets, in length, capacity, or size, can then be enumerated to give total capacity and scale (Figure 2).

3. *Density:* Next, the intensity with which spaces or channels are packed into a given unit area can be stated—as a single quantity, if uniform, but more likely as ranges of intensity and as average and typical intensities. This idea is familiar when applied to adapted space, particularly enclosed space, as is exemplified in the concept of the floor–area ratio (Figure 3). The same idea could be applied to the circulation system, calculating intensity as the flow capacity which passes in any direction through a small unit area and mapping the variation of this ratio (as in potential vehicles per hour/acre).

4. *Grain:* The extent to which these typical elements and densities are differentiated and separated in space can be defined as coarse or fine, in terms of the quantity of a given type that is separated out in one cluster, and sharp or blurred, in terms of the manner of separation at the boundary. Thus, house and factory building types might typically be separated in one city into large, pure clusters, sharply differentiated at the edges; whereas in another town the grain might be very fine and the transitions generally blurred. Again, the outdoor spaces might be blurred and undifferentiated or, in the circulation system, footpaths and vehicular pavements might be sharply and coarsely separated. Essentially, this quality refers to the typical local interrelations between similar or dissimilar elements, but without reference, as yet, to total pattern (Figure 4).

Figure 3

Figure 4

5. *Focal organization:* The spatial arrangement and interrelation of the key points in the total environment can be examined. These might be the density peaks, the concentrations of certain dominant building types, the key open spaces, or the termini or basic intersections of the circulation systems. Consideration of the arrangement of such key points is often a shorthand method of expressing total pattern (Figure 5).

6. *Generalized spatial distribution:* This category could be taken as a catchall which includes the entire analysis. What is meant by the term is the gross pattern in two- (or three-) dimensional space, as might be expressed on a greatly simplified map or model, which would include such items as outline (or the shape of the city with reference to the noncity) and the broad pattern of zones occupied by the basic element and density types. One city might have a single, central, density peak; another a circle cut by pie-shaped zones of "factory" buildings; another a flow system on a rectangular grid; still another might have a uniform pattern of small, interconnecting, enclosed outdoor spaces surrounded by a deep belt of free-flowing space punctuated by tall masses. Such a description would be needed whenever the notation of type, quantity, density, grain, and pattern of key points was insufficient to describe the significant total pattern (Figure 6).

Figure 5

Figure 6

Finally, of course, it would be necessary to interrelate the two basic categories—for example, to show where the flow termini came with reference to the density peaks, or to relate the pattern of the flow system to the general open-space pattern.

The method outlined above is proposed as a basic system of analyzing a city's form in accordance with the original criteria. It does not try to cover all the physical features of a city, which are endless, but concentrates on those considered significant at that scale. Only systematic testing in real cities will indicate whether all the important features are included.

AN EXAMPLE OF THE ANALYTICAL SYSTEM

Since this system may be difficult to follow in the abstract, it will perhaps clarify the proposal to use it in describing an imaginary settlement named Pone. Like any town, Pone is best described by the use of both words and precise drawings, but here words and a simple sketch must suffice.

1. Pone is made up of six types of adapted space: dirt-floored rooms, 20 × 20 ft, roofed with thatch and enclosed by adobe, each structure free standing; concrete-floored shed spaces, 75 ft × up to 300 ft, in corrugated iron, sometimes single and sometimes in series horizontally; multistory concrete structures containing from 50 to 200 10 × 10-ft rooms; walled-in, cultivated spaces of rectangular shape, varying from ½ to three acres; walled, stone-paved spaces pierced by paths; and irregular, bare, dust-covered spaces which take up the remainder of the area. Pone has four types of flow channels: 4-ft dirt paths, unenclosed; 30-ft cobbled roads, enclosed in semicircular tubes of corrugated iron; an interconnecting, waterproof system of four-inch pipes; and some telegraph wires.

2. There are 10,000 adobe rooms, totaling four million square ft; 50 shed spaces, totaling one million square ft; and four multistory structures, with 40,000 square ft of floor space. There are 5,000 cultivated spaces occupying 5,000 acres, two walled and paved open spaces of 10 acres each; and the leftover dust covers 1,200 acres. There are three miles of cobbled road, each

with a capacity of 400 mulecarts per hour in both directions; and 60 miles of dirt path, each able to carry 2,000 persons per hour in either direction. There are 20 miles of pipe and two miles of wire.

3. Density of adobe rooms varies continuously from a floor-area ratio of 0.003 to 0.3; that of the sheds from 0.3 to 0.9 (with a tendency to group at the two extremes), while the tall structures are uniformly at 5.0. Road-capacity density varies from a peak of 1,600 carts per hour/acre to a low of 20; path-capacity density varies from 4,000 persons per hour/acre to 50.

4. The three types of enclosed space are sharply differentiated and separated in plan. Cultivated spaces are mixed coarsely with the adobe rooms, while the irregular dusty areas are finely distributed throughout. Roads and paths are sharply separated and do not interconnect except at the shed spaces. Any intersections are at separated grades. They are also coarsely separated, since the roads are associated with the shed spaces.

Wires and pipes follow along paths. Pipes are dispersed, but wires serve only sheds and the multistory structures.

5. Focal points in this organization are the two rectangular, paved, open spaces. The first is central to the area of adobe rooms and is the focus of converging paths. It corresponds to the peak of room density and to one of the peaks of path density. The other focal point is flanked by the multistory structures, occurs at another convergence and density peak of the path system, and is touched upon by the road system. Here occurs the major terminus and interchange point of that road system. The wire lines all pass through a central switchboard in one of the multistoried structures. The pipelines have a single source just beyond the town boundary.

6. The settlement is round and compact, with no holes. The multistoried structures and second focus occur at the center, with the sheds occupying a narrow, pie-shaped sector outward from this point. The focus of room density is slightly off center. The road system is a rectangular grid of irregular spacing, tying to the sheds, to the second focal point, and, by a single line, to the outside. The path system is irregular and capillary, but converges and intensifies at the two focal points, as noted above (Figure 7).

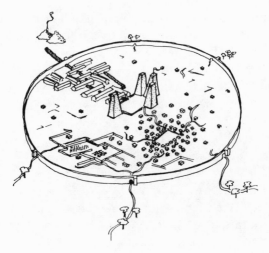

Figure 7

In theory (and particularly if we could use more drawings)
we now know enough of the physical form to judge its value for
various basic purposes at the city level of significance. One is
tempted to object that this is meaningless if one knows nothing of
the life that is going on within that form. Lifeless, yes, and saying
little or nothing about the society of Pone (though one may make
some guesses); yet adequate, if one wants to test its cost, or
productive efficiency (given some productive system), or comfort
(given some standards). Certainly it is the first step in trying to
disentangle the effects of physical form *per se,* and the first step
even if one wants to study the results of physical form in relation
to activity pattern, or social organization, or politics. (To describe
New York City in this way would, of course, take a few more
pages.)

PROBLEMS OF GOAL FORMULATION

What will be the goals against which we will test this city?
Unfortunately, for a neat and workmanlike job, they might be
almost anything. One group might find inhabiting Pone highly
satisfactory, another might find it useless or even dangerous, all

depending on their several purposes and the variations in their cultures. Is there any method by which relevant goals might be set out and related to these environmental shapes? To consider the problems of setting up such a goal system we must digress. Only after we have done so will it be possible to return to the implications of the forms themselves.

First, the possible goals must be considered. This matter may cause some confusion, since such a collection is not likely to be consistent or unified. It must be distinguished from a goal *system*, that is, a set of selected objectives which are coherent, unified, and capable of guiding action. Construction of such a system is the desirable result of considering goal possibilities, but it can only be brought to completion by a particular group in a particular situation. Thus the possible range of goals might include both the preservation of individual life at all costs and also the maximization of sacrifice by individuals. A particular system would have to choose, or, more probably, settle upon some intermediate stand; and this stand should be related to its other objectives.

Probably the most confusing aspect of this question is not the infinite number of goal possibilities but rather their range of generality. Some objectives, such as "goodness," may seem to regulate almost every action, but to do so in such a vague and generalized way as to be of little help in choice. Others, such as the goal of having all children say "please" when asking for things at the table, are very clear in their implications for action but limited in their application and their consequences. These two goals are interconnected only by a long chain of explanations, situations, and interactions. It is difficult to be sure that one follows from the other and hard to weigh their relative importance in relation to other goals.

To avoid such confusions, it is important that any one goal system should contain only objectives which are at approximately the same level of generality. We may smile when someone admonishes a child to "Be good, and keep your fingernails clean!" But we are also exhorted to build city additions that will be good places to live in and will keep valuations high. In many cases, of course, there may be no real confusion, as when the second point is the true objective and the first is only a verbal blind.

Similarly, it is meaningless to consider beauty and fresh paint as alternative objectives: they do not operate at the same level. Each objective may in its turn be regarded as a means of attaining some objective higher up the scale of generality. Shouting at recruits may be considered a means of overawing them, with the goal of developing obedience, which is itself directed to the building of a disciplined military force, having as its objective the winning of wars, which may be thought of as a way to gain security. When constructing a rational system for guidance in any particular situation, what must be built up is a connected hierarchy of goals, considering possible alternatives only at the same level of generality and checking lower levels for their relevance to upper levels of the system.

The more general objectives have the advantage of relative stability: they are applicable to more situations for larger groups over longer spans of time. They have the corresponding disadvantages of lack of precision and difficulty of application to any specific problem. Very often, in goal systems of real life, such general objectives may have very little connection with objectives farther down the list, being, rather, top-level show pieces, or covers for hidden motives. The operating goals are then the intermediate ones, those which actually regulate action. To develop a rational set of goals, however, the connection must be sought out, or the motives that are the true generalized goals must be revealed. The aim is to produce a system that is as coherent as possible, although such a result is rare in reality.

Since reference back to very general goals is intellectually painful, most actions must be guided by intermediate, more concrete objectives which can be referred to more quickly. Only the most serious steps warrant reference to fundamentals, whereas everyday decisions depend on customs and precepts that are actually low-level goals. City building is important enough to be referred back to more than simple precepts; but even here decisions cannot always be brought up to the highest level of generality, since the analysis is so complex. Therefore reliance must be placed on goals of an intermediate level. But these intermediate goals should be periodically checked for their relevance to more general objectives and to the changing situation, as well as for consistency among themselves.

It is a besetting sin to "freeze" upon rather specific goals and thus risk action irrelevant to a new situation. If it is observed, for example, that growing cities have been prosperous ones, attention may focus on increase of population size as an objective. Actions will be directed toward stimulating growth, regardless of any consequences of dislocation, instability, or cost. Industries may be brought in which will depress the wage level and the general prosperity, because no one has stopped to examine the objectives that lie behind the growth objective—that is, to ask the simple question: "Why do we want to grow?" Because of this continuous tendency to fix upon goals at too specific a level, it is a wise habit to challenge current goals by always pushing them back at least one step up the ladder of generality.

CRITERIA FOR THE CHOICE OF GOALS

What will be the criteria for the choice of goals in our case? If they are rational, they should be internally consistent. There should, moreover, be some possibility of moving toward their realization, now or in the future. Otherwise they are simply frustrating. To have operational meaning, they must be capable of being contradicted, thus permitting a real choice. And finally, the goals must be relevant to city form, since there are many human objectives which are little affected by environmental shape. Therefore, given one's basic values and the values of the culture in which one is operating, it is necessary to develop a set of useful intermediate objectives which are consistent, possible, operational, and relevant to the task at hand.

Devising such objectives is difficult; and it is not made easier by the fact that planners are individuals responsible for actions or recommendations in an environment used by large numbers of people. They are not concerned with their own values, nor how they interact with the values of another individual with whom they can communicate, which is the situation of the architect with a single client. The planner's client is a large group, a difficult client to talk to, often incoherent, and usually in some conflict with itself.

To some extent planners can rely on democratic processes to establish group objectives; to some extent they must use sociological techniques to uncover them. Often they are forced, or think they are forced, to rely on their own intuition as to group objectives—a most hazardous method, since planners are likely to be members of a rather small class of that society. In any event, they must make every effort to understand their own values, as well as to uncover and clarify the goals of the society they are working for.

Their troubles do not stop there. Even if they had perfect knowledge of group goals, and these goals proved to form a completely consistent system, planners would still be faced with the issue of relating them to their own personal values. They cannot be solely the handmaiden of the group, but have some responsibility (should they differ) to urge upon them a modification of their goal system or to acquaint them with new alternatives. As is the case with many other professional groups, they have a complicated role of leader and follower combined.

And should the public goals, as is most likely, prove to be internally inconsistent or in transition, then planners must mediate these conflicts and changes. They must find the means of striking a balance and the way of preparing for the new value to come without destroying the old value still present.

But at all these everyday woes we can at the moment simply shrug our theoretical shoulders. Give us a consistent and operational system of objectives, a system possible and relevant and organized properly by levels, and we will show you the environmental forms to achieve these objectives. If your goals are superficial or shortsighted, so much the worse. That is your concern, not ours.

In Western culture, general and accepted goals would probably cluster around the worth of the individual human being, around the idea of man as the measure, with an emphasis on future results and yet on the importance of process as well as final achievement. Basic values for the individual might include: (a) health, equilibrium, survival, continuity, adaptability; (b) coherence, meaning, response; (c) development, growth, stimulus, choice, freedom; (d) participation, active use of powers, efficiency, skill, control; and, (e) pleasure, comfort.

On the basis of such generalities, one can formulate for oneself (or for one's group) a set of broad goals. One way of conveniently organizing such goals may be the following:

1. Goals regarding the relation of men and objects; or those goals (a) having to do with direct functioning: biological or technical goals, such as the achievement of an environment which sustains and prolongs life; and (b) having to do with sensuous interactions: psychological or aesthetic goals, such as the creation of an environment which is meaningful to the inhabitant.

2. Goals regarding the relation of men and men; or those goals (a) having to do with interpersonal relations: sociological and psychological goals, such as constructing surroundings which maximize interpersonal communications; and (b) having to do with group functioning: social goals, such as survival and continuity of the group.

It is important to see that a mere listing of objectives is insufficient even at this generalized level, if a policy of relative emphasis is not also included. Any real action may work for one goal and against the other, or be more or less helpful in relation to another action. Yet the choice must be made. Therefore, a statement of objectives must be accompanied by a statement of relative importance: for example, that group survival is valued above individual survival, although both are valued. More precisely, it will have to be said that, in a given circumstance, group survival is more valued.

Since attainment of human objectives almost always entails the use of scarce resources, the next level of objectives is that of the economic. In their most general form, these objectives involve the attainment of ends with the maximum economy of means, while keeping or making the resource level as high as possible. In all these general objectives, moreover, there is an

intertwining of means and ends, of process and final achievement. Particularly where "final" achievement may be as long
delayed or even as illusory as it is in city development, the attainment of objectives may be affected more by the process itself
than by the final form that is being sought.

But the goal system at this level, however consistent and
relevant, is still too general for effective application to city-form
decisions. Moving down to lower levels for specific illustration,
how can one define a "meaningful environment," for example, or
the limits within which interpersonal communication is to be
maximized?

It would be possible to move down the ladder step-by-step,
ending with some such rule as "All buildings should by their
exterior form reveal to any adult inhabitant of average education
and intelligence their principal internal use," or even "to accom-
plish this, the following building types shall have the following
shapes." The latter is undoubtedly an example of "misplaced
concreteness"; but even the former rule poses problems in relating it back to the general descriptive categories of city form that
were developed above. How does the "meaningfulness" of structure relate to density, or grain, or focal organization? In coming
down the ladder of specificity, we may find we have slipped away
from relevance to form at the city scale, or have developed precepts which have multiple and complex effects on the various
categories of city form.

Since the formulation of specific objectives is unavoidable, it
would be preferable that they be reorganized by being grouped
in terms of their relevance to the descriptive categories. Such
organization is simply a tactical move, but a crucial one. It involves running through the list of descriptive categories of city
form, and choosing (by intuition or prior experience) those general objectives that seem most relevant to that aspect of form.

For example, the following general goals are probably affected in some important way by the "grain" of adapted spaces in
an urban settlement: (a) optimum interpersonal communication;
(b) maximum choice of environment for the individual; (c)
maximum individual freedom in construction; (d) optimum

aesthetic stimulus; (e) maximum productive efficiency; (f) maximum productive flexibility; (g) minimum first cost; and (h) minimum operating cost.

By thus selecting and grouping our general goals, a hypothesis is being asserted—for example, that "the grain of city facilities has significant (if unknown) effect on the first cost of constructing them." Such hypotheses may prove untrue, in which case the group of goals must be revised or, equally likely, some other objective not originally listed is also significantly affected and must be added to the list.

One objective may be significantly affected by more than one form quality and will thus appear in more than one group. Another objective may be little influenced by any one quality alone, but rather by the nature of the combination of two or more, such as the total effect of grain and density together. This point is a separate one to which we will later return.

The critical nature of the form categories previously selected now becomes apparent, since they impose their pattern on the entire investigation. If they are not in themselves highly significant, or if they are inconsistent or poorly organized, the work must be redone. Nevertheless, by thus bringing in the relation to form early in our consideration of objectives, a much more economical and systematic attack is possible. The objectives not only contain hypotheses of relevancy, but are really turning into action questions: for example, "What grain of spaces gives a minimum first cost?"

It must be made clear that, if physical forms are considered in isolation, such action questions are not answerable. No relation between grain and first cost can be established until a construction process is postulated. Or, for another example, the impact of the grain of spaces on interpersonal communication depends also on the activity occupying those spaces. Nevertheless, once given a construction process or an activity distribution which is held constant during the test, then the differential impact of various grain alternatives can be analyzed. Thus, in a given activity context, the results of various physical patterns might be studied. Often, a principal result of a given physical pattern may occur via the manner in which it changes an activity distribution, given an assumption as to a fixed association between certain forms and certain activities.

The same limitations apply to the study of activity patterns in isolation, which are meaningless without reference to the facilities available for communication, insulation, and so on. Eventually, there would be a more complex level of analysis, in which both activity distribution and form might be allowed to vary simultaneously. Even here, however, a general cultural context is still required.

Once the general goals are arranged in terms of the type, quantity, density, grain, focal organization, and pattern of the adapted spaces and the flow system (and in the process just those objectives have been selected which may be most critically affected by these qualities), and once a general context of culture and activity has been chosen, a more concrete level of analysis is possible. The level should be specific enough to say that "City A is closer to this objective than City B." The meaning of terms must be put in an operational, and often quantitative, way. For example, the question "What density of spaces allows a reasonable journey from home to work?" might become: "What density (or densities) allows 75% of the population to be within 30 minutes time distance of their place of work, providing no more than 10% are less than five minutes away from their work place?" Different city models could now be tested by this criterion.

Not all goals could be put in this quantitative form, of course. But they could at least have a testable wording, such as: "What is the density at which there is maximum opportunity for interpersonal communication within the local group, without destroying the ability of the individual to achieve privacy when desired?" Such formulations are likely to contain the words "maximum," "minimum," or "optimum."

The caution must be repeated that, although satisfyingly specific, such goals require continual rechecking for relevance to the general goals and the changing situation. The home-to-work objective, for example, is simply a definition of the original word "reasonable." Next year, or in India, it might be different.

GOAL–FORM INTERACTION

Having established an analytical system of urban form and groups of objectives cast in relevant operational terms, the next problem we have is the interaction of form with goal. One might begin either by considering the grain of adapted space and the objectives significantly related to it, or, alternatively, a fundamental objective and the form aspects related to it. If one of the goals is minimum first cost, then, for example, are the shed spaces of Pone cheaper to build when concentrated as they are in a coarse grain than if they were dispersed throughout the adobe spaces in a fine grain? Or, perhaps, does the grain of dispersion make no difference whatever? Undoubtedly, the effect of grain on cost may differ for different types of space. For example, whereas the grain of shed spaces was critical because they were built by mass site fabrication methods, the grain of adobe spaces might be indifferent, since they were put up singly by hand in any case. Or it might be found that dispersion of the multistory spaces among the shed spaces did not affect their cost, but dispersion among the adobe spaces did. Only in certain cases could generalizations be made as to grain *per se*. More often, the grain of a certain type of adapted space would have to be the subject of a conclusion.

The grain of the shed spaces may also affect productive efficiency. To test for this possibility, one may assume a type of activity, a given productive system, similar to the assumption of construction methods to test the cost implications. To do so does not mean that activity distribution slips in by the back door; we are still testing the impact of one or another physical quality upon the functioning of an activity which is held constant during the test. That is, given a factory system of production, which operates more easily in the wide-span shed spaces of Pone than anywhere else in the city, is that productive system more efficient if all the sheds are close together or if they are dispersed?

In this manner, the goal implications of grain could be analyzed, testing each for relevance and effect, and ending by a search to see if significant goals have been left out. If this system is successful, one should be able to say that, in a given culture, this particular grain gives best results if one's goal system has these particular elements and emphases, and another grain would be better for another system. Alternatively, the objective of minimum first cost could be explored throughout all its ramifications, resulting in a statement that, given a certain culture, this particular total urban form can be constructed at a minimum cost.

These are final-stage results, difficult to attain. Partial and still useful conclusions are more likely, such as: If this is the contemporary American society, and if the *only* goal is productive efficiency, then here is the grain to use for this type of adapted space (or: there are several equally good distributions, or, perhaps, the grain is of no consequence). Of course, the answer is likely to be still more qualified. One may have to add that this grain is best in a city of small size, another in the larger city; or that optimum grain cannot be separated from density or pattern.

One further note must be made. The *process* of achieving goals or of reshaping form is, in cities, as important as the long-range goal or form. Building a new city of a specific shape may have vital side effects on the administrative acts and organization required; sequence of development has as much to do with cost as final density. Moreover, one may have important goals which have to do mainly with the process itself, for example, that development decisions be arrived at democratically, or that people be allowed to participate in planning their dwellings, regardless of the final result.

The goal–form method, then, consists in ordering form analysis and definition of objectives so that their interrelation can be considered in a systematic and rational manner; it also helps to pose the problem. The method blesses the investigator but drops him in the mud; it has no further bearing on the analysis of any given interrelation. Each such analysis is likely to be unique and to demand its own method of solution. One might be amenable to mathematical methods; another, to sociological tools; a third, solvable only by subjective analysis; a fourth, by full-scale field tests. There is no guarantee, of course, that the fifth may be solvable at all. What is proposed is merely a way of attacking the central problems of cities in a methodical fashion.

This "merely," however, may in time open up new possibilities, simply because the problems are more precisely put. If the important physical properties of cities can be clearly defined, and if an operational standard can be set, such as one regarding commuting times, we may be able to study the implications of complex forms by means of new mathematical methods or with such aids as the high-speed computers.

COMPLEX FORM AND GOAL RELATIONSHIPS

If form qualities and goals could be analyzed and disposed of one by one, then in time a complete structure could be built with relative ease. Unfortunately (and this is perhaps the most vulnerable point of the system), physical patterns and goals have a habit of complex interaction. There is not one goal, but many; and the presence of other goals influences the force of the original one. The city forms, which we have herded into arbitrary categories to make our analysis possible, in truth make one pattern. It is not always easy to discuss the impact of grain without specifying density or size. The consequences of the distribution of adapted spaces rest partly on the flow system allied with it.

Thus there are frequently situations in which a given goal may not only be influenced by more than one form aspect but may also at times be affected by such an intimate interaction of aspects that there is no separable cause. A convenient system of notation (see Figure 8) for such a situation might be as follows, imagining that we are concerned with five goals, A, B, C, D, and E, which have these relationships with form.

Achievement of goal is influenced by:
    A—(1) space type; (2) flow-system size
    B—(1) space, density, and grain combined; (2) focal organization of space and flow system combined

C—(1) space size and flow-system pattern combined
D—(1) grain of flow system; (2) density of space and flow
     system combined
E—(1) grain of space, and density and focal organization of
     flow system all combined

The appearance of a goal in the top diagonal (shaded squares) of Figure 8 indicates that it relates to a single form quality at a time. Elsewhere its appearance shows that it is influenced by a pair of form qualities that must be considered together. One goal that it shows (E) is affected by an inseparable combination of three and must therefore be shown as a connected triangle. If a three-dimensional notation system were used, it could occupy a single solid cube. Higher interactions would require more complicated notations.

The shape of Figure 8 would change, of course, as the system of descriptive categories was modified. It is simply a convenient way of reminding ourselves what must be taken into account in studying goal-form interaction. Incidentally, the figure indicates that in this particular case two aspects of form (space pattern and flow-system type) happen to be the ones that have no bearing on any goal. All the rest are involved in one way or another.

These analytical methods would probably be sufficient for situations in which pairs of qualities were involved. Triads of qualities become much more difficult, and many more are likely to make analysis impossible. Some questions may therefore be answerable, and others may resist our best efforts.

To complete the example, consider again the city of Pone. The people of Pone are unsophisticated; they have few wants. They have only three goals relevant to city form: (1) maximum individual privacy when not producing; (2) maximum defensibility in war; and (3) maximum productive efficiency. In case of conflict, Goal 2 takes precedence, then Goal 3. The Ponians are a simple and a rather grim people.

These goals are set in the following situation: the town produces various kinds of simple consumer goods, which it exports to the surrounding countryside in return for raw materials. This

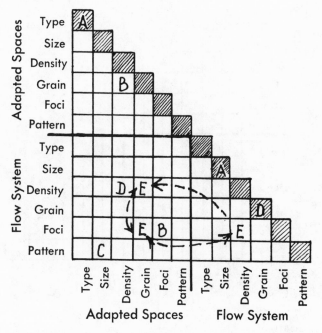

Figure 8

production is most easily carried out in the shed spaces, directed by control functions in the multistory spaces. But the town also produces a large part of its food supply in the cultivated spaces within its limits. Other life functions, beyond production and distribution, are traditionally carried out in the adobe rooms or in the paved open spaces. Wars are fought by ground action, with simple, short-range weapons, and may occur suddenly.

The matrix in Figure 9 indicates the probable relevancy of various form aspects to the three goals. That is, Objective 1 is affected by the type, density, and grain of adapted spaces, all acting singly. Objective 2 is influenced by the pattern of spaces and by the density, grain, and focal organization of the flow system, acting singly. It is also the prey of the combined action of the size and density of the adapted spaces. This is the case because, although the larger the city the greater the defensive army that could be raised for war and the higher the density the more

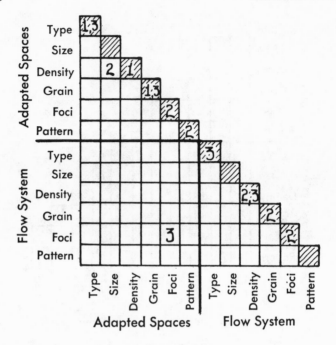

Figure 9

compact the defensive perimeter, yet in combination these factors may work in another way. A large, very dense city might quickly succumb to food shortages, owing to the lack of adequate internal cultivated spaces. Therefore, the optimum solution is likely to be a function of size in relation to density. Finally, Objective 3 is related to the type and grain of spaces and the type and density of the flow system, acting singly, plus the combined effect of the spatial and flow-system focal organizations. The matrix indicates that the size and pattern of the flow system are meaningless to the Ponians.

The analysis of all these separate points could then be carried through and the total balance struck, comparing the actual form of Pone with any other forms within the reach of this people. One might come out with some such conclusion as: Given these goals, the actual form is probably the optimum available, with the following modifications: (a) For the privacy objective, a new type of space should be substituted for the single-room adobe space. (b) For the defense objective, a better balance of size and density could be struck, particularly if the unused dust spaces were eliminated. Furthermore, if the capacity density of the flow system were increased and the system dispersed at finer grain throughout the settlement, then defense would be simplified. (c) For the production objective, an increase in flow capacity/density would also facilitate efficiency.

As was stated at the beginning, the high planners of Pone would also have gone on to a study of the consequences of the activity distribution in the city, and they would have ended with a higher-level study of the interrelation of activity and form.

EVALUATION

Application of this method to a modern metropolis would obviously be far more complicated and, necessarily, more frag-mentary. But the basic technique should still be applicable, though it would call for descriptions at a larger scale and goals less precisely formulated. Since the whole technique is analytical—a study of isolated parts—it will tend to give first approximations rather coarse conclusions bristling with "ifs," which would nevertheless be the elementary knowledge upon which much more refined and, in particular, much more fluid and integrated methods could be constructed.

To the student of the physical environment, perhaps the most attractive features of goal–form studies are the new pos-sibilities for research and theory. Regardless of the inadequacy of our present formulations, there is a need to test and explore both the range and appropriateness of form categories. Hardly any-thing is known of how they interact and what possibilities for substitution exist. And instead of fragmentary notions, such as the differentiation of traffic networks, the separation or mixing of land uses, and the organization of neighborhood units, there is the prospect of a general theory of urban form for the city as a whole. If some measure of success is achieved in developing such a general theory, it should not prove too difficult to fit these miscellaneous doctrines into this broader framework, especially since these doctrines purport to modify city form in line with some more or less definite objectives.

Goal-form studies also suggest a new lead for examining city-planning history. Instead of the traditional historical survey of civic-design accomplishments, the adequacy of urban forms might be examined in the light of some of the major goals of different cultures. The same approach might be applied with profit to current history. Inquiries into how adequately the goals are formulated and how explicitly they are related to the physical forms proposed may provide significant insights on contemporary plans for communities.

The essence of progress for most disciplines lies in finding ways of systematizing as well as extending present knowledge. Goal-form studies offer a springboard for city and regional planning to achieve this extension and synthesis.

But aside from the elegance or logic of the theoretical framework, such an analytical system may find its ultimate usefulness in providing the raw material for planning decisions. Eventually it should tell the planner: "If your only aim is productive efficiency, and if other elements are like this, and if your society does not change, then this form is the best one yet found to do the job." This is the underpinning for what must remain, in part, a complex art, an art still beyond the determinability of scientific knowledge in three ways: first, in that the more complex interactions are most likely to elude rigorous theory and depend on personal judgment; second, because the method is indifferent to the choice of values, and the choice or clarification of objectives is a fundamental part of the art of planning; and third, because the method can do no more than test form alternatives previously proposed. The creative task of imagining new form possibilities, as in all other realms of art and science, lies beyond it, although the analytical system in this work may be suggestive.

CHAPTER FIVE

Images of the City in the Social Sciences

WITH ROBERT HOLLISTER

The city is a palimpsest on which man's story is written.... It is a composite of trials and defeats, of settlement houses, churches and schoolhouses, of aspirations, images and memories. A city has values as well as slums, excitement as well as conflict;—a personality that has not yet been obliterated by its highways and gas stations;—a voice that speaks the hopes as well as the disappointments of its people.
—*Charles Abrams*

Two decades ago, Kevin Lynch began to transform thinking in the field of urban design by exploring images of the city held by different people. These differences—never systematically explored before—produced some fruitful research by Lynch and by a number of other people who were influenced directly and indirectly by the main lines of these investigations: in essence, by the differences between the images held by professionals and non-professionals (such as children, older people, women, and persons in different occupations); and by the differences in design and in psychological, sociological, anthropological, and other methods of conducting these studies and of interpreting the findings.[1]

Another neglected area of investigation is that of images of the city which writers in different disciplines and professional fields and policy discussions have developed over the past generation. Although there exists a substantial literature in several disciplines conveying images of the city, there has been no careful effort to identify and compare some of these images of the city in the social sciences. It is easy to conjure up plausible reasons for

61

this absence. The subject is elusive and methodologically frustrating. There is no common definition of "image," and there are
a frustratingly disparate set of meanings of "city." Aside from
these difficulties, there is the scholar's inclination to regard images as decorative or suggestive but of very limited and possibly
even of negative value for analysis or policy.

Although the difficulties are real, we are attracted by the
uncommon interest of the subject and the likely benefits of
greater knowledge about these matters. In our judgment,
Geertz's observations about symbols hold for images of the city,
too:

Although the general stream of social scientific theory has been deeply
influenced by almost every major intellectual movement of the last century and a half—Marxism, Darwinism, Utilitarianism, Idealism,
Freudianism, Behaviorism, Positivism, Operationalism—and has attempted to capitalize on virtually every important field of methodological innovation from ecology, ethology, and comparative psychology to
game theory, cybernetics, and statistics, [yet] it has, with very few exceptions, been virtually untouched by one of the most important trends
in recent thought: the effort to construct an independent science of what
Kenneth Burke has called "symbolic action."[2]

One way to explore these matters is to look at current examples of urban images in public-policy discussions. Another way is
to examine the image of the city as it has been developed by
writers in different disciplines and professional fields. We did
both: we tried to sort out the different ways of thinking about
urban images in public policy and the social sciences and to draw
some conclusions and tentative explanations about them. Our
efforts have been exploratory, and our findings at this stage are
quite tentative.

IMAGES OF THE CITY IN PUBLIC-POLICY DISCUSSIONS

The city itself is often summed up in a metaphor, and the
most trenchant of these metaphors generally reflect Picasso's dic-
tum that "art is a lie to tell a truth." They depict or caricature a

condition, a function, a trend, a problem, or an injustice. The idea of the educative city is made powerful not so much by the perceptive or witty or biting brief as by the unforgettable image of a "school without walls";[3] similarly powerful is a communications view of the city as an efficient switchboard "to enlarge the range and reduce the cost of individual and social choice";[4] or the biting view of the inner-core city as sandboxes to occupy people who would be nuisances or otherwise likely to get into trouble;[5] or the comparable characterization of inner cities as the equivalent of (Indian) reservations for the people and their guardians (and those profiting from their presence) who cannot function in the larger society.[6] Powerful, too, is the image of parasitic cities which perform no useful or essential functions;[7] or the neo-Marxian conceptualization of metropolitan (or imperial) power to characterize capitalist urban enclaves which exploit the population of their cities and their hinterlands in behalf of local or expatriate ruling groups;[8] or the shrewd manipulation of tough-minded, realistic, yet basically romanticized conceptions of the life and death of cities.[9]

So far as specific public-policy issues are concerned, there is abundant evidence that urban images often orient or influence public judgments as well as the judgments of opinion makers and scholars. By way of illustration, we cite below a few examples:

The New York City Financial Crisis of 1975

This crisis aroused both an intensely hostile and vigorously sympathetic public response. The images conjured by newspapers and political figures as they addressed the crisis exposed some of their distrust, dislike, even loathing, on the one hand, and attraction, admiration, or glorification, on the other. The *Daily News* printed the blunt headline, "Ford to City: Drop Dead." A West Coast politician opined that New York City "symbolizes a lot of things that are going wrong with the country." *Newsweek* reported a "coast-to-coast current of free-floating hostility" against New York.[10] The *Arizona Republic* railed against the "labor unions who've turned the New York City budget into their personal cornucopia" and "welfare beneficiaries who owe their idle way of life . . . to blindly generous City Hall spending." Countering the critics of New York as a center of avarice, profligacy, and corruption were others who heralded the city as a creative entrepot, as a traditional haven for the immigrant, the underprivileged, and the poor, or as the irreplaceable marketplace of ideas and goods, now in temporary difficulties partly because of mismanagement, partly because the city gave more than its fair share of revenue to serve the needs of the nation.

To be sure, the crisis itself was brought to a head by a complex mélange of problems—those that were budgetary and intergovernmental, as well as shifting population composition, a declining economic base, and issues of the quality and management of public services.[11] But the emotional reactions and debates which swirled around the policy options reflected also hostility to the big city, as well as conflicting beliefs about its appropriate functions and viability and the ultimate effects of its scale and values on people and the economy. The fact is that for many Americans, New York City symbolized what is wrong with modern cities, with the United States, with contemporary life. These deep feelings, organized as images, constrained the possibilities for national assistance; and—although the technical mechanisms of financial rescue or bail-out were the subject of protracted debate and negotiation among city, state, and national government—the need for public support for the outcome made it almost mandatory for the maneuvers to take the guise also of public chastisement, penance, tutelage, and rehabilitation.

Urban Decline, Maturity, or Revival

In the recent past, some scholars and policy makers have confidently predicted the declining economic functions of central cities; others have viewed the shifts of population and activities as evidence of the pace of the future—that is, more characteristic of maturity; and still more recently, some have expressed admiration or bemusement with regard to the commercial revival being enjoyed by several older United States cities.[12]

The assurance behind the pronouncements is intriguing because all of us know (although we infrequently behave as if we do) that prediction of trends is unusually hazardous in the social sciences, especially when the models are gross and aggregative, the data skimpy, and the relevance, behavior, and relative importance of particular variables unclear. These constraints are simple "ABC's" to knowledgeable urban scholars—especially in interpreting the impact of such phenomena as future changes in values and technology, the importance of face-to-face business contacts, the location of service activities, and the locational preferences of changing households—not to mention the character of future "externalities" and of "exogenous" factors such as the energy crunch. All of which reminds one of the sage observation of Spinoza that what we say generally tells us more about ourselves (and, we would add, our images of things) than about the subjects we presume to explain.

United States National Urban Policy

In early 1978, President Carter announced his long-awaited urban policy, followed by an ambitious legislative package to aid "cities and people in distress." A year later administration officials acknowledged that the policy was not really operational, and it ultimately was labeled a failure; it had become the subject of occasional "Whatever happened to... ?" follow-up media accounts.

Explanations for the fiasco vary. Analysts cite Carter's personal weakness as a leader; changed urban realities; competing political priorities, both international and domestic; and rivalries among federal departments and cabinet secretaries. No doubt these considerations were important. But successful policies generally require images that will appeal to the mind and the heart. Skeptics might contend that there was not enough substance behind the programs to do either. But we suggest that, in addition, the edge of public responsiveness was dulled to the symbols and vocabulary of urban crisis. In any case, it is a fact that the clichés of the administration about the diseased city failed to fire the imagination of anyone in or outside of the government, despite what appeared to be impressive potential public support for urban-policy initiatives.

This example is an instructive one for further exploration of urban images. Do new images reflect shifts in public mood or media demands for novelty? Or are they a product of fresh analysis and new understanding? In preparing the national urban policy, Carter administration officials documented continuing fiscal and human distress in central cities, seeking to sustain the Congressional (and popular) perception of crisis. Their product did not sell. In fact, to the alarm of federal officials, media accounts began to challenge the crisis analysis, either declaring that a crisis no longer existed or heralding the advent of an urban renaissance. One observer noted:

These articles were based on a thin thread of fact—the very limited reinvestment in selected older neighborhoods—plus a desire for novelty. HUD officials heard that the new image of an urban renaissance would kill their chances of getting interagency and Congressional support for measures to help the still-troubled central cities.[13]

The Department of Housing and Urban Development's response was to question the accuracy of the critical media accounts.[14] This strategy turned out to be a fine instance of the futility of using naked fact to do battle with an image. Regardless of how well or how poorly grounded it was in fact, the image of urban renaissance struck a responsive chord, whereas the image of urban crisis met with limp indifference.

The urban-policy debacle points up the challenges images pose for policy makers. Other responses might have been feasible. After all, crisis-mongering is only one way to build public support for policies designed to help still troubled central cities. Although the "renaissance city" was feared as a rationale for jettisoning present programs of central-city revival, it could also provide a social-psychological underpinning for popular confidence in the efficacy of maintaining federal urban programs.

IMAGES OF THE CITY IN VARIOUS PROFESSIONS AND DISCIPLINES

So much for some of the well-known public-policy discussions in the United States in which urban metaphors and other images have figured in different ways. But, as we have already noted, there exists a substantial literature in several disciplines—which go beyond these popular images of the city. Because the specialists in different fields tend to approach the problems of the city from distinct intellectual traditions, and with different concepts and tools, we invited several of them to participate in a seminar on this subject.[15] Their task was to spell out how images of cities have been presented in the fields they knew.

Before we discuss some of our findings, a word about the scope of our efforts is in order. The fields we examined included several branches of the social sciences—geography, economics, sociology, and political science; as well as some subfields or new fields—population studies, communications, and ecology; as well as the most centrally and directly concerned professional fields—urban design and city planning. In addition, we added two other categories of views—the perspectives of the Marxists and of the less-developed countries—because distinctive images and special literatures are emerging in these domains. On the other hand, we did not include several other appropriate fields such as law, anthropology, or the arts and humanities; and although we touched on history and literature in the seminar, we did not include them in our subsequent evaluation because we did not know how to characterize even roughly the image of the city of the historian and the writer.[16]

The responses varied greatly, as might have been expected, but they are of sufficient interest so that we are considering publishing some of them independently. For our purposes here, we are using the responses as general background information to help us summarize (below) the nature of these images and some of their more salient characteristics.

Issues of Definition

For better or worse, research about images of cities has proceeded without a clear definition of "image." In some respects, prevailing traditions of studying images in different disciplines have sharpened, but may also have limited, the apparent potential of such inquiry by focusing it too narrowly. For example, in urban planning, images of the city involve primarily visual image and environmental design; but in social science, images include concepts, ideas, similes, and metaphors.

The shorter Oxford English dictionary offers several shades of meaning of "image": a likeness; a mental representation of something, especially a visible object; a mental picture or impression, an idea, conception; a vivid or graphic description; a simile, metaphor, or figure of speech; an optical appearance or counterpart. For our present purposes, any of these definitions could indicate how people in different fields viewed or chose to characterize the city; but we deem it useful for our purposes to treat images and concepts as synonymous and to distinguish them from similes and metaphors, which we consider specific expressions of the more general urban images.

More specifically, by "image" we mean a *mental representation*—more than a fleeting picture—that significantly influences or structures thought or reflects the influence or structure of thought. Our use of the word "images" overlaps with meanings attached to "ideas," "views," "ideologies," or "models"; but our main focus is on the ways these concepts and images sum up the distinctive points of view of different modes or systematic ways of examining urban phenomena.

In retrospect, we could perhaps equally well entitle our review "Ideas of the City," but "images" is more apt because the term is used more broadly. Although "images" runs the risk of overemphasizing the visual, the mental processes of *visualizing* are more generally accessible to people than are, for example, the ascribed processes of metaphor. And this initial understanding of the role of images—in the sense of visualization—can be a solid building block for understanding images in the broader sense we are utilizing.

Urban Images of the Social Sciences

What were some of the images that emerged from the cross-disciplinary exploration that we organized? We cite 10 examples culled from the professional literature and from our seminar discussions.

1. *The numerical city.* Census and population specialists and some sociologists provided an easy starting point. They identify different types of cities by number, by statistical indicators which lead to analyses and inferences about activities, functions, behavior, values, and other matters. "SMSA" (Standard Metropolitan Statistical Areas), "census tract," and numerical magnitudes symbolize a scale and density of settlement and trigger mental associations with absolute size of population. Although census categories and demographers' classifications identify and help to explain urban phenomena, they have come to stand for the phenomena themselves, and sometimes even misrepresent these phenomena.

2. *Gravitational and hierarchical urban systems.* Geographers and regional scientists have produced at least three well-known images: gravity, central place, and hierarchy.[17] The gravitational metaphor, drawing directly on concepts of physics, led to the exploration of a large number of direct and inverse distance–population relationships between urban areas. The central-place image suggested a system as well as an array of cities which could be ordered in a variety of ways, particularly on the basis of market areas, size, function, and influence. All these images evidenced the direction of search for empirical regularities.

3. *Competitive urban systems.* From one perspective, cities are what they do; and what they do, from the point of view of economists, is to develop competitively viable basic activities in

strategic locations. This view is familiar enough: Who has not on occasion summoned up images of manufacturing, commercial, capital, or institutional cities and attempted to explain their origin? Appreciating these relationships is indispensable for understanding "what makes a city tick." Growth or decline of cities depends on whether the markets and/or the comparative advantage of the strategic location of these basic economic functions are being enhanced or lost, just what factors are responsible, and what can be done about them.[18]

Competition also accounts for the internal order of cities, at least to the extent that there is a market arena. Here, too, the key image involves those activities which can turn accessibility into a profit and can survive or prosper in the preferred locations with the resulting land-use patterns simply reflecting these preferences and capabilities.

4. *The city as turf, melting pot, and mold.* Quite different images of the city are employed by sociologists to account for similar as well as different phenomena. Thus, invasion and succession, a favorite metaphor of the "Chicago School" of sociologists, has been used to depict the changes in "turfs" of different groups and activities in the city.[19] Still other images have been emphasized to interpret changes in behavior and social characteristics. For example, sociologists attach far more importance today to the "molding" of behavior by the social and cultural systems of different urban groups than to the previously accepted image of the dissolution of ethnic and cultural systems by the urban melting pot.[20]

5. *The juridical, the efficient, and the unheavenly city.* Still other images have evolved in the analyses of urban government and urban political behavior. First came the shift in the older conception of the *juridical entity* to the *managerial-service view* of a public enterprise: the former was concerned with the appropriate territory for the discharge of its functions; the latter (akin to a large private firm) focused on efficient planning and management. This perception was later followed by the close-up view of the pluralistic cleavages within the real, not altogether heavenly, city—with tough-minded realists translating the con-

flicts of interest into a struggle to control rule making and the bureaucracy, and cynics highlighting, in particular, the violation of the rules, the ugly infighting, and the increasing problems of governability.[21]

6. *The city as communications collage.* The transformation of the urban designer's image of the city was no less striking. The perceptions as well as the aims of the traditional designer turned out to have negligible relevance to what people saw and liked. Many factors contributed to this shock of recognition. One of the more important was the sudden realization that almost no one really knew or cared—until Lynch reported the results of his initial research findings—how people of different social and economic backgrounds and of different occupations, ages, and cultures saw or interpreted the city; or if they did know or care, they saw no way of doing something about it.[22]

Another development contributing to the change in perceptions was the rejection by Venturi and his postmodernist colleagues of the aesthetic norms of contemporary design and his fulsome praise for the "vulgar" vernacular of Las Vegas. In manipulating symbols to communicate with urban residents, the postmodernist designers view the city as an eclectic communications façade.[23] No one is quite certain what the new look of the "collage" city might ultimately be, but it bids fair, at the very least, to be both a rejection of many of the values of current design and an effort to understand and react to how different people do in fact apprehend their urban environment and the ways in which they attach meaning to it.[24]

7. *The city as habitat for the urban organism or the urban consortium.* The urban planner's conception of the city evolved quite differently, albeit in the same direction taken by the city designer. The earlier conception viewed the city as an organism requiring a habitat of appropriate space, forms, and services to serve its needs. In this view, only the professional planner understood the critical needs and interrelationships; and only the planner could diagnose resultant problems and prescribe plans to ensure efficient, attractive, and comprehensive environmental solutions. But this view has been successfully challenged and is in

the process of being supplanted by the conception of the city as—in effect—a very loose consortium of interests and clients (with changing membership and powers) whose views will (and should) control the making or implementing or changing of the physical arrangements for their habitat.[25]

8. *The city as a resource-conserving ecosystem.* The shift in the focus from the urban designer and the planner to their social clients, actual or neglected, did not take place without some discomfiture for the physical planners. It led to the downgrading of their roles and (it appeared for a time) even to the downgrading of the relative importance attached to the organization of the physical environment. Ecologists, however, arrested the wholesale retreat from environmentalism with their images of a fragile, delicately balanced resource base and physical setting unable to sustain profligate urban growth or pollution of various kinds. These trends, in their scenario, not only imposed high social costs but threatened the sustainability of life as well as the functioning of the urban system. However, such was the indecisiveness of our knowledge of what was necessary to avoid these outcomes that it was still possible for ecologists to favor big cities or decentralized cities, or even an "urban civilization without cities." Of all of these varying perspectives, the most systematic and comprehensive was Meier's picture of the resource-conserving cities, which was based on the assumption that in the future knowledge would serve increasingly as a substitute for resources. In Meier's words, the metropolis must be "a self-repairing, homeostatic social reactor that can, when necessary, obtain from its hinterland or from other cities whatever it needs in the way of natural and human resources," in order to conserve and add to the general stock of knowledge which "constitute[s] the ultimate output of civilization."[26]

9. *Primate, overurbanized, and exploitative cities.*[27] In many quarters (not only in the less-developed countries) there was outright hostility to "primate" and overurbanized cities (in terms of functions, available jobs, densities, and/or relative allocations of public services) and resentment for what was considered their inevitable corollary—stunted urban systems and lagging regions

elsewhere. Despite the fact that the images were obscure and controversial,[28] for the field of regional planning and development the technical problem appeared to be what, if anything, should be done to offset the advantages of concentrated purchasing power in these big cities and the allure of their more varied public services and wider job and social opportunities. But there is as yet no consensus among the reformers whether this requires (a) more effective strategies for decentralized concentrations of urban and regional development; (b) measures to combat urban bias; (c) the encouragement of appropriate technology and support of the more traditional, neglected, "informal" urban or rural sectors; or (d) something far more ambitious—the establishment of "a new international order."

10. *The socialist city.* Marx deliberately avoided spelling out his image of the socialist future; and so there is no clear "Marxian" image of the future socialist city. But the contempt of Marx (and of Marxists) for the "idiocy" of the countryside reinforced the determination of key Soviet leaders to squeeze savings from agriculture in order to industrialize the country as well as to industralize and collectivize agriculture. The latter was hardly a conspicuous success. And the bold notions of some Soviet planners (explored in the decade or so after the Russian Revolution) of decentralizing and reorganizing the form of the city withered away with limited resources and as the party clamped down on unorthodox views. In China, where rural and small-town bias appeared ineradicably entrenched and a policy of containment, if not ruralization, of the great cities appeared to be in the offing, a major reversal appears to be in the process of occurring with the death of Mao. The impulse for urban transformation has not disappeared, but it is no longer one of the more visible, "privileged" items on the national agenda. So—at least in the two mammoth realms where feudal capitalism had collapsed and revolutionary Marxism came to power—the form as well as the image of cities ended up to be, if anything, more conventional than elsewhere.[29] No doubt this eventuality was reinforced by the severe housing shortages and limited resources. But when more resources became available and the pressures to build could be satisfied, the

building and other policies led in the main to a mushrooming of high-rise flats, and a sameness (as well as drabness) of "look" in most socialist countries—which at any rate conformed to the prevailing rhetoric of equalization.

SOME CONCLUSIONS AND TENTATIVE EXPLANATIONS

Summing up our first round of investigation, what can we say, in general, about these urban images?

Scope and Function

At present, we have no adequate model or conceptual framework to help us to explore systematically the critical elements and common denominators of different urban images; and until we make some progress in developing appropriate models we must hobble along with somewhat coarse, ad hoc categories. Meanwhile, we simply observe that the urban images we have examined have dealt with some of the features of the city listed below:

1. *Urban trends and perspectives:* Urban evolution (worldwide and for different subnational, national, and world regions); the significance of these trends for individuals, groups, organizations, cultural development, innovation, etc.
2. *Urban characteristics, functions, and behavior:* Systems and subsystems of cities; their sizes, hierarchy, functions, and patterns of influence; strategic linkages and interactions within and between cities.
3. *Urban sectoral activities and interactions:* Public services, transportation, housing, industrial and other land uses, etc.
4. *Urban control and governance:* Leadership, influence, management, control, and power in cities.
5. *Urban "look":* How cities are perceived and understood, and by whom and why.

6. *Urban inequities and problems:* Who is benefited and
   disadvantaged within cities; how and why

With reference to these features, the images themselves,
even the small selection we have examined, have an enormous
scope. The reasons are understandable enough. Urban images do
not simply mirror, they interpret an extraordinarily complex reality, and very often quite different features of that reality. They
also provoke controversy when the interpretations are considered distorted, wrong, or otherwise unacceptable. The urban
images we have examined deal with different urban subsystems
(gravitational, hierarchical, competitive or economic, social,
political, and physical); with different functions (habitat, communications, melting pot); with different roles (educative,
exploitative, parasitic); with different governmental or developmental processes (juridical, managerial, bargaining or growth,
maturity, decline); and with different focuses on physical elements (physical form as well as perceptions and attributed meanings). But the images also mirror differences of interpretation of
the urban phenomena: for example, the shift from melting pot to
mould; from the legitimacy and relevance of elite to that of none-
lite perceptions; and from an emphasis on managerial to bargaining and infighting processes for urban policy making.

What must be emphasized is that each of these images was
employed by some well-known analyst to sum up what a city
does, or is thought to do, from the point of view of *the* central
subject matter, or *a* central subject matter, of his field. All these
images—whether technical or popular, visual or analytical,
positivistic or normative, persuasive, perceptive, or neither—are
essentially characterizations of, or theses about, strategic features
of the city. Each is intended to underline or to clarify critical
functions, neglected problems, or directions for policy. And our
list, of course, is hardly exhaustive.

The Prospects for a Synoptic Image

We know more today about cities than ever before, but we
do not have an image, or synthesis, of all of the disparate ele-

ments, one which illumines and goes beyond the components. We are probably not ready for such a synthesis; and perhaps it is not even possible or desirable. A quarter of a century ago Robert Oppenheimer argued against the expectation that science would be all the more "deep and important if only it could be made relevant to our time, our life, the human problems generally; if only it could be brought back intact and integral into the common knowledge of man."[30] Instead of "architecture of global scope," Oppenheimer anticipated more numerous but limited syntheses in the world of science, more "dining together" at the interfaces of different fields leading to "an immense intricate network of intimacy, illumination and understanding."[31] In this world, he argued, everything could not be connected with everything, but "everything could be connected with anything." Perhaps this also applies to the contemporary images of urbanism.

Popular, Literary, and Social-Science Images

At first blush, the urban images of the social sciences seem to have little in common with popular and literary images. Throughout urban history there have been mixed popular attitudes to the city. For many persons, the city has meant escape, variety, sophistication, modernity, opportunity; for others, loss of roots, anomie, dependence, vice, poverty, congestion, and corruption. Louis Wirth summed up the ambivalence well by observing that

the city has become indispensable to civilized existence, but at the same time subjects man to so many frustrations of his deepest longings [that] the notion of an ideal mode of life lying somewhere between the two extremes has been a force ever since cities have been in existence.[32]

Novelists, too, have often contrasted these pastoral ideals and antipathies; and literary scholars have assiduously documented the different varieties of pastoralism, and of urban romanticism and revulsionism. These scholars have led other disciplines toward the importance of examining not only explicit statements of attitude toward cities, but also the sentiments embedded in the structure and form of creative expressions.

In apparent contrast, social-science studies have taken two forms: analyses of how the interrelated urban systems function, and analyses of the effects of possible or proposed changes. The former try to sidestep explicit value judgments; the latter presumably go beyond a brief and do not necessarily involve a commitment to a particular policy. Yet we know that implicit in most social sciences are inescapable values which influence what is studied and what is taken for granted, how evidence is evaluated and how conclusions are arrived at. And few persons doubt that many, if not most, of the controversies—such as the pros and cons of different sizes for cities; rural versus urban bias; or the issues of migration, urbanization, and the flight from or the return to the city—as well as a host of other subjects, reflect these varying inclinations and mental sets.

The "Collage" Urban Image of the Social Sciences

Even if we concede these powerful influences, the fact remains that the aim of the social sciences is to increase knowledge and understanding and to temper emotional reactions and judgments through more rigorous analyses, methods, and data. How much the social sciences may have succeeded is still uncertain; but they have rechanneled questions about the city into three directions: (1) tracing more specifically what is happening through macro and micro studies; (2) identifying underlying systems or subsystems and by, analysis of interrelationships of components, showing how things work (behavior); (3) reformulating and evaluating problems, models, and policies and predicting trends and consequences of exogenous changes.

From this point of view, the major changes of image introduced by social science are the broadening of the perception of the phenomenon of urbanization, and the deepening of the understanding of the mechanisms and processes involved in urbanization, in the functioning of cities and urban systems, and in their broader sociopolitical and structural relationships.

The Worldwide and National Urban Image

In addition, there appears to be increasingly a shift in the view of both scholars and policy makers of the scope and character of urban problems and the need to do something about them. The current image—quite novel in historical perspective—is that urban problems are not just short-term, sectoral, and local, but long-term, multisectoral, and worldwide, and national and even megapolitan in scale; also, that international organizations as well as national governments will often have to help cities to strengthen their economies and upgrade the quality of their public services and environment; and that assistance for nonservice policies (e.g., use of taxation and eminent-domain powers) as well as sectoral service programs (e.g., transportation, housing, welfare, education, or other public services) must be given within an area-wide and international policy framework. In short, the image of the city is no longer one of local political entities coping with a limited number of relatively routine land-use and growth problems but rather more in the nature of quasiautonomous public entities serving as administrative vehicles for the realization of many complex national, international, as well as local aims.

PART TWO

The Metropolis and New Communities in the United States

CHAPTER SIX

Problems of the Metropolis

Changing Images and Realities

CHANGING PERCEPTIONS OF METROPOLITAN PROBLEMS: THE 1950s AND THE 1970s

What is striking about current perceptions of the problems of the metropolis in the more-developed countries are the ways in which they differ *in emphasis* from the notions held on these matters only 25 years ago. In the main, the perceptions are less naïve, perhaps less optimistic, and certainly less one-dimensional. Consider some characteristics:

1. The issues are no longer seen largely as growth problems associated with economic and population expansion, but also as retrenchment problems associated with decreases in population, economic activities, and the tax base.

2. They involve not only problems *of the metropolis*—of functions and land uses (in inner and regional areas) of public services, transportation, housing, and community facilities—but problems of people *within the metropolis*—of crime, social welfare, and social conflict.

3. They are broader than former concerns about slums and blight, for they have been refocused to embrace areawide problems involving the quality of life and of the environment.

4. They involve pressures to ensure not only more explicit metropolitan and national roles in coping with the problems of the metropolis, but also to produce more decentralization, autonomy, and participation in the decision-making process.

The problems have still another common denominator: the changes in relationships stemming from the recent downward

trends in population growth and economic activity of the great
metropolises in the United States, Western Europe, and Japan.
That is what will be examined here in a number of different
contexts: between and within regions, between central and local
governments, between local governments in the metropolitan
region, and between key actors and decision makers and the poor
and disadvantaged.

THE CONVERGENCE OF DOWNWARD ECONOMIC AND
POPULATION TRENDS

Shifting Economic Functions

A metropolis grows (at least in our culture) when it is a
relatively favorable place to produce goods and services, and is
simultaneously a satisfying place for people to live and to enjoy
themselves; and it loses economic activities and population when
these circumstances no longer hold. The growing importance of
market-oriented activities during the first half of the nineteenth
century gave the metropolises of Western Europe and the
United States—particularly the economic and political
capitals—what appeared to be almost unassailable additional advantages. Aside from a favorable location and the advantages of a
head start, these included a large labor force and skilled manpower; public and private services; increasing capital and credit;
a variety of economic opportunities; a milieu stimulating to enterprise and innovation; the seductive appeal of success; great
concentrations of purchasing power; and a rich array of shops and
of cultural and recreational resources.

These characteristics obtained in varying degrees for most
metropolitan areas—some of which served mainly their regions,
others a national market, and a very few of which operated on an
international scale. There were, to be sure, ailing or lagging
regions and metropolitan centers—often poorly located in relation to the new markets and bogged down with declining
activities—where special policies appeared necessary to amelio-
rate the conditions. In general, these policies involved some ap-

propriate mix of the following ingredients: (a) the promotion of investments and special activities linked to the human- or natural-resource endowment; (b) the improvement of the infrastructure; and (c) the encouragement of movement of resources to areas of greater economic opportunity. What needs to be underlined, however, is that the problem areas—within the metropolis and in the lagging regions outside of the metropolis—were considered marginal concerns: no doubt painful to the groups involved, and certainly expensive to deal with, but likely to work themselves out in time with sufficient subsidies and patience.

However, a new trend appears to have emerged in the United States, Western Europe, and Japan, consisting not only of a slowing down of economic growth within the metropolis, but also of a decline of economic activities and a loss of jobs in some of the great metropolitan centers and capital cities, which occurred more quickly and drastically than policy-makers had anticipated. The ultimate dimensions and implications of the changes are only now being analyzed, but it is increasingly clear that the difficulties and challenges associated with these trends are likely, because they affect the main economic centers and capital cities, to be critical problems of the metropolis of the future.

Ironically enough (for planners at least), the changes in these patterns of metropolitan economic growth should not be new or surprising, for they have been developing for several decades. They involve, first of all, a steady decline in the growth of manufacturing activities. For example, the changes between 1967 and 1976 in manufacturing and total employment in 32 large cities in the United States indicated

that manufacturing, the prototypical basic industry, is no longer the pacemaker in metropolitan employment growth. There is no case where manufacturing jobs increased at a faster rate than total jobs, and no case where manufacturing jobs declined less than total jobs.[1]

Second, there has been a secular shift of these activities—away from central cities and even from metropolitan areas—to other regions.

Third, there is some additional shift outward of a portion of the service activities, particularly retail and wholesale trade, certain business and consumer services, and even some corporate headquarters. This shift is of great concern, because the growth of these service activities, particularly the FIRE group (finance, insurance, and real estate) was counted on to offset the drop in manufacturing employment.

In Western Europe, unlike the United States, the bulk of these relocations are occurring in peripheral areas and in small communities within 40 to 50 miles from the main metropolises;[2] also, some of these changes have been planned as part of an explicit national urban policy. But the view is now spreading that the rate of the outward movement has gone much further and more precipitously than anticipated.[3]

For example, the five largest cities in Britain—London, Birmingham, Manchester, Liverpool, and Glasgow—have experienced substantial losses in manufacturing and some losses in service jobs. (Greater London alone has lost a half-million jobs since 1961, a large portion of the losses owing to plant closure, and not simply to outward movement.)[4] The drop in employment and revenue is causing considerable inner-city unemployment as well as difficulty for the cities in maintaining public services. Some observers say that Amsterdam, Brussels, Stockholm, possibly even Paris, and other older West European cities may face a similar situation.

In the United States, the process has gone further, even in the absence of an explicit decentralization policy. A large percentage of the relocation of firms was to areas well outside the boundaries of the metropolises in the northeast, north-central, and western regions, to smaller nonmetropolitan areas, or to metropolitan areas in other regions, particularly the South and Southwest. New York City's problems were especially severe, with a 40% drop in manufacturing employment between 1967 and 1976. The city lost not only 43,000 manufacturing jobs per year, but also 30,000 service jobs per year between 1969 and 1974.[5] The trends were similar (although not quite as dramatic) in Philadelphia, Baltimore, Buffalo, Pittsburgh, and other cities.

In Japan, too, a decentralization of economic activity and the relocation of investment to less-developed areas and regions outside the congested Pacific belt (and particularly the Tokaido megalopolis) seems to have taken hold in the early 1970s, or perhaps even earlier.[6] However, these trends have been less prominent because of the very high rate of national economic growth.

Shifting Population Trends

Changes in the patterns of population growth are an additional complex and critical component which both causes and reinforces the above trends. An almost unquestioned premise in the 1950s and 1960s was the need to do something about the increased growth and densities of the great metropolitan regions. Imagine, then, the stunning surprise of finding mounting evidence not only of a declining rate of growth but also of a decline in total population, not just in the inner areas but in most or all of the territory of the giant metropolitan areas. This proved to be the case in the United States, parts of Western Europe, and possibly Japan, and it constituted a reversal which the efforts of the metropolitan planners had little to do with. Indeed, it stems from several interacting and converging trends, the basis for which has yet to be explained adequately.

With regard to population trends, too, the evidence concerning their secular character extends back over the past half-century or more. In the past, there were some plausible push-and-pull explanations for the out-migration of firms and families: encroaching business, a deteriorating environment, the anticipation of an eventual shift or a succession of more intensive uses, lower rents, more space, a higher-quality environment in the outer areas, etc. These explanations were persuasive as long as the population of both the metropolitan region and the areas directly adjacent to the boundaries of the metropolis expanded. These increases in population supported the view that the losses in some areas of the region were, in reality, shifts in location within the metropolitan region, and that the dominant attractions of the metropolis—its purchasing power, personal contacts, basic services, variety, and accessibility—would sustain its general growth and its role as a center for innovations of new activities. But what is arresting about the new trends is that the population losses in the aggregate hold for the entire metropolitan area, including a generous portion of the areas adjacent to the conventional boundaries of the metropolis.

More specifically, previous migrations of the metropolitan population to outer areas or elsewhere were offset by relatively high birth rates and substantial migrations from rural or other areas, so that metropolitan areas grew at the same or at a larger rate than the national average. Now, however, the reduction of both birth rates and migration from rural areas seems to be the case for most of the largest cities in the more-developed countries. In Japan, for example, the century-long shift of population toward the Pacific coast of central Honshu has dropped precipitously from 430,000 persons (net) in 1970 to 9,000 (net) in 1976.[7] In Sweden, all three metropolitan regions experienced negative or next-to-negative net in-migration from other regions by 1970.[8] In the United States, 25% of all metropolitan areas were losing population, and over half of the country's metropolitan dwellers lived in areas of population decline.[9] Indeed, 11 of the 18 countries studied by Vining and Kontuly (Japan, Sweden, Italy, Norway, Denmark, New Zealand, Belgium, France, West Germany, East Germany, and the Netherlands) showed either a reversal in the direction of net population flow from periphery to core, or a drastic reduction in the level of this net flow.[10]

To be sure, there are many metropolitan areas which are expanding and which will continue to expand in the future. But the convenient assumption of the past—that movements outside the metropolis would be offset by new population recruits and higher birth rates of migrants in the most fertile age brackets—is less likely to be the case for an increasing number of metropolitan areas in the future, particularly the largest ones. What is more, natural growth trends are likely to reinforce the decline of migration from rural areas because the migrants are predominantly young; therefore an area "experiencing positive net in-migration will see its age distribution shift towards the younger or more fertile age groups."[11]

In the United States, the reduction of the natural population increase by about two-thirds (i.e., from 1.6% per year to 0.6%), and the concurrent reduction of increase by migration to one-ninth of the total population increase, is pointing up the secular pattern of sustained out-migration from the metropolitan areas.[12] Alonso observes that "in the 1960's nearly 40 percent of the metropolitan areas of the United States had more people leaving than arriving. By 1974, 44 percent of the metropolitan areas had net outmigration."[13] Most of the population shifts, however, are not to rural areas but to other metropolitan areas or to communities in the hinterlands of the giant metropolis. What appears to be happening—in the main by the action of market forces—is a shift of population and economic activities to other areas, or what a recent Japanese study has characterized as "dispersed concentration,"[14] and the result seems to be what some planners have advocated, namely, concentrated decentralization. But there are also some interesting growth trends even in the least urbanized and more remote nonmetropolitan regions which have yet to be adequately explained.

Impact of Convergence

As already mentioned, losses of economic activities were not a critical problem for the metropolises of the past. There were always declining and expanding activities as well as new firms taking the place of those failing. Metropolises functioned like large, diversified firms, constantly dropping less profitable activities and taking on new ones. The ability to offer incentives and stimuli to firms and individuals with entrepreneurial and innovative capabilities is one of the undisputed strengths of the metropolis. What distinguishes the new trends is a widening "vicious circle" of negative pressures and an increasingly inflexible set of constraints which limit effective responses. The key factors are rising costs for households and firms and a deteriorating environment over a larger part of the metropolis, coupled with lower

costs and a more attractive environment elsewhere. With far
fewer firms and families taking up the slack created by the departures, the gap substantially increases inner-city unemployment
and slashes the revenues necessary to maintain even basic services, let alone those required to reverse or retard the process.
Reductions of services, higher taxes, and powerful union resistance to wage cuts only hastened the outflow.

In the past, the forces which decreased the need to be in the
center of the metropolis, or even within its boundaries, had limited impact as long as many firms and many people had strong
incentives or inclinations to remain there. But these incentives
and inclinations are being attenuated by the mounting concerns
about increases of crime and about problems of pollution and
environmental quality; and by the preference for more space,
better schools, more attractive surroundings, and preferred
neighbors (not to mention the fear in some countries of racial and
ethnic conflict). With these departures, the central city—the traditional haven of the poor, the unskilled, the rural migrants, the
minorities, the foreign-born, and the disadvantaged—has begun
to accommodate these groups in relatively greater numbers than
in the past and at far lower densities; and this change has been
facilitated by the relatively larger welfare payments in the big
cities.

One result is that the slum pockets of the past have expanded into broad swaths of poverty and depressed working-class
areas—further spurring the outward movements of moderate-
and middle-income families. Still another consequence (which is
seen principally in the eastern-seaboard metropolitan areas of the
United States, but is visible also in London and Liverpool) is the
abandonment of housing and other structures taking up substantial areas of the central city. Early warning signals about the
problems of finding future uses for these expanding "gray areas"
were detectable more than a quarter of a century ago—perhaps
the most well-known were the studies of the New York metropolitan region by Professor Raymond Vernon and his
associates[15]—but there were no easy solutions available, and
there was no visible crisis spurring officials to act. The problems,

after all, were the problems of success—problems generated by rising income and rising standards for many moderate- and even low-income families—which were worsened by the ease with which the disadvantages of the central city could be avoided simply by moving.

No doubt the specific character and relative gravity of these trends vary significantly in different countries and in different metropolitan areas within the same country. Much will depend on multiple variables, including (a) the composition of the economic base; (b) the quality of local leadership and management; (c) institutional arrangements for financing particular services (for example, welfare and education), (d) the national policies for income maintenance and employment; and (e) the specific policies for housing, transportation, etc. Nonetheless, variations of these general trends are now quite visible and likely to become more so. Great Britain, for example, decided in September of 1976 to reverse its policy favoring decentralization from London, and is now trying to reverse the outward flow.[16] The sustained financial crisis of New York City and the bankruptcy of Cleveland in December of 1978 have dramatized the consequences for some cities in the United States. If these trends persist, there is likely to be a reassessment of metropolitan policy in growing and "unwinding" cities in many of the major regions of the world.

Let us now consider the implications of the above-mentioned changes for (1) local diagnosis and action, (2) the role of national policy, (3) the issues of metropolitan organization, and (4) the possible discrepancies between the aims and values of planners and the needs of the underprivileged.

PROBLEMS AND IMPLICATIONS

Local Diagnosis and Action

Surely one of the most difficult problems posed by these trends will be the recasting of attitudes about the great metropolises. Only a quarter of a century ago metropolitan planners felt that the high-priority problems were how and where growth

should occur, and how much growth was desirable. Their focus
was on such matters as land uses; appropriate densities; internal
patterns of physical development; the efficient movement of
goods and services; methods of organizing or influencing the
growth of outer areas through national policy; the most appropriate or feasible means of organizing metropolitan and intramet-
ropolitan government; and planning, scheduling, financing, and
coordinating the necessary investments for water, roads, schools,
housing, and other infrastructure and public-service requirements. There were other concerns as well, such as the costs of
welfare and the problems of blight and of poverty areas; but these
problems, however important, were not considered critical elements affecting the future of the city—on the contrary, they were
dealt with as the flotsam and jetsam of development. The principal intent behind all these efforts was to enhance the efficiency,
the amenities, and the general "look" of the metropolis, subject
to a stiff set of constraints; that is, to do so in a way that would
augment revenues and simultaneously not hurt (and perhaps
even help) poor and disadvantaged residents.

Now the tide has turned, or so it appears. The surge of
growth in population and economic activities has ended, at least
for the next decade or two, and perhaps longer. But it is too early
to gauge the contours and impact of the new trends. There is a
wide consensus that their outcomes will be greatly influenced by
the nature and location of the growth in the service activities. On
this score, however, opinions vary.[17] The more pessimistic
analysts think large reductions in employment are likely, because
of (a) the huge losses of population and therefore of income and
purchasing power in the metropolis; (b) the probable continua-
tion of the outward shift of retail and wholesale trade and of many
business and consumer services; (c) the growing pressures to cut
local "public sector" budgets; and (d) the expectation that more
and more "brain" and service jobs can be handled in other areas,
because of extraordinary progress in information processing and
telecommunications. The more optimistic analysts think that
with rising income, there are likely to be many new activities and
jobs in the knowledge-based and learning industries: in the new

health, learning, and other paraprofessional services, and in the arts and related cultural services.

Whether the pessimists or optimists prove right will depend on the relative importance of these diverse trends in different metropolitan areas. In any case, we can expect many studies of the expanding activities in these metropolitan areas to the end of ensuring that the reasonable requirements of these expanding activities are met; we can also expect many studies of more marginal activities, which might find it advantageous to stay in the metropolitan areas if their reasonable requirements were met. The odds are, however, that even if all which should be done is done, there will be fewer people and reduced economic activity in the older metropolitan areas for the next two or three decades, and perhaps for a much longer period.

Of course, we have always known that at some point the largest metropolises could develop enough negative features—relative to other locations—which could in turn generate a downward trend in population and economic activity; but there was no agreement on when these "negative externalities" would reverse the net balance of growth and of real income. We now appear to have reached the threshold at which many great metropolitan areas are experiencing declining growth, but still have higher-than-average income as well as rising real income. To a large extent, the maintenance of these income levels occurs because the population of many of the older and larger metropolises receives a significant portion of its revenues from property income and transfer payments.[18]

No one can predict with certainty what the future holds. There is, however, good reason to believe that despite the outflow of firms and families, most of the great metropolitan areas will display great resiliency because of their exceptional assets: their location and infrastructure, their high income potential, their wide range of services. Even with due recognition of these elements of strength, there is no escaping the fact that there is a vast drop in demand (and in some cases no demand) for many of the buildings—residential, commercial, and industrial—from which the families and firms have departed. In comparison with other alternatives, these structures have inferior locations and their costs—economic and social—are too high. According to the traditional "competition of use" doctrine, the household or income-producing activity which could extract the highest satisfaction or returns from use of the site should pay for it and get it: other things being equal, this would be the most efficient means of allocating land uses. Whatever one may think of the doctrine, the poor—both families and firms—are getting many of these buildings at prices they can manage, often in carved-up, run-down, and inferior condition because of previous conversions and overcrowding. These changes in the structure and the nature of occupancy may change the quality of the unit and the neighborhood, and may reduce its price to levels that can be afforded by the new users; and where the demand exists, the modifications can often generate enough income to cover maintenance costs, taxes, fixed charges, and in some cases may even yield handsome returns.

There are many buildings, however, which nobody wants—not unless prices and values tumble drastically, or subsidies are available; however, even these inducements are sometimes insufficient. These unwanted houses, factories, and warehouses are being closed and boarded up; some are being abandoned and vandalized—stripped of almost anything of any value which can be removed by scavengers. Often, subsequent razing of these structures is not even worth the expense, for it means throwing "good money after bad."

There is no question that one of the highly visible problems for the declining older metropolitan areas will be what to do about these areas. There are no easy answers. One possibility is to do nothing: simply to wait until a new demand appears; and if for some areas this is a very long wait indeed, so be it: why risk significant resources trying to reverse deep-seated trends?

Another possibility is to analyze the problem areas with some care. They are not homogeneous. They vary in their locations, their infrastructures, the character of the surrounding areas, and the values and characteristics of the local population. Some are best left alone, for they will develop their own regenerative processes: for example, imaginative conversions of some of the more accessible abandoned factories and warehouses into exciting residential, office, commercial, and entertainment facilities. There are already many instances (in London and Paris as well as in Boston, New York, and Washington, D.C.) where this has occurred. Still other areas and structures might be left as is—serving the needs of marginal or new firms at relatively low rents. Some might be rescued or restored for housing by a combination of neighborhood-conservation, "sweat equity," and development strategies linked with modest improvements in community facilities and public services.

Still other structures are in areas that might lend themselves, either now or in the future, to more extensive uses: new public parks, new versions of Tivoli Gardens, and perhaps in-town vacation areas, golf courses, rural retreats, airports for small planes or whatever else might be appropriate. In a very few cases there might be bold public enterprises; but in most circumstances, it may be wise, as William W. Wurster once suggested with regard to paths in university grounds, not to create them until one has seen where people prefer to go, and whenever possible, to let them be created by the people themselves.

The Role of National Urban Policy

The recognition of the new realities facing the mature metropolis in the United States, Western Europe, and Japan is bound to produce new pressures and alliances, as well as a rethinking of many of the problems and policies now affecting metropolitan areas. The outcome will be new or greatly modified national urban policies.

Take, for example, the differences between inter- and intra-regional movements of population and economic activities. The former will be welcomed—at least nationally. Reduction of inequalities of income between regions has been one of the major development aims of most countries for several decades. This effort is still an important one, even though it has constituted less of a problem in more-developed countries (for example, the

United States, Western Europe, and Japan) than in Third World countries largely because these inequalities tended to decline in the more-developed countries once certain thresholds of economic development were achieved.[19] Even if some of the more economically advanced areas and regions are adversely affected, there would have to be some solid evidence of national disadvantage before policy makers could be induced to do something to counter the dramatic growth now occurring in the formerly "stagnant" or lagging regions, such as the South and Southwest of the United States. At some point, no doubt, a review of the national policies and actions now favoring the formerly lagging regions against the more "mature" regions is bound to occur; and the outcome of this debate is apt to be influenced more by sectional coalitions and regional politics than by planning—which is perhaps as it should be.

On the other hand, the continued spread of the actual metropolitan regions, as well as the movements of firms and families outside the corporate jurisdiction of the central cities to neighboring jurisdictions within the region, involves well-known fiscal problems associated with fixed boundaries and institutional arrangements. The nature and relative gravity of the problems vary in different countries. The problems appear to be less acute (but still serious) in Britain, France, and possibly Japan, when compared to the situations in the United States, the Netherlands, and West Germany. This is because the former countries have expanded the jurisdiction of their local governments and have also relied more heavily on transfer payments and/or corporate rather than local property taxes.[20] It is not at all certain, however, that this problem will or must be dealt with—as formerly supposed by many metropolitan planners and specialists in local government—by extending government boundaries or by some form of metropolitan or regional federalism, for reasons we shall consider in more detail shortly.

But as the mature metropolitan areas experience increasing financial difficulties because of boundary issues, there will be sharp questions raised about the indirect effects of national sectoral policies on the inner and outer areas of the metropolitan region. The experience of the United States offers one of the most dramatic examples of how independently formulated housing-finance and road-building programs facilitated outward movement to the outer areas of the metropolitan region, and also facilitated the avoidance of problems of poverty and crime in the inner areas.[21] Wherever there are such policies favoring the outer areas against the inner areas, there are sure to be powerful pressures and conflicts in the future to change them. The pressures will take many forms: to facilitate the rehabilitation or conversion of existing housing in the inner areas; to make commuting by car more expensive; to devote more resources to crime prevention and detection, including, especially in the United States, the development of youth- and other special-employment and family-income tax-maintenance programs. How successful such policies may be, once agreed on, is another matter. It is always possible that raising the price of commuting and stressing the need for conservation of energy may (in cases where the process of development in the outer areas is well advanced) only make the peripheral communities more self-contained, and even less of a direct contributor to the sales volume and tax revenues of the central city.

Sooner or later, these issues will find expression in national fiscal policy for one basic reason: the local options—cutting services and costs, increasing taxes and productivity, or obtaining a share of national revenues—are so limited![22] Without doubt, most mature metropolitan areas will be under great pressure to cut or stabilize services and to spend less. But this course is quite risky: it may indeed be necessary, but it will run into great resistance. Similarly, raising taxes may make sense in countries and metropolitan areas where the local tax shares are low, and where local power and independence are limited. But this option, too, is politically unpalatable in most countries. There is a good chance that both options, however unpalatable, may have to be employed, but their initial effects may only further accelerate the outward movement.

There will also be powerful incentives to increase productivity, and many persons will applaud this possibility. But this is a severely limited option for the local public sector, especially where there are strong union organizations. Success may also impose a high price on some groups: for example, the local public sector is often an opportunity area for some of the poor and the minorities.

That leaves national revenue sharing and transfer payments. This option, too, will be quite limited in a period of inflation with mounting pressures to curb national spending. Nonetheless, the great battles for redressing the balance between inner and outer areas—and between growth and nongrowth economies—will be fought as much on the national as on the metropolitan level.

Metropolitan Organization

Another inescapable issue is the organization of government for the mature metropolitan areas. The arguments are now less intransigent on the subject, and the evidence is limited and mixed.

Most planners have favored some form of metropolitan government on the grounds of efficiency and equity. But their views have proved to be most persuasive to those who welcomed efficiency because costs were increasing, as were the demands for services.

In point of fact, the cluster of communities in a metropolitan region constituted one city in terms of management and services. Aggregation, it was felt, would make it easier to reach the minimum critical size to achieve economies of scale, to increase the variety of resources, and to reduce the duplication (in whole or in part) of some (but not all) services. It was considered essential that a consensus be achieved on development policies for the region. This implied an "intelligence" mechanism for evaluating the nature and trends of the metropolitan economy, and for determining the measures that might be taken to correct weaknesses, to encourage desirable developments, to decide on the variety and location of different infrastructure investments, and to decide on how to share the costs.

To design and secure backing for such a metropolitan system, however, turned out to be extraordinarily difficult in practice. To work effectively, the system would have to take adequate account of the wishes and needs of the central city, the larger metropolitan community, and the smaller local community. A single metropolitan government with decentralized components, or some form of federalism with effective representation and "checks and balances" would be necessary. Either system would need to be responsive to pressure politics and bargaining; it would have to safeguard local autonomy and not threaten the power of the provincial or regional authority or state legislature; it would be required to balance the costs of welfare and other services in the central city with the costs of development in the outer areas; it would need to give these central-city, suburban, and other groups reasonable trade-offs between losses and gains; and it would have to work well enough over time to achieve its aims. Even if successfully innovated. the maintenance of such a system would be anything but simple—as we can determine by reviewing some of the difficulties encountered in situations where such systems have been implemented.

Most proposals for area consolidation or metropolitan organization have been rejected in Canada and the United States.[23] Some communities wanted a higher quality of services; still others saw the need for joint financing, but not necessarily unitary management: they preferred local control, particularly over land use and decisions affecting the status or character of the community. The opposition, incidentally, did not come only from the affluent communities trying to keep taxes down or certain people and uses out: some communities did not value certain services or felt they could not afford them. Very often, there was a traditional conflict of suburban communities resisting the politics, problems, and control of the central city. Not surprisingly, few persons with experience expected metropolitan organization to come easily, if at all.

Frequently, central, state, and provincial governments have been persuaded that broader areawide responsibility for planning and development was desirable, particularly from the point of view of encouraging more effective and equitable allocation of grants. Their support and influence, and even direct financial assistance, have often played a decisive role in getting local governments to agree to form metropolitan areawide organizations, federations, coordinative councils, or, at the very least, special-purpose authorities. In the past 25 years, Canada and Western Europe (in particular, Britain, France, Denmark, Norway, and Sweden) have moved much further in this direction than the United States.

Two recent evaluations reflect the more sober contemporary views. Alan K. Campbell, who can be considered a cautious proponent, thinks "metropolitization as a structural change will offer small relief for those areas where decline has spread from city to suburb"; but he emphasizes that metropolitan areas in the United States (e.g., Minneapolis, Indianapolis, and Jacksonville) which have adopted metropolitan forms of organization "have weathered fiscal difficulties better than those cities which have not utilized metropolitan government [thus] reinforcing the impression that [metropolitan] government does make a difference in stemming the economic erosion of a region."[24]

Toronto's experience, however, provides less reassurance on this score.[25] Formerly regarded as one of the more successful experiments in metropolitan government, the views of the key actors and scholars today are far more guarded. The Metro-organization experienced considerable success in providing and financing (with the help of municipal Toronto taxpayers) water, sewage-disposal facilities, roads, and other public and private transportation; indeed, the accomplishments led later to the shifting of library, police, solid-waste disposal, and other functions to the Metro jurisdiction. But this very shift in functions has led many people to fear the progressive weakening of the local government through attrition. The Metro government has also been least successful in such redistributive areas as ensuring the availability of services on the basis of need; securing a consensus on how to shoulder the costs of welfare for "the working poor or indigent who congregated within the central city (a problem which required intervention by the Ontario legislature to solve)"; or in handling the more general problems of social planning: housing rehabilitation, neighborhood conservation, and a general improvement of the services of central Toronto.[26]

To date, however, we have far too few assessments of the accomplishments of these metropolitan organizations, and almost no first-rate comparative analyses. The information now available does not lend itself to simple generalization; perhaps in another decade or two we will have enough adequate evaluations from which to draw firm inferences. The current studies suggest that the pressures for more and better services and for more consistent and effective development policies are the driving forces behind the reform efforts, and that such efforts are more likely to be innovated in countries with hierarchical and elitist governmental structures, legal institutions, and patterns of social behavior.[27]

The evidence is substantially more equivocal as to whether such metropolitan organization has produced the hoped-for economies of scale or more equitable division of the costs of services. There is, at best, ambiguity as to whether a metropolitan organization can expand sufficiently to deal with the spreading megalopolitan complexes. Finally, the evidence is indecisive or negative as to whether metropolitan organization has led to more responsive or democratic local government.

Values, Planners, and the Poor

A major assumption with regard to our metropolitan policies and programs is that we know enough or can learn enough about the nature, functions, and problems of the metropolis to intervene skillfully *and equitably* at critical points to achieve intended effects. This is an axiom of hope: it sums up the faith by which most planners live. But one of the frustrating lessons learned repeatedly by the past few generations of planners is that what we know often turns out not to be so, or at least much less right or relevant than we supposed. These frailties are particularly evident if we consider three well-known, and more or less misguided, efforts to come to grips with the housing problems of the metropolis in the United States—indeed, efforts and errors sometimes made by other countries as well.

Well-intentioned housing specialists thought they could solve the inner-city housing problems of low-income families by having local housing authorities build subsidized housing for them at rents they could afford; but, with rare exceptions, the "projects" turned out to be expensive, neglectful of the needs of the families, and generally unacceptable. Similarly, although the innovations in housing-mortgage finance and the terms of repayment (together with ample credit and rising real income during that period) often helped middle-income families to own homes and often lined the pockets of the project developer, they also often had the effect of exacerbating the problems of the central city. And as almost everyone now is aware, redevelopment authorities subsidized, bulldozed, and renewed many urban centers—often with the undeclared aim of evicting the poor, the minorities, and other groups and activities in the areas which were despised or deemed inappropriate.[28]

In each of these cases, the problems were viewed through the lenses of the housing specialists, the planners, or other technical specialists, who fancied they were jousting with blight, slums, and crowding. We now know—or should know—that these policies often neglected or gave short shrift to the values and needs of the groups most affected by them. Critics—right, left, and center—did not overlook the discrepancies between the presumed and actual beneficiaries; or the callousness of giving first priority to programs of area development rather than the needs of the people who lived in the areas; or the sensitivity to fundamental class interests, values, and structural relationships which shaped the basic course of events.

Some of the critiques may have been exaggerated. In particular, the crude generalizations of the neo-Marxists could hardly compare in subtlety and detail with the more sophisticated behavioral studies of community influence, styles of leadership, and the power structure.[29] The neo-Marxists' analyses ignored or glossed over the roles of different actors—important because of their control of either resources or decision-making structures—and the quite different outcomes possible when dealing with public or private goods, or when operating in centralized or decentralized environments. They were also likely to run into great difficulty in explaining such subtle and intriguing details as how important elite groups in cities like New York could have so little influence (as Professor Vernon pointed out) in protecting the core areas they sought to preserve.[30] However, for all of their failings, the neo-Marxist critiques did make clear the differences between the values of the planners and those of the groups disadvantaged by their plans; and they did emphasize the danger of focusing only on the fiscal and physical problems of the metropolis, while neglecting questions of equity and of reasonable participation in the basic decision-making processes by the groups who were likely to be most affected by these processes.

These experiences may be easy to gloss over, but they provide evidence of the clear and present dangers in addressing the problems of the metropolis more as "technical" than "human" problems. The dangers continue to be real and pressing, because both the mature and the growing metropolis present powerful demands which give short shrift to those whose needs stand in the way of their realization.

CHAPTER SEVEN

Conditions for a Successful New Communities Program

WITH LAWRENCE SUSSKIND

It took the British just about 25 years from the inception of the New Towns Act of 1946 to build 25 new towns. With a population four times greater and a per-capita national income more than twice that of Britain's, the United States ought to be able to build more. Of course, we will not do half as much; but why quibble about numbers, especially since it is the scale and quality of these towns that will be so important. Let us consider instead what the more articulate and perceptive critics might—and probably would—be saying about these communities, assuming they were built.[1]

PROSPECTS FOR NEW COMMUNITIES

We venture to predict that more than half the new communities completed 25 years from now would be suburban-type new communities, closely dependent on older urban centers. These communities, built in the style of Columbia, Maryland, Jonathan, Minnesota, and Lysander, New York, would probably end up with populations of 100,000 to 200,000. Although most of the federally assisted new communities are presently being planned for somewhat smaller numbers of people, most of them

This article was written shortly after the enactment by the United States Congress of what Senator Hubert Humphrey called "an historic piece of legislation concerning 'new towns,'" that is, Title VII of the Housing and Urban Development Act of 1970.

are in rapidly urbanizing areas and our expectation is that they may well exceed their population targets.

Less than a third of the new communities would be self-contained cities with population levels between 50,000 and 100,000. Independent new communities in lagging areas are most often thought of as large, self-contained developments. This assumption is dead wrong. Unless very special steps are taken, new communities designed as growth centers in lagging areas are likely to be smaller rather than larger. Lacking an existing economic base and being too distant from the central city to permit a substantial portion of the labor force to commute, such cities would face the difficult problem of attracting employers (because of the absence of a labor force and business and consumer facilities), and residents will be hard to attract unless jobs are available. Even with substantial federal support, such new communities would grow very slowly.

A small number of the new communities might be of the "new town in town" variety. Cedar-Riverside (Minneapolis) and Roosevelt Island (New York City) are examples. Basically, such developments would seek to revitalize sagging inner-city economies. They would also try to attract high-income residents back to the central city and to promote racial integration.

How would these communities fare? Some of them, financed largely by private investors, would be abandoned halfway through the development process because they failed to yield a handsome profit. They would go through the financial wringer and simply fade into the usual pattern of speculative developments.

A few, as might be expected, would be straight-out economic failures. In some cases, development costs would exceed the returns on the sale of housing units and the leasing of industrial and commercial properties. In other instances, the pace of development would be too slow, or the "turnaround" time on investment would drag out long beyond the point at which repayment of borrowed money is expected to begin.

What might be surprising, and sad, is that many of the new communities completed 25 years hence would not fail; they would succeed in a moderate and dull way, yielding a small profit, providing a modicum of low- and middle-income housing, managing to stick fairly closely to the original development plans (having overcome the objections of various pressure groups), and presenting no particular threat to the natural environment. The way of life for residents of these new communities would not be too different from that of other suburban dwellers. More persons might live comfortably, walk to work, have easier access to assorted recreational facilities, and perhaps even feel a greater sense of "belonging" because of their participation in a "social experiment." What is far less certain, though, is whether these new communities would serve the poor and disadvantaged, achieve a reasonably greater socioeconomic mix, spur significant innovations or, even more importantly, serve broader ends: that is, would these new communities have a critical impact on the larger population in areas outside the communities themselves?

The future of most new communities completed during the next 25 years would no doubt depend on their financial, political, and social feasibility. In terms of financial feasibility, privately sponsored new communities would prove successful only if they have paid careful attention to a number of such factors as *location* (selecting a site easily accessible to growing markets); *front-end financing* (making sure that considerable financial support is available at the outset); *federal loans and grants* (working closely with federal, state, and local governments to secure whatever supplementary funds are available); *reasonable tax agreements* (securing favorable assessments, easements, tax credits, or other abatements if they can be arranged); and the *pace of development* (working to achieve as rapid a "turnaround" time and positive cash flow as possible).

The plans for most new cities completed 25 years from now would have run the gauntlet of various community groups and politicians. "Abutters" trapped between various parcels pieced together to form a new community would have expressed vociferous views about what the proposed development should be like. So, too, would local, county, state, regional, and federal officials. Each would have exerted whatever influence was exercisable over zoning, tax rates, assessments, utility extensions, transportation plans, and industrial-location decisions. The first residents would also have demanded a meaningful role in decision making. And, at some point, the developer would have been forced to turn over some of his decision-making authority to an elected body. With authority and control so fragmented, we can take for granted that the majority of new-community projects would not have developed according to plan.

Successful communities, to be sure, would have benefited from a managerial team able to gain zoning- and building-code clearance by arguing for new approaches such as density zoning and planned unit development, and able to deal with political opposition by building a coalition of local, state, and perhaps national supporters. The team would also have devised an effective bargaining strategy, by offering to be responsive to local needs and by offering something in return for local support. But there will be few such teams; and, in retrospect, we might wonder why we ever thought that the homebuilders and large-scale developers of the 1970s (even those with successful track records and support from diversified business enterprises) were equipped to manage the complex process of new-community development.

To meet financial strains during the early stages of development, even the best-intentioned developers would decide to build a high percentage of high revenue-producing housing first. Once the initial wave of high-middle and middle-middle income families has been served, however, resistance to the construction of housing and facilities for low- and middle-income families would heighten. And so, most new communities 25 years hence would have ended up catering to a clientele not much different from that of the customary suburban development. Glorified suburbs, they would have had a negligible impact on the problems of providing decent low-priced housing and easier access to new jobs for low- and middle-income families. This is likely to be true despite some low-cost, and even public, housing tucked away behind or alongside industrial parks, or a few scattered subsidized units physically indistinguishable from the units of moderate, unsubsidized cost.

To better cope with the problem of providing a broader economic mix, a few communities would have sought help from public entities, such as the Urban Development Corporation (UDC) in New York, which would have built housing for all economic classes by using a quota system[2]—not because quotas are desirable, but because they were the only means of eliminating "de facto apartheid" housing patterns.

One could continue this accounting, but what it all adds up to is that some 25 years from now, we would find critics of the new-communities program arguing that public investment in these projects merely diverted resources from inner-city redevelopment efforts and that our largest central cities are worse off than ever. They would be pointing out that our new communities accommodated a tiny fraction of our population growth over the last quarter of the twentieth century, perhaps only 5%, possibly even only 1 or 2%.[3] Other critics would be reminding us that back in the early 1970s, it was pointed out that new communities would never provide us with significant alternatives to conventional urban development. And the more radical commentators would be asserting that new communities are not (and could not be) a solution to urban problems since fundamental shifts in the distribution of resources and power are prerequisites to effective social change, and the new-communities program certainly does not imply a significant redistribution of money or power.

GOALS OF FEDERAL INTERVENTION

This scenario is not altogether fetching. But perhaps it may provoke a hard-boiled reconsideration of what governmental intervention in the design and development of new communities can be expected to achieve. Suppose we were in the unenviable position of those federal decision makers responsible for the administration of the New Communities Program.[4] How would we run the program to ensure that we get the kind of cities we need and want? There are at least seven criteria that would govern our decisions:

1. *New communities ought not to be built when the expansion of existing communities will serve the same purposes.* But they will be built when they should not be if our principal focus is on new communities and not on the urban-growth objectives that we are trying to achieve.

2. *New communities ought not to lose money.* Yet they are likely to unless a reasonable proportion of the appreciation in land values or of earned income (realized through the sale or lease of commercial properties and the rise in land prices) can be captured by the developers. This also holds true for new communities built by public-development corporations.

3. *New communities must provide a choice of jobs for all primary and secondary wage earners.* But they will not unless the number of new-community developments is restricted and each is large enough to support a diversified set of economic activities, businesses, and social services.

4. *New communities have to be socially acceptable in the second half of the twentieth century.* But they will not be unless they directly serve a reasonable proportion of disadvantaged minorities and middle-income families, and also create reasonable economic and social opportunities for other disadvantaged groups in the surrounding metropolitan area.

5. *New communities should help to reduce congestion in our biggest cities and to reorganize development patterns in metropolitan areas.* They will not contribute much to meeting these objectives, however, unless they are consciously conceived as a means of achieving them. Until a special effort is made to relate new-community development to such things as national, state, and regional planning for transportation, capital-improvements programming, welfare policy, and industrial-development strategies, metropolitan growth patterns and current development trends are unlikely to be changed much.

6. *New communities should help to encourage the development of growth centers in lagging regions, especially in regions with a large unemployed and underemployed population.* Clearly

they will not begin to do this difficult job if undue emphasis is placed on maximum returns to the developer or if new communities are planned without full recognition of the forces which impel migration and the location of economic activities,

7. *Aside from the six above-mentioned criteria, it would be wonderful (and astonishing) if we could somehow produce two or three brilliant showpieces: breathtaking examples of more responsive and elegant ways of organizing our physical environment.* For example, new communities might reflect the "educative city" of the future: that is, (a) they could demonstrate a number of ways in which client groups of all income and educational backgrounds might participate in the design of services and facilities, such as schools, health programs, day-care centers, and possibly even shape the decisions affecting the financing and day-to-day management of programs at the neighborhood level. (b) They might provide unique educational workshops outside the traditional "classroom" (nature and wildlife observatories, opportunities to observe building and planning processes, etc.). (c) They might even offer a number of opportunities to experiment with unusual building, highway, street, or area designs, as well as alternative models of entire communities.

The hitch, however, is that it is incredibly difficult to ensure a brilliant performance. An unusual blend of initiative, rare ability, and hard work (as well as a good measure of luck) will be required to produce two or three outstanding new communities. Pennypinched programs and a fear of anything too different or too out-of-the-ordinary will tend to wipe out even these slim chances.

Which leads us once again to wonder about the likelihood of realizing these aims—any of them, prosaic or extraordinary. We find ourselves in a dilemma. From the conditions we have set, it looks as if we are guilty of advocating the best and making it the enemy of the good ("*le mieux est l'ennemi du bien*"), and in the process vitiating the entire New Communities Program. It just is not so. We want a program that will work and that we can be proud of. The conditions we have posed cannot be met overnight; we acknowledge that. Nevertheless, the prospects for the future are uninspiring unless we can muster considerable political support for the following key ideas.

1. The desirable focus must be on the expansion of existing communities as well as the building of new ones. Planners, designers, and politicians cannot be allowed to use new communities as a shield to fend off the problems of the central city. They must collaborate with local, regional, and state officials.

2. There must be a need for a limited but strategic increase in the public ownership of land to harvest the full economic and social value created by new-community projects. Public land ownership is hardly a cherished institution in this country, but we have got to learn how to use the tricks of the private developer to serve the public interest.

3. The importance of limiting the number and augmenting the size of new communities must be realized. Given our egalitarian system and the normal pattern of political pressures, it will be quite a feat to develop a significant program in which costs are shared nationally but the visible benefits to particular regions are sharply limited.

4. The obligation of new communities must be to serve the needs of the disadvantaged elements of our population—both as consumers and producers, which means reversing or overriding prevailing suburban attitudes.[5]

5. There must be an immediate as well as a long-term awareness of relating new communities to the needs of the existing metropolis. Most new-community planners and developers think their problems are harrowing enough without having to take on the burdens of existing central cities; but unless new-community development on the metropolitan fringes and in lagging regions is linked to the depopulation or redevelopment of inner-city neighborhoods, efforts to build these communities will be trivial.

6. The reminder that new (or existing) communities must serve as chosen instruments to help spark the growth of selected urban centers in Appalachia or in the depressed areas of the deep South should not be overlooked. Most planners rarely see the need, let alone the desirability, of getting entangled in the prob-

lems of lagging regions, for it is much easier to build new communities in high-growth areas where there is a more assured market.

7. The need to spend generously and imaginatively, even in the face of a tradition and a culture that tend to deplore a consistent and long-term public policy in pursuit of the objectives should be implied in the first six items above.

Finally, before concluding the section we would like to voice some additional hopes and forebodings which ought to be inscribed in the minds of new-community enthusiasts.

New communities will become odious symbols if they are identified as devices for diluting the power of emerging innercity majorities. There must be provisions for neighborhood government and local control over key public services in each new community if we expect to convince large groups of people to move from the inner city to new communities.

On the other hand, many new communities can become attractive territory for investment in the minority enterprise. They can provide capital-investment opportunities as well as markets for goods and services. The vehicles by which this can be achieved are federal contracts and purchasing agreements which can encourage minority-run businesses, and ought in fact to do so. The new markets for inner-city entrepreneurs should be the lure not to entice them out of the inner city but to allow them to generate additional resources for reinvestment.

TURNING THE PROGRAM AROUND

When goals are set too high, they must be trimmed down. In our case trimming goals means recognizing that new communities will simply serve as another string in the planner's bow, another way of organizing growth and developing resources in the suburbs, in the central cities, as well as in poorer regions; and that we will be very lucky indeed if the tools are used well or at least not misused. We know that in a new program the language of hope is more appealing than the language of regret; but we would remind those whom we disappoint that the disillusioned generally suffer from illusions to begin with.

Department of Housing and Urban Development (HUD) officials have expressed a keen desire to ensure the financial success of federally supported new-community development efforts, hoping that a few early successes will attract the long-term support and the involvement of the private money markets. At the same time, various administrative spokesmen have encouraged new-community developers to undertake socially and technologically innovative experiments designed to test new ways of designing, building, and organizing urban service systems. It may well be, though, that these two objectives are incompatible; and, in the long run, a policy that pursues both objectives may be self-defeating. The factors which determine financial success may inhibit or even prohibit innovation, and the new communities most likely to be financially successful may also be those least suited to producing socially significant results.

It has taken almost 10 years for the New Communities Program in the United States to evolve.[6] Along the way, many of its strongest advocates have felt obliged to embellish the potential advantages of new communities and to exaggerate the contribution they might make to the resolution of various urban problems. There will be a substantial mismatch between the claims of the most avid new-community proponents and the actual results of our first round of development efforts under Title VII.

For this reason in particular, we caution against exaggerating or deluding ourselves as to the prospects for innovation. It is not that we do not welcome or appreciate the need or apparent opportunity for such innovations. But, contrary to the conventional wisdom, we do not think the circumstances under which new communities are built are altogether conducive to innovation. The pressure to make a killing or to avoid a disaster drives out most high-risk activities and provides powerful reinforcements for hard-boiled, conservative, not to mention backward and prejudiced judgments as to what will work. Despite this forbidding reality, we believe—or hope—that at least some public-development corporations will support limited risk taking in a few areas. In one case, the focus may be on the design and delivery of novel health and educational services; in another it may be on experimentation with new approaches to urban design and transportation; in still another it may be on innovative factory- or site-fabrication methods for building housing. In all these cases the risks are real, but so are the prospects for some success or for minimizing failure, provided the experiments are few in number and that in each case a careful effort is made to monitor and evaluate the results.[7]

Another easy mistake we warn against is to assume that the government, because it is providing some backing for new communities, will guarantee the kind of benevolent and enlightened leadership that can sustain the program through periods of difficulty that might lie ahead. On the contrary, there is much disconcerting evidence to show that even in the short run, changes in government policy and administration can cause perilous lurches and lags in patterns of development. Changes in leadership, values, and purposes can, as Charles Abrams often reminded us, convert measures of reform into instruments of reaction. Without unremitting vigilance the New Communities Program is hardly likely to be the exception; and the danger is real that if new communities become the symbol for the government turning its back on the problems of existing cities, or diverting resources from lagging regions, then new communities will become as unpopular as public-housing projects are today, and rightly so.

Finally, because the idea of new communities is becoming fashionable and national officials now intone many of the more euphonious phrases about what such communities are all about, we ought to point up the fact that the government still has no national urban-growth policy.[8] We applaud—mildly, to be sure—the current draft regulations accompanying the 1970 Urban Growth and New Community Development Act recently released by HUD, for the regulations outline a host of sensible criteria that will be taken into account in selecting projects for governmental assistance. We cannot quarrel with indices such as economic soundness; contribution to the social and economic welfare of the entire area affected; increasing the available choices for living and working; making provision for housing of different types and income ranges; serving a wide range of families; and taking account of the location and the functions of new communities with regard to combating sprawl, reorganizing inner-city development, or helping lagging regions.

The size of the community, the adequacy of transportation connections and services, the quality of planning, and the capabilities of the developer are additional considerations (among others) which are appropriately underlined when administrative regulations have to be applied "across the board." But this facade of knowledgeable and comprehensive regulations is hardly adequate if the government has no sense of direction. Regulations in these circumstances are like the sky: they may cover everything and touch nothing; and meanwhile, in an effort to get the program off the ground, the range and multiplicity of criteria can easily offer more rhetoric than results.

What is needed to change this situation is an unrelenting focus on the relationships between the reorganization of our inner cities and the organization of growth in our outer areas; between the slowing down of growth in our largest megalopolitan areas and the spurring of growth in a few key portions of our lagging regions. When we say that the program ought to be turned around, we mean that instead of building 60 new communities, mostly in suburban locations at somewhat lower densities, we ought to be building only about 10 to 15 new communities but much larger ones, with higher densities, designed to deal with interregional development problems. Instead of funding mainly new communities under the control of private-development groups, we ought to be favoring public-development entities. Instead of supporting new communities that promise to test a great number of technological innovations, we ought to be encouraging efforts which will monitor only a few well-designed experimental approaches to the delivery of services; and we ought to put a premium on experiments in citizen participation. Moreover, we ought to provide special assistance for those efforts which focus on the needs of the poor and the disadvantaged and which emphasize the processes and strategies by which the development of new communities can reinforce national urban-growth objectives.

CHAPTER EIGHT

The New Communities Program and Why It Failed

WITH HUGH EVANS

First authorized in 1968, then significantly expanded in 1970, the New Communities Program was, according to its former administrator, "reduced to a salvage operation in exactly four years."[1] The program was dismantled in the fall of 1978, three years after even its modest objectives had been jettisoned in an effort to bolster the precarious financial positions of individual projects.

Under the best of circumstances the New Communities Program probably could not have met the grand objectives promised in the rhetoric of its less cautious supporters: accommodating much of an estimated United States population increase of 75 million from 1970 to 2000, encouraging more efficient use of resources and methods of design, improving social and economic opportunities for the disadvantaged, and the like. Yet not just the highest hopes were dashed. Despite occasional bold experiments—such as a car-free transportation system devised for Roosevelt Island in New York City, and comprehensive-health-care programs in two other projects—the United States New Communities Program was a disaster the magnitude of which surprised even the program's harshest critics.[2]

Throughout the 1950s and 1960s, housing and planning specialists chafed at the narrowness and inadequacies of housing

We are indebted to Hilbert Fefferman for incisive comments and generous assistance on the legislative history of the program, and for frank and helpful responses to our questions by several knowledgeable officials in the HUD administration.

and urban programs. They were determined to broaden the basic policies and programs for financial assistance, and worked with great persistence, and some success, under Republican as well as Democratic administrations. By 1965, the national housing programs provided categorical grants not only for housing and urban renewal but for public works, community facilities, open space, and mass transportation. Still later, additional and more generous categorical grants were made available for programs involving "area-wide"—that is, metropolitan or regional—planning.

Yet the new-community planners sought to go beyond this ad hoc federal assistance for water, sewage, open space, transportation, housing, and community facilities. Many proponents thought building costs could be lowered, and high standards of design promoted, through modern site planning, economies of scale, and utilization of research breakthroughs in technology and public and social services. Others nursed still more ambitious aims: they were persuaded that new communities could provide alternatives to "metropolitan sprawl," foster diversified mixtures of income, ethnic, and social groups, while reinforcing government efforts to promote depressed rural or abandoned inner-city areas. Though public understanding and support of these ideas were negligible, these aspirations generated a series of legislative and administrative initiatives that aimed at the building of such communities.

Congress's first major thrust insured mortgage loans for the purchase and improvement of land, in 1965 for large-scale subdivisions, then in 1966 for community development in metropolitan areas. Federal guarantees of debentures, issued by private new-community land developers, and not necessarily backed by mortgages, followed in 1968 with Title IV of the Housing and Urban Development Act—an attempt to tap the bond market as a new source of financing for the principal community-development costs, namely, site acquisition and improvements. Title IV also provided supplementary grants in the form of an increment 20% above the level of existing categorical grants for water, sewer, and open-space projects, in order to encourage local governments to work closely with new-community developers and make the necessary investments for public facilities.

Four communities were launched under this legislation: Jonathan, Minnesota; St. Charles, Maryland; Park Forest South near Chicago; and Flower Mound, Texas. The Urban Growth and New Community Developmental Act (Title VII of the Housing and Urban Development Act of 1970) extended the federal guarantees to state and local public organizations acting as new-community developers. To make the incentives even more attractive, the act provided for additional "infrastructure" programs (in addition to water, sewer, and open-space projects) which would be eligible for supplementary grants,[3] and authorized three specially targeted grants designed to facilitate financing and innovation, and to cover the higher costs of operating public services for the small number of residents during the early years of development. The federal government was also empowered to plan and carry out large demonstration projects, if it chose to do so.

There were only two public initiatives of any consequence—both of them programs of the New York State Urban Development Corporation. This paucity resulted, in part, from widespread skepticism that the federal government would play any but a supporting role, and, in part, from the fact that few state or local agencies had the requisite experience or were properly organized to undertake such efforts. But there was as well a widespread preference for the private builder, reinforced by some fairly recent massive failures in public housing and large-scale community development (such as Jersey Meadows) and by some private-sector successes. In particular, numerous large suburban divisions (for example, the Levittowns of New York and New Jersey) and early "new towns"—such as Park Forest in Chicago, built in the 1950s, and Irvine, California and Columbia, Maryland in the 1960s—were relatively successful ventures financially, and were developed with little or no assistance from the government.

In any case, the 1968 and 1970 legislation aroused high ex-

Table 1. Federally Assisted New Communities in the United States[a]

Community[b]	Location	Date of HUD commitment	Guarantees committed ($ millions)	Development period (years)	Acres	Projected population	Population December, 1977	Current status[a]
Jonathan Minnesota (S)	20 miles SW of Minneapolis	2/70	21.0	20	8,194	50,000	2,860	B
St. Charles Communities Maryland (S)	25 miles SE of Washington, D.C.	6/70	38.0	20	7,408	75,000	9,500	A
Park Forest South Illinois (S)	30 miles S of Chicago	6/70	30.0	15	8,163	110,000	5,800	B
Flower Mound Texas (S)	20 miles NW of Dallas	12/70	18.0	20	5,156	64,000	1,605	C
Maumelle Arkansas (S)	12 miles NW of Little Rock	12/70	25.0	20	5,319	45,000	503	A
Cedar-Riverside Minnesota (NTIT)	Downtown Minneapolis	6/71	24.0	20	101	30,000	3,100	C
Riverton New York (S)	10 miles S of Rochester	12/71	23.0	16	2,437	26,000	1,000	C
San Antonio Ranch Texas (S)	20 miles NW of San Antonio	2/72	18.0	30	9,318	88,000	—	D

The Woodlands Texas (S)	30 miles N of Houston	4/72	50.0	20	17,000	150,000	3,606	A
Gananda New York (S)	12 miles E of Rochester	4/72	22.0	20	4,733	56,000	—	C
Soul City North Carolina (FS)	45 miles N of Raleigh	6/72	14.0	20	5,180	44,000	94	A
Harbison South Carolina (S)	8 miles NW of Columbia	10/72	13.0	20	1,740	23,000	176	A
Radisson New York (S)	12 miles NW of Syracuse	c	—	20	2,670	18,000	900	A
Roosevelt Island New York (NTIT)	East River between Manhattan and Queens	c	—	7	143	18,000	3,500	A
Shenandoah Georgia (S)	35 miles S of Atlanta	2/73	40.0	20	7,200	70,000	110	A
Newfields Ohio (S)	7 miles NW of Dayton	10/73	32.0	20	4,032	40,000	122	C

[a] *Source:* HUD, New Communities Administration: unpublished memorandum.

[b] S = satellite; NTIT = new town in town; FS = free standing.

[c] New York State Land Development Projects not guaranteed by HUD but eligible for benefits.

[d] A = development to continue; B = to be acquired by HUD: development to continue; C = to be acquired by HUD for disposition of assets; D = development halted, pending resolution of lawsuit.

pectations. The administrators of the program, confident of a positive private-sector response, counted on processing about 10 projects a year if all went well. In fact, of the nearly 100 applications submitted for federal assistance—many of them from utopians, eccentrics, or devious operators—only 13 submissions, over the whole course of the program, received the "go-ahead" from the administration.[4] Eleven were "satellite communities" on the periphery of metropolitan areas, one a "new town in town," and one a "free-standing community" in an economically depressed rural area. For the projects, federal guarantees ranging from $5 million to the statutory limit of $50 million were made (see Table 1). (The two new communities undertaken by the New York State Urban Development Corporation rejected the federal guarantees but sought other benefits of the program.)

In January, 1975, the Department of Housing and Urban Development (HUD) closed the door to further applications. This was not because projected targets had been reached, but in order to concentrate resources on those projects already under way, which were by then clearly in trouble. Following an embarrassing reassessment, HUD decided to recapitalize six projects—Harbison, South Carolina, Maumelle, Arkansas, St. Charles, Maryland, Shenandoah, Georgia, Soul City, North Carolina, and Woodlands, Texas—and to acquire the other seven from the original developers. Two, Gananda, New York and Newfields, Ohio, were considered to lack adequate development potential.

Of the 13 projects (see Figure 10) six—Cedar-Riverside, Minnesota, Jonathan, Minnesota, Park Forest South, Illinois, St. Charles, Maryland, Woodlands, Texas, and Riverton, New York—eventually managed to get off the ground and, after periods of two to six years, reached populations of 1,000 to 6,000. Most of them had constructed a range of community facilities, several had attracted commercial and industrial firms offering job opportunities, and a few provided subsidized housing for moderate-income families. Development in the other seven projects started late and progressed slowly or not at all.

The loan guarantees for the 13 communities came close to

Figure 10. New communities in the United States approved under Title VII, the Housing and Urban Development Act of 1970. Cedar-Riverside, Minneapolis, Minn.; Flower Mound, near Dallas, Texas; Gananda, near Rochester, N.Y.; Harbison, near Columbia, S.C.; Maumelle, near Little Rock, Ark.; Newfields, Dayton, Ohio; Jonathan, near Minneapolis, Minn.; Radisson, near Syracuse, N.Y.; Riverton, near Rochester, N.Y.; Roosevelt Island, New York City, N.Y.; Park Forest South, near Chicago, Ill.; St. Charles Communities, Charles County, Md.; Shenandoah, near Atlanta, Ga.; Soul City, Warren County, N.C.; San Antonio Ranch, near San Antonio, Texas; The Woodlands, near Houston, Texas.

$300 million; other grants and assistance totaled $72 million. No one knows what the total losses will be until the liquidation program is completed. Congress, the administration, and friends of the program asked, "What happened?" And, "Why?"

SIX FLAWS

A spate of studies surveyed the faltering program, including inquiries by Congress, HUD, the Comptroller General, university scholars, and others—including the former administrator.[5] The evidence points to six flaws.

Defective Financial Arrangements

The financial arrangements for the program were defective. The essence of the financial problem of the program is that for several years before there is any offsetting income, the developer is burdened with heavy fixed charges both in the form of interest on the massive initial debt incurred for site acquisition and improvement, as well as state and local property taxes. Although expenses are large and fixed, revenues from the sale and lease of improved land are highly volatile and subject to a host of factors beyond any developer's control; hence many responsible developers shy away from such investments. The problem, therefore, is to minimize the gap between fixed charges and income and to reduce the number of years before the project breaks even and begins to show a profit.

The new-communities legislation included a whole complex of measures addressed to specific start-up problems. There were, for example, loan guarantees to assure credit, grant assistance to cover the unusual planning and technical requirements for communities of this nature, and supplementary categorical grants to induce local authorities to make infrastructure investments in areas then without population, revenue, or political power. Similarly, public-service grants compensated localities for providing services to areas as yet without an adequate property-tax base to defray the costs. Repayable-interest loans (for periods up to 15 years) covered the shortfall between interest charges and revenues. Yet even with this potpourri of helpful measures, many financial pitfalls remained.

Though federal guarantees removed the element of risk to lenders (usually insurance companies, investment banks, and later the Federal Financing Bank), little was done to reduce the need for massive initial outlays of capital for land acquisition and infrastructure. The legislation omitted any possibility of freezing land values or holding it in publicly funded new-community "land banks," to be released to the developer when required. Moreover, the absence of federal powers of eminent domain handicapped private developers in securing key "hold-out" parcels—except when states specifically provided such powers. This omission meant that unless there were an ongoing urban-renewal program, large-scale assemblage of in-town locations was virtually precluded. But HUD regulations stipulated that in order to be eligible for assistance, developers must already possess, or have an option on, at least the essential acreage required for the proposed new community!

A further source of delay and friction was the HUD staff's distrust of developers, compounded in part by the staff's relative inexperience in real-estate development—and an altogether justified suspicion of the rich potential for financial legerdemain. The new-community developers, as is common practice for private developers, formed separate companies for different stages of the development process: for the initial acquisition and assembly of land parcels; for the subsequent planning, improvement, and preliminary development of the land; and for "above ground" construction, such as housing, shopping centers, or industrial buildings. There are many reasons for doing this. Institutions lending money for different activities often insist that these transactions be kept separate; also, the developers conducting these operations may want to minimize risk by isolating potential losses, or they may wish to combine entities for tax purposes so that losses in one may be offset against profits in another. On the other hand, HUD officials were wary of the potential abuse of such practices. In the several stages of development, purchases and sales and service contracts were from and to affiliates or subsidiaries of the same companies. In such cases, there is enormous potential for excessive profit as a result of the less-than-arm's-length sales between affiliated companies. HUD's new-community officials felt a special need to be on guard because, under Title VII legislation, guaranteed loans could only be used for land development; "above ground" construction, except where related to public facilities, was specifically excluded.[6]

The most risky period for the developer was the intermediate or improvement stage because of the heavy investments, the unpredictable negotiations with diverse public authorities, complex program requirements, the lack of significant revenues, and the necessity of repaying the principal sums borrowed plus the interest loan according to the terms worked out with the loan institutions and the New Community Development Corporation.[7] (The legislation was deliberately silent on these matters to permit tailoring of terms suited to the particular circumstances of each new community.) But if the "front-end" financing was steep—for example, if the entire site was acquired at one time or if expensive investments for roads or sewage or other facilities had to be undertaken at the outset—and heavy debt charges were incurred, considerable and steady revenues would be required to repay the loans.

Since the loans commonly took the form of 20-year debentures or bonds, with provisions for postponement of interest payments during the early years, and with the possibility of extensions of moratoriums on repayment, the problem of heavy fixed charges was ameliorated. But not so the debt-service costs, which alone—excluding repayment of principal—were projected to be greater than 60% of revenues anticipated to 1975 in eight cases out of 12, and in practice exceeded 100% of revenues in all cases but two.[8] Thus there was little or no cushion to absorb the impact of changing conditions in the local market and the national economy, errors of market analysis, and other unforeseen contingencies. In addition, the characteristic behavior of developers involved in high-risk activities only compounded the difficulties.

The guarantees covered the loan institutions, not the developers, and so experienced developers "mortgaged out," that is, put up the minimal equity and sought the maximum in loans—with the hope of retrieving at the very start of the program whatever funds they put into the venture, not to mention some profits as well. So the projections underlying loans were apt to underestimate costs, overestimate land values, and be optimistic about revenues and future contingencies, and the records and documentation were likely to be obscure and meager.

An outside study commissioned by the New Communities Administration found that only two of the developers participating in the New Communities Program had extensive experience and national reputations.[9] Most of the developers lacked adequate equity. Though the legislation specified that developers should contribute 20% of the equity investment, the New Community Administration—anxious to get a decent-sized program quickly off the ground—did not rigidly enforce this requirement. And even if it had been enforced vigorously, developers could get away with much less by substituting an "urbanization-appraisal increment" on the value of the project's land of up to half of the required equity contribution.[10] At best, therefore, the developer's financial commitment to Title VII operations was tenuous. At Shenandoah, Georgia, where HUD's initial guarantee amounted to $25 million, the developer put up $10,000 in cash and subordinated debt of $5 million.

In conclusion, the developers borrowed in massive amounts, which increased the burden of fixed charges and reduced the projects' abilities to withstand periods of revenue shortfalls.[11] Costs were systematically underestimated, revenues overestimated, and both the developers and the supervising officials were lax in evaluating the consequences of less favorable assumptions.[12] Subsequent analyses by consultants evaluating the projects in 1975 and 1976 on the basis of more realistic assumptions indicated that six of the communities (Riverton, Gananda, Flower Mound, Jonathan, Shenandoah, and Maumelle) had acquired land "in areas with significant market-acceptance problems,"[13] and that six communities (Riverton, Gananda, Park Forest South, Maumelle, Soul City, and Newfields) would never pay back their original investment.

A Lack of Acceptance

New communities served no major strategic aims or special constituency; they did, however, require a lot of money. One estimate by the League of New Community Developers puts the capital requirement for 20,000 units—a city of 70,000—at approximately $1.5 billion. If scheduled over a 15-year period, that would approximate $100 million a year. But even if we cut the figures by half, these are substantial sums, and so the number and scale of new communities could not have achieved much impact without serving important national or regional development aims. Otherwise, as one of the authors of this article wrote in 1971, critics of the program would argue that public investment in these projects had diverted resources from inner-city redevelopment, that our largest central cities were worse off than ever, that the new towns accommodated a tiny fraction of our population growth, and that they would never provide significant alternatives to conventional urban development.[14]

The new communities actually built invite precisely these attacks. Even had they been fully completed according to plan, they would not have served any substantial middle-class group. They did not extend or reinforce the concept of growth centers; they were not particularly well located; they were not successful financially; nor did they contribute to the reorganization of their metropolitan areas. Except for a handful of middle-income blacks whose entry was facilitated by the newness of the community, neither did they provide any noteworthy advantages to blacks, the poor, or any other disadvantaged groups.

The legislation gained the support of Congress through ingenious bipartisan compromises and skillful maneuvers negotiated by two congressmen, Thomas Ashley, a Democrat, and William Widnall, a Republican, with Senator John Sparkman, and aided by HUD's legislative counsel who had been deputized to discourage features of the legislation especially distasteful to the administration.

But the fact is that the New Communities Program never had any solid constituency: at best it was a fragmented coalition of planners, architects, a few public administrators, builders, and mayors. (The mayors, who were originally hostile—since new communities involved no votes and might divert funds from their bailiwicks—were reluctantly persuaded that the program might help decaying inner cities or the sprawling periphery of their metropolises.) Is it any wonder that whatever political support it had simply evaporated as soon as the program encountered difficulties?

Inadequate State and Local Support

Inadequate arrangements were made to ensure the backing of new communities by state and local governments. New communities confronted local authorities with three problems: whether to provide infrastructure and services for a new population which was an uncertain quantity politically and possibly an unwelcome burden financially; if provided, how to finance the necessary roads, water, and sewage facilities, schools, and the like, given the needs of the existing population and the constraints imposed by state debt restrictions; and a dearth of local experience in dealing with these complicated matters.

Nevertheless, for developers state and local cooperation was essential. Delays in providing roads, sewers, water supply, or schools would inflate costs and block or undermine the whole program. And from the vantage of the federal government also, state and local backing was critical, for the federal government assumed the principal risks of the enterprise. In addition, federal sponsorship of and investments in new communities would seem all the more justified if—as state and local cooperation might have made it seem—the new communities served some paramount regional need. Unexpectedly, local authorities became indispensable "third partners": the program was sure to founder without their active support and cooperation.

Though one method of guaranteeing local enthusiasm would have been to make the approval of the new-community proposals contingent on their serving some high-priority local or regional concerns, just the opposite assumption was made: namely, that the new communities should be built according to the judgments and calculus of private entrepreneurs. The necessary collaboration, it was thought, could be negotiated by HUD's new-community planners, with the help of sweeteners provided by the federal government. This formula generated a maze of problems, later exacerbated by the failure of federal agencies to make available the promised sweeteners.

We cite only a few examples of the lack of coordination. The Genesee Expressway, linking Riverton, New York, to downtown Rochester, New York, was merely a recommended component of the Rochester Metropolitan Transportation Study published in 1969—and remained a mere recommendation. At the Flower Mound, Texas, project, the developer relied heavily on the expected completion of the Mid-Cities Freeway by 1980—although it was never even included in the Texas Highway Department's official plan. And necessary road improvements at Jonathan, Minnesota—despite support from the Federal Highways Administration and assurances of priority ranking from the Minnesota Highways Department—were postponed 10 years. In addition, the lack of clear agreements with local authorities not only delayed progress but sometimes left the developer to foot the bill for items normally undertaken by public agencies. At Cedar-Riverside, Minnesota, a "new town in town," the developer expected the Minneapolis Housing and Redevelopment Authority to take responsibility for relocating displaced residents, but after protracted disputes was forced to do so himself to avoid holding up the project further. At St. Charles, Maryland, the developer was held up 19 months waiting for the county commissioners first to approve a necessary zoning ordinance and then to grant approval to the new community. At Riverton, where improvements were needed for off-site utilities, the developer undertook on behalf of the town of Henrietta the process of grant application to the Environmental Protection Agency, assisted the town in supervising construction, and when grants fell short of costs, wound up paying the difference.

Naïve Assumptions

There were naïve assumptions concerning the political support, and, therefore, the continuity of the new-communities policy. It was perhaps understandable but nonetheless dangerous to assume that the federal government, because it was providing some backing for new communities, could guarantee the kind of benevolent and enlightened leadership that would sustain the program through periods of difficulty.[15]

In fact, key programs authorized by Congress were curtailed or never implemented. William Nicoson, the program's administrator, has catalogued how repeated efforts by HUD to acquire authorized funds were thwarted by the Office of Management and Budget (OMB) or by Nixon-administration policy changes. For example, funds to help developers meet interest payments during the early stages of development were initially apportioned but later withdrawn.[16] Tax-waiver grants, designed to encourage the participation of public developers, were rejected by OMB on the grounds that public bodies should not be accorded preferential treatment—despite HUD's argument that the grants were needed to reimburse states and localities for the higher interest they would have to pay out as a result of a Treasury Department ruling that federally guaranteed bonds, issued by states and localities, cannot be tax-exempt.[17] Public-service grants, to help meet operating costs during the formative stages of new communities; planning grants to state and regional agencies for the development of rational urban-growth patterns; and planning-assistance grants to encourage innovative approaches among developers were also turned down by OMB. When Congress nevertheless appropriated $5 million for planning-assistance grants, OMB impounded the funds.

Another blow was the new federal revenue-sharing policy, which was designed to replace categorical grants for a wide variety of purposes. This policy had a paralyzing effect. It terminated the basic grants, as well as the supplementary grants for public facilities, which were indispensable to local support and cooperation. In addition, the administration took advantage of some scandals associated with profiteering in subsidized private housing to suspend indefinitely the subsidies for low- and moderate-income housing (provided under Sections 235 and 236 of the housing legislation) which were essential for a balanced mix of housing in the new communities.[18]

Nicoson blames bureaucratic inertia for the administration's attitude, but it is more likely that the decisions reflected the administration's hostility to a program it never wanted. What better excuse could it offer than the need to cut spending in a period of inflation? And to add that the program was inconsistent with the new revenue-sharing policy! Lacking significant political support, the New Communities Program was an easy target.

Faulty Assumptions

The legislation assumed a stable national economy, and that should all else fail the government's special-grants-and-guarantee program could offset the traditional risks of undercapitalization of large-scale community development. Alas, those assumptions were wrong on both counts. No doubt more is known now than in the past about how to manage a national economy, but the additional knowledge was hardly enough to anticipate or to cope with the double-digit inflation and economic recession that whipsawed the economy from 1973 to 1975. The consequences of this "stagflation" are a matter of record.[19] Quadrupled oil prices boosted the costs of fuel, asphalt, and plastics. Other material costs followed the upward spiral. Then, in April 1974, removal of the Construction Stabilization Committee controls led to widespread wage increases. Housing costs rose 11% in 1973 and nearly 20% in 1974, while homebuyers found mortgages more expensive and harder to come by. Sales prices increased and sales sharply declined.

Developers seeking loans for industrial and commercial purposes—activities not covered by the initial HUD loan guarantees—found them almost unobtainable, even at record-high interest rates. The downturn in the property market prompted investors to withdraw their funds from Real Estate Investment Trusts, which had been ready sources for loans. Most serious of all, the recession forced business firms to postpone or cancel plans for opening plants in the new communities.

The sharp drop in sales and rentals, coupled with heavy front-end costs and cash-flow projections wildly off schedule, left developers with no way of meeting their fixed charges. Short of funds—the classic danger of frozen long-term investments with no short-term revenue base—they faced reorganization or bankruptcy as the only alternatives. This in turn raised the perennial questions of new-towns programs: whether even big private builders could ever shoulder the short- and intermediate-term risks of such massive enterprises.

Overreliance on the Private Sector

By casting the private sector in the leading role the main social aims of the program were jeopardized. It seemed only fair to ask for a significant quid pro quo from the private developers if they were to receive public loans and subsidies. But it is common in such cases that the list of requirements tends to expand, as government officials overlook the fact that private developers' principal concern must be profitability. The results are often frustration and bitterness. Failure to meet commitments is regarded by the officials as prima facie evidence of bad faith, while, on the other hand, insistence on the conditions simply confirms the hard-pressed developer's sense that he is being harassed by simpletons and bureaucrats who do not understand the most elementary requirements for business survival. Finally, apprehensive officials and the outsiders often fear that relaxation of the requirements will be taken as a signal that all sorts of hanky-panky will be tolerated. Alas, there is evidence for each of these views.

One of the aims of the program was to "encourage the fullest utilization of the economic potential of the older central cities, smaller towns and rural communities."[20] However, the private developer's criteria for choosing a location are based first and foremost on market demand (for housing, and commercial and industrial facilities), availability of attractive, reasonably priced land (preferably land already in his possession), and the proximity to already-developed areas (thus minimizing development costs). Inner-city locations—in the absence of land-cost "write-downs" under urban renewal—tend to be ruled out by high land costs and land-assemblage problems, distant rural sites by inadequate infrastructure, and lagging regions because they are economically and socially unattractive. The developers' preferred locations are fast-growing metropolises—but these are the areas least in need of federal assistance.

As one might have supposed, most of the new communities were in suburban areas. With the exceptions of the privately developed Cedar-Riverside project and Roosevelt Island, developed by the New York Urban Development Corporation, none of the new communities were in-town because of the difficulty and the lack of eminent-domain powers. Only one of the new communities, Soul City, North Carolina, though beset with severe financial difficulties, tried to serve a lagging region. One reason—perhaps not the only one—was that no provision was made in the legislation for federal help in establishing an economic base for new communities so that they might function as growth centers. Since the government never formulated a clear urban policy, despite a legislative mandate and a feeble, ineffectual effort to do so, there was no way the new communities could serve the aims of such a policy.

The Title VII legislation also stipulated that new communities should make "substantial provision for housing within the means of persons of low and moderate income"[21] and aim to "increase for all persons, particularly members of minority groups, the available choices of location for living and working."[22] The case for providing federal assistance to new communities on the periphery of metropolitan areas was based in part on the anticipated potential of such developments to help the disadvantaged population of these big, fast-growing regions, but this assumption ignored the pressures on the private builder for high yield and relatively safe activities, for more middle- than low-income housing, and for prudence with regard to controversial and potentially destabilizing mixtures of families with different social or ethnic backgrounds.

The New Communities Administration's goal for low- and moderate-income housing was 27% of all units, and on the basis of housing completed by October 1976 they claimed to be on target. But two-thirds of these units were at Cedar-Riverside and Roosevelt Island, the two projects located in inner-city areas, where most of the disadvantaged are living anyway. With the exception of Park Forest South, which in 1974 had a black population of 16.4%, considerably higher than most Chicago suburbs, the racial mix of Title VII communities was reported as being "roughly parallel to the minority profile of the metropolitan area as modified by the specific area in which the new town is located."[23] In short, federally assisted new communities in suburban areas did not much widen for the poor and disadvantaged the choice of a place to live and work.

HUD regulations also required developers to "provide for an ongoing planning and implementation process with local public bodies, residents, community groups, and private agencies."[24] The private developers, however, anxious to preserve the long-range trajectory of development and to protect the financial viability of the project, set up community associations in such a way as to ensure their controlling interest until the land was substantially developed. Partly because of the inadequacy of these processes and partly because of their inadequate representation in the elected chambers of county or municipal government, the main recourse of residents with grievances was dilatory and expensive legal procedures. This is what happened at Park Forest South, where lengthy disputes broke out over the preservation of woodlands, and at San Antonio Ranch in Texas, where a lawsuit involving conservationists concerned about possible pollution of the main source of water effectively torpedoed the project before it started.

Aside from all of these problems, there was evidence that

the program and the supervisory administration had sadly deteriorated. Thus, two new communities (Gananda and Riverton) were in the metropolitan area of Rochester despite expectations that the region's economy would remain relatively stable for the foreseeable future; and Newfield was in the Dayton area, "which during the period 1970–75 experienced an out-migration of jobs and very slight or even negative growth."[25] Further, the scrutiny by the Comptroller General disclosed that market feasibility studies were out-of-date and based on inadequate information; that financial feasibility studies were improperly evaluated and in some instances failed to show that enough money would be generated to retire guaranteed loans; and that the financial progress of the projects was poorly monitored, thus failing to reveal approaching difficulties.[26]

WHEN ARE NEW COMMUNITIES JUSTIFIED?

We do not conclude that there is no case to be made for a new-communities program, but clearly new communities are not panaceas for the problems of housing costs, social integration, urban growth, or lagging regions, if only because of the limited scale of the possible efforts. In no country has the number and the size of new communities been large enough to accommodate more than a minuscule fraction of the growth in population and economic activities of cities and regions; and this situation, given the size of investment in existing cities and the sheer difficulty and cost of building new communities, will not change.

We should also know by now that building new towns is highly unlikely to be a viable proposition for the private sector. Because they require enormous outlays of capital with almost no prospect of adequate financial returns for many years, new communities have to be built quickly and efficiently to keep costs, prices, and even subsidies reasonable. But they cannot be built without complicated and very time-consuming and costly collaboration between the developers and the public officials (at local, state, and federal levels), and between the new-community planners and the residents of the area. Add also (a) the enormous difficulties of raising sufficient capital even by the largest private developers; (b) break-even and profit-making points some 10 to 20 years in the future; (c) the perennial ups and downs of the economy; and (d) the twists and turns of local and federal policies, and it becomes clear why the odds for privately sponsored new-communities programs are heavily tilted in the direction of financial disaster.

Surprising as it may be, we do not conclude from the experience of Title VII that the new communities are necessarily financial losers. True, they are most unlikely to be viable propositions for the private sector. But in circumstances where there is an assured economic base, some form of quasipublic-development corporation could be set up with the capacity to carry heavy waiting costs during the long, risky development period. Were this supplemented with measures for land banking or freezing land prices, it should be possible to reduce considerably the initial front-end investment costs, and to obtain reasonable if not handsome returns from some of the middle-class residential areas as well as from the commercial and other economic activities and the increases in land values.

Nor ought one to suppose that public-development corporations would exclude the private sector from the development of new communities, although the roles of the public and private sectors would be redefined. The private sector would be largely relieved of functions properly the responsibility of public authorities and would be left to do what it knows best: develop real estate. Leadership would come from the public agency, which would be better placed to pursue the social objectives of the program, to obtain access to the substantial funds and subsidies required, to coordinate planning between federal, state, and local authorities, and to recapture much of the increase in land values arising from public investments.

It goes almost without saying that the demise of the 1970 version of the New Communities Program and the lack of interest in or backing for a national or state urban policy will smother further efforts along these lines, at least for a decade or so. But the idea of building new towns will revive in a new guise, for there are circumstances where more conventional forms of urban growth are impossible or inappropriate. For example, in the event of a need for speedy development of an exceptional resource in an undeveloped region, a new community could help attract the firms and the high-level staffs and labor force required for the undertaking (e.g., Los Alamos, New Mexico). A second opportunity for the new-towns concept would be the building of a new capital city, a decision sure to generate many extraordinary problems of site planning, urban design, housing shortages, soaring rents and sales prices, and increases in land values and land speculation. Still another opportunity might be a "new town in town" involving the rehabilitation of an extensive, problem-ridden inner area of the metropolis such as the South Bronx in New York City. Not least might be the possibility of reinforcing at strategic points a national urban-growth strategy if a significant consensus developed on the need for such a policy and on feasible ways of carrying it into effect.

By offering these possibilities, new-communities legislation adds a string to the bow of planners, although, alas, a frail one. There is little prospect of new communities serving the high-priority needs of our existing cities and especially of the poor and disadvantaged population who reside in them, much less of serving as an "essay in civilization," as their most ardent proponents once envisioned. More is the pity, then, for surely new communities are the stuff idealists' dreams are made of.

PART THREE

The Metropolis and City Planning in Third World Countries

CHAPTER NINE

Realism and Utopianism in City Planning

A Retrospective View

It is becoming almost respectable, if not fashionable, to go beyond the traditional tools of scientific research to deepen or to enlarge our understanding of experience. Literary techniques, and, in particular, some of the elements of "story" have been emphasized as one means of achieving these ends. As in the case of suggestive models, this approach may illuminate different, unsuspected, and unimportant features of the subject. Mindful of this possibility, I propose to present a collage of ways in which the "story" of regional planning and development over the past 25 years can be interpreted. I will contrast the "reality" of regional planning viewed as a professional problem with the "reality" of regional planning when examined from political, technological, and what, for want of a better term, I will call the empirical "realities." Then I shall draw some inferences from these realities to some less well-known aspects of regional planning: the shifts over the years from a "technical" to a "sociopolitical" emphasis; the potential conflicts between equality and decentralization; the novelty of the regional characterization of inequality; the movement from and interdependency between the regional, national, and autonomous versions of regional planning; and the quasi-utopian features of both the professional and the political perspectives.

THE PROFESSIONAL REALITY

Ask a regional planner what the big issues and developments were in regional planning in less-developed countries with mixed economies over the past quarter of a century, and he is apt to tell you roughly the following story.

Some 25 years ago, the problems of the big metropolitan regions and of the poor, declining, or undeveloped regions began to loom large in regional planning in most developing countries. Pressures to do something about congestion, land speculation, housing shortages, slums, makeshift settlements, poverty, inadequate public services, and real or disguised unemployment in these cities mounted. There were at the same time growing pressures to find ways to promote economic activities and job-creation strategies in the poorer regions or in regions with untapped resources—partly to reduce, partly to redirect the massive shifts of the poor from the rural hinterlands.

The major central-planning agencies were hardly of much help. They had pursued aggregative approaches focusing on investment, savings, output, employment, and income. They had little interest in where growth should occur, on what scale, or over what period. The main concern was with capital use. There were few regional plans or priorities although investments for roads, ports, river-valley programs, and irrigation schemes had specific location tags. There were no migration policies and almost no adequate housing or other infrastructure or public services to accommodate the migrants moving mainly to the larger cities or development areas where the prospects (or illusions) of jobs and other opportunities beckoned.

The local authorities were not much help either. They had very little power and negligible experience or staff for dealing with the problems. There were very few trained physical planners, almost no trained urban or regional economists, sociologists, or other types of social scientists knowledgeable about or even interested in these problems. Those with training were steeped in the policies of Western, industrialized countries and the tools designed to deal with the problems of these countries, but were rarely familiar with either the policies or the tools appropriate for the needs of less-developed countries. In most countries a ministry of public works or a separate urban-regional planning department handled the problems by quickly preparing area plans—more often honored in the breach than in the practice. Resources were too inadequate to provide more than minimal facilities—perhaps some rudimentary water service, some open-sewer arrangements, or sometimes (at a later date) a water tap or even electricity.

In this welter of change, what was most required were some clear, or at least agreed on, ideas of how to cope with the problems. This consensus did not exist. Some planners and policy makers thought there should be more investment in rural areas, and that the existing migrants into urban areas should be relocated, perhaps even pushed out, and new ones forcibly discouraged. Such a policy, it was thought, would avoid the slumming of cities and the extraordinary levels of unemployment, real or disguised, in urban areas. These views appeared naïve to others because of the limited opportunities in agriculture and the limited scope and effects of land reform, not to mention the possibilities of resistance. Other planners favored development of small urban centers, arguing that these were less expensive to build and provided a more satisfactory physical environment. Still others favored movement to medium-size and even larger urban centers on the grounds that improvements in agriculture were sure to require less people on the land and that more varied jobs and other opportunities were available in the larger cities. There were also the perennial eclectics who pressed for action in all of these directions to whatever extent it might prove feasible.

Before the 1950s, the field of regional planning was too undeveloped to provide significant leads for a strategy of development. The basic doctrines, derived in the main from experience with ad hoc metropolitan and resource-development programs, took for granted that comprehensive development and land-use plans would encourage activities that would exploit the resource endowment, enjoy comparative advantages, and satisfy exchange, employment, and income requirements and other relevant economic criteria. The plans were also supposed to identify the complementary requirements of the principal sectoral activities, public and private, and to provide leads on the necessary infrastructure investments. The function of the land-use components was to ensure both the spatial accommodation of all major activities and more efficient physical patterns of development. One other point is intriguing in retrospect: There was hardly any question on the part of the practitioners but that the ideas could be applied and could be helpful in all sorts of regions—big and small, lagging and growing, subnational and subregional.

However, wrestling with concrete problems in less-developed countries led to a gradual evolution of these ideas into some more detailed and characteristic ways of conceptualizing and attempting to cope with regional-planning problems. In the period roughly from 1950 to 1965, the most important of these ideas and tendencies were:

1. *A reluctance to rely unduly on the market or on public management.* The regional planner fancied that his job was to correct or to avoid the inadequacies of the market economy, but few persons could work in developing countries without losing some faith in the efficiency and benevolence of public ownership and management.

2. *An emphasis on ways in which land-use planning could promote and not simply accommodate economic development.* A variety of measures were involved: control of growth in congested areas, the programming of infrastructure and basic public services, and the provision of financial and other incentives.

3. *A preference for encouraging urban development in medium-size centers outside the region in which the capital city or the large urban centers were located.* This aim seemed sensible, indeed obvious, namely to avoid the diseconomies of large, congested cities and to promote development in poorer regions and regions with significant resource endowments.

4. *A preference for modern, capital-intensive, import-substitutive industrial development (in addition to the customary consumer-oriented industrial and raw-material-processing activities).* There were several reasons: A key aim was modernization; imports suggested viable entrepreneurial possibilities for closely related native producers as well as native importers, distributors, and servicers; also, industrial development was more income-

elastic, diversified the economy, lowered the trade deficit, and therefore reduced risk and dependency.

5. *An acceptance of shantytown housing settlements with minimal services for the poor.* It proved impossible to block most of these settlements. Later, there was also belated and grudging recognition that these settlements, for better or worse, provided effective ways of coping with the housing requirements of low-income families, especially given the patent inability or unwillingness of builders or governments to provide these families sufficient housing of the right type, location, and price.

6. *An acknowledgement, at least in principle, of the need for stress and sacrifice, that is, of the need for an explicit choice of selected areas for development.* The reason was faultless: Even if growth were slowed down in the big cities, it could not be promoted everywhere.

7. *A dependence on national strategies of urban and regional development.* On this score, there was the view that such strategies had to be consistent with national economic-development policies; besides, the prevalence of centralized administrations almost everywhere as well as limited staff resources reinforced the weaknesses of local and regional organization. There was hardly any chance that these relationships would change very much in the near future.

8. *A budding interest in participatory processes.* A basic premise of the "sophisticated" planner was that there was more to planning than just making plans: there was the need to take account of or even to obtain the participation of key interests and groups, nationally and within the region. Some planners even felt that this was one of the most critical but difficult to achieve of all of the goals of planning.

9. *A search, sooner or later, for linkages and integration between national, subnational, and subregional plans.* To avoid laissez-faire bureaucracy, there had to be consistency between micro and macro plans and between their sectoral components.

Given the constraints and the state of the art, most regional planners realized that they had to learn a good deal of what they did in the process of doing it. But this did not stop them from believing (and even from persuading many of their colleagues in related professional fields) that regional planning could help to make sectoral and inter- and intraregional development more efficient and more responsive to basic needs: more efficient in the sense of organizing better spatial arrangements for the most important activities within the city and region and devising spatial-development strategies to do the same on a national scale; and more responsive to basic needs by identifying priorities for remedying the inadequacy of infrastructure and of public and social services in the different regions of the country, including the poorer regions with development possibilities and the poorer segments of the metropolitan region.

SOME DISSENTING VIEWS

There are other ways of interpreting the deeper story behind these events, of explaining what was really happening. For example, consider (1) how the tough-minded "realist" of the right might have written the script; and how this view might compare with (2) the cynical "realism" of the left and with (3) the ecological "realism" of the technocrat.

The Tough-Minded "Realism" of the Right

We can be sure conservatives would point up the illusions of planners, especially with regard to human motivation and behavior.[1] They would argue that the planners' efforts would prove naïve and misguided, because the planners had not taken adequate account of the diverse political and private pressures and do-gooder sentiments, which were apt to push through quite different ideas (many of them popular but not sound) and to divert resources in costly ways. Also, the efforts would be ineffective because there was little likelihood of accomplishing very much with underpaid, inefficient, growing, and often corrupt bureaucracies. Shrewd conservatives would scorn the usual market critique of the planners. True, they would argue, there were social and market restraints, unsatisfactory income distributions, and limited information and factor mobility, and, to be sure, these hobbled market prices and opportunity costs as allocative devices, but these limitations were trivial compared with the planners' ambiguous and inadequate criteria for guiding the location of activities and capital investments. Worse still were the hopelessly inadequate information systems, "intelligence" mechanisms, and implementation tools the planners proposed to substitute for the traditional market indicators and allocative mechanisms—all of which only increased the danger of marginal economies and firms being shored up by endless government subsidies. The conservatives might sum it all up in one basic question: What greater misjudgment could there be than to place still heavier burdens on the limited administrative capabilities and initiatives in the public sector rather than to tap the deep, powerful motives of private interest—supplemented, to be sure, by some limited public measures to accommodate, spur, and reinforce these initiatives and to curb the worst excesses of private action?

The Cynical "Realism" of the Left

If the script were written by the left, the efforts of the regional planners would appear all the more illusory. Their error would lie not in a naïve faith in the public sector, as the conservatives claimed, but in their failure to understand the structure and impulsions of the socioeconomic-political system and the power of the private sector to manipulate individuals and institutions to serve its ends.

On the left (perhaps more than the right) the scripts would vary in emphasis depending on which group did the writing. On some aspects there would be a consensus. For example, all would reject the view that with increasing investment and production in regional-development centers, jobs and income would not only increase but spread throughout the region, eventually blanketing the landscape. This expectation they would stoutly challenge not simply on the grounds that the urban system in most developing countries was stunted, but because the critical economic linkages were with the more-developed areas and the privileged groups in the main regional core and abroad. It is these areas and groups that would receive the benefits and not the periphery.[2]

Save for a consensus on matters of this sort, the scripts of the non-Marxian and Marxian left would interpret the roles of key actors and groups quite differently. The non-Marxian left, mainly the modern dualists, would impugn the whole modern, highly capitalized productive sector.[3] They would object to its dependence on favorable exchange rates, tax concessions, licenses, infrastructure, and other privileges of the state; they would object to its linkages with multinational and other foreign firms; and they would take exception to the role of a Western-educated elite, serving the needs mainly of upper- and middle-income families, devising the basic policies of the state, and living in and biased in favor of the development of a very few large urban centers (particularly the capital city, the commercial metropolis, and one or two industrial or other enclaves). Summing up, they would charge that the economic interests in these centers not only exploited the hinterland's resources, but their economic activities plus the policies of their administrative elites undermined the traditional economy in the rural areas as well as the small-scale, less productive, low-wage, labor-intensive, "informal" sector in the urban areas, thus creating mass unemployment.

How do the regional planners fare in this script? They simply exacerbate the difficulties because they formulate the problems altogether incorrectly. They assume that the informal sector is marginal and bound to disappear as development occurs and that the modern sector, including the foreign and multinational firms, has to be "bribed" by tax, licensing, exchange, and other privileges in order to obtain the necessary capital, technology, and products. As a consequence they neglect two key problems: how to reorganize procurement, infrastructure, and other public policies to encourage the use of appropriate technology, indigenous resources, and the growth of the informal sector; and how to eliminate subsidies (tax and other benefits, duty-free purchases, low exchange and interest rates) for the formal sector, reduce the leakage of their exorbitant investment returns, and curb their formidable economic and political power.

The script of the Marxian left, however, would scoff at these ideas. It would simply reject the notion that the capitalist state is neutral and that matters could be changed by seeking greater autonomy, more appropriate technology, and policies which serve the needs of the informal sector. It would be scornful of the assumption and of the apparent reality of dualism, because both ignored the interdependence of the capitalist and colonial economies and the basically exploitative nature of the market economy which produced and perpetuated a state of underdevelopment. By slighting these basic realities, it would be charged, the policies of the dualists and of the regional planners, directly or indirectly, simply serve the needs of influential economic interests, whether in commerce, industry, or agriculture, and at best provide only negligible benefits for the rank and file in the cities or the countryside. From this angle of vision it is simply naïve to impugn any particular actor or sector rather than the whole system of market institutions, which disadvantages the bulk of the population, requires unemployment for equilibration, and generates class conflict and war. It would be all the more naïve to expect real change before those on the bottom obtained political power and the basic economic activities were publicly owned and managed.[4] No doubt once this major institutional transformation occurred the urban and regional system would reflect these changes, but to envision just how beforehand would be dismissed as not altogether realistic.

To be sure, there would also be other scripts. For example, one dissenting version would expect the Chinese model to prove more appropriate in nonindustrialized economies, where the impoverished peasantry would provide the revolutionary force. Still another would argue that the increasing "tertiarization" and creation of an urban "lumpenproletariat," when coupled with growing disparities of income, might well produce the nonproletarian revolutionary force envisaged by Franz Fanon. This would not occur in the short run, to be sure, since urbanization, because of

the process of "involution" (or fractionalization of jobs), is a potential safety valve which would stave off discontent by creating
petty enterprises, jobs, and the illusion of progress. However,
this respite would end with the commercialization of agriculture
and its penetration by capital, which would displace even more
population and push involution beyond the tolerable threshold.
In either case, it would be held that the regional planner who did
not grasp these realities (and that most of them, alas, did not)
simply mouthed or swallowed bourgeois dogma and served the
interests of the status quo.[5]

The Ecological "Realism" of the Technocrat

There would be even more striking differences if the script
reflected the technocratic view of the ecological reality behind
the economic and urban transformation.[6] From this vantage
point, nothing could be more superficial than the antipathy to the
large metropolis and its technology expressed by resource-
conserving environmentalists and dualists. They simply fail to see
that this new, man-made physical and social environment offers
the opportunity, particularly for developing areas, to escape the
hazards and persistent threats of disaster of the natural environment by developing new knowledge and capabilities, more effective communication, and more and better multifaceted and
multinational organizations. Far from inhibiting progress, metropolitan and multinational organization provides the vital innovative seedbeds of the future for resource development as well
as resource substitution and conservation.

Throughout the world, the technocrats would maintain,
there is evidence of increasing technical capabilities, often in the
most advanced form in the metropolises of the poor countries,
especially in South and Southeast Asia. The progress made is
erratic, but its secular character is clearly evident in the steady
increase of the population, food, other outputs, and technological
innovations which have made it possible for large segments of the
population to move from minimum-subsistence levels to an approx-
imation of an evolving set of norms of basic needs, perhaps better

expressed as a minimum adequate standard of living. This trend will most likely continue, because the metropolis builds up markets and marketable skills, augments knowledge, attracts outside capital, enhances managerial capabilities, and diffuses ideas over wide areas. It even transforms the countryside with its innovations—for example, pumps, machinery, fertilizer, roads, credit, price intervention, changing patterns of demand, and seductive inducements for escaping from tradition. To be sure, many problems result from increasing size, age, and resource depletion, but the metropolis generally develops analytical and feedback mechanisms to examine and eventually to cope with these problems. Progress is also often arrested or deflected by misguided judgments. Sometimes these produce movements to the right because of the obsession of the ruling classes with middle-class values, but such shifts lead to rigidity, curbing of liberties, and the persistent threat or outbreak of civil strife. Sometimes the movement is to the left because of dogmatic commitments to ideologies of equity: this kind of shift may reduce unemployment and gross inequality, but it generally leaves agriculture depressed, innovations hampered, and openness, exchange, and diversity sacrificed. Sometimes the stagnation results from the sheer complacency of moderate, centrist regimes which have satisfied the preferences of the affluent and near-affluent while ignoring the needs of the masses. However, success breeds imitation. The chances are good that visitors and refugees reporting on achievements elsewhere are likely to stimulate policy emulation in those nations which have lost the way or have not yet found the way to cope with these various problems.

THE EMPIRICAL REALITY

For many persons this range of discordant views will only confirm their worst suspicions about the nature, or at least the current state of regional planning, but the situation is not untypical of the most advanced of the social sciences. Thus, with few changes we could substitute Franklin M. Fisher's comments on four papers dealing with tax incentives and capital spending. He observed:

> The four analyses... are all marked by high quality. Each applies sophisticated econometric tools to the empirical and theoretical analysis of an important problem; each sheds light where before there was darkness. If it were not for the inconvenient fact that the four analyses happen to concern the same problem, and happen to contradict each other's findings, there would be little to discuss.[7]

In the case of regional planning, the differences reflect different paradigms, values, and goals. That is why getting more and better data will not help very much. For example, the 1978 *World Development Report* of the World Bank emphasizes the ways in which the progress of developing countries has exceeded early expectations.[8] Its data show not only rises in growth rates from 2.0% to 3.4%, but even more favorable growth rates than those experienced by the more-developed countries during their periods of industrialization, as well as clear increases in real per capita income. The data also show other notable changes accompanying these general trends: mobility of production factors (e.g., significant capital transfers and labor migration), rapid growth of education systems, increasing literacy, improvements in nutrition and health conditions, modernization of agriculture, and creation of new, important institutions, for example, extension agencies, vocational training programs, and development banks. Heartening as these changes may be to some persons, we live in a world of rising expectations and there is much impatience with the view that it must take several generations or more for the impact of these efforts and changes to become manifest. Other facts underlined by the World Bank's report reinforce this impatience. For example: Some 40% of the world's population, about 800 million people, are now living in the most miserable kind of subsistence (what the World Bank calls "absolute" poverty). There is also evidence of growing inequality of income between countries; the gap between rich and poor countries since 1950 has tripled. Worse still, it is far from certain whether the limited progress of the past will necessarily be sustained in the future.

For the poorer countries and the poorer regions and for many intellectuals there is increasing skepticism whether economic growth will necessarily reduce poverty. Take as an example the uncertain attitudes and evidence on what was once considered an authoritative empirical study in the field. Williamson concluded from his data that

Rising regional income disparities and increasing North-South dualism is typical of the early development stages while regional convergence and a disappearance of the North-South problems is typical of the more mature stages of national growth and development.[9]

This observation reinforced a well-known conjecture of Kuznets[10] and a study by Oshima with specific reference to Asia.[11] It was also in line with conventional neoclassical views that the regional income differentials reflected "market imperfections and institutional obstacles [which] will disappear in the process of economic growth."[12]

Hirschman and other growth theorists doubted whether the powerful negative forces could be corrected except by vigorous government action.[13] Still others like Myrdal[14] and, of course, leftists[15] like Frank, Sunkel, and Amin flatly questioned whether government policy could or would reverse these trends. Some recent empirical research appears to support these views and to raise doubts about Williamson's thesis. For example, Gilbert and Goodman have observed that in Williamson's cross-sectional analysis of 24 countries there were only five Third World countries, and in his time-series data only one; so the conclusions, if valid at all, apply mainly to the more-developed countries because of the variations in the income concepts and indicators, the range of error in the data, and the quite different definitions of regions.[16] In addition, more recent and comprehensive evaluations by Gilbert and Goodman of regional income data for 15 less-developed countries do not confirm the convergence trends.[17]

To point up the reality behind their data, Gilbert and Goodman show by a case study of Northeast Brazil that real income of the poorest groups has declined, and that personal-income inequalities within the region have widened with measures of social deprivation remaining high. They emphasize that these results have occurred despite a massive industrialization and infrastructure investment program and tax transfers since 1959, followed by agricultural credit programs and the development of rural infrastructure after the drought of 1970. To help the poor in less-developed areas, they conclude, the policies must aim directly at increasing their access to gainful employment opportunities, extending coverage of social services, and reducing inequality of income.

These conclusions back up earlier, more general rather than regional studies, such as Adelman and Morris's analysis of the experiences of 74 developing countries.[18] They are also both reinforced and extended by other studies, especially Stöhr and Tödtling's comprehensive evaluation of regional policies.[19] Stöhr and Tödtling sum up the findings of a wide range of secondary studies dealing with the experience with regional policies in both more- and less-developed market and mixed economies. Collating these studies posed many problems, for they differ in many respects: some analyses are quantitative, others qualitative; some deal with the policies' effects on broad regional trends, others on their effects on firms or small geographic or economic areas; and, for all practical purposes, it is impossible to distinguish the separate impacts of regional policies, market behavior, and other factors. Nonetheless, Stöhr and Tödtling argue that the evidence in these studies can help us understand the self-defeating characteristics of existing regional policies, and the basis for their extremely serious, unanticipated negative effects. Theirs is clearly an economic brief, but one that is shrewd, sophisticated, always tentative—and persuasive.

At the outset Stöhr and Tödtling concede much economic progress, as measured by the traditional quantitative indicators, for example, number of jobs created, amount of investment, level of regional unemployment, regional per capita income, and gross or net out-migration. They also note evidence in the secondary studies of some reduction of spatial disparities in living levels, or at least the stabilization of these disparities in some countries.

THE JEWEL — embodies a pure, striking, superb visual and architectural ambiance, still relatively unspoiled by subsequent development.

Florence, Italy: Ponte Vecchio, view toward Palazzo Vecchio.

THE SUBJECTIVE CITY— preserve this extraordinary medieval environment, while fostering its inhabitants' welfare? People living there would tear down the walls and buildings, hostile to the concept of a museum for international tourists.

Fez, Morocco: Street and local mosque.

THE AMORPHOUS CITY—the blob, dark, satanic mills, poverty and human exploitation; ugly and polluted environments; breeding places of misery and degradation.

Manchester, England.

Twentieth-century, omnipresent, gas stations, food parlors, honky-tonk developments around the edges of cities in the United States.

Denver, U.S.A.: Colorado Boulevard.

Mushrooming makeshift settlements—shacks, favellas, bustees, bidonvilles, barrios, jhogees, gecekondus, ranchitos.

Bogotá, Colombia: Barrio in transition.

Grim realities of some places around the outer fringes of cities in poorer countries.

Elisabethville, Zaire: Refugee camp in the outskirts.

THE HISTORICAL CITY—strategic points in the campaign of history; accumulation of arresting artifacts and residues of the past, conjuring up visions of their place in history.

Salzburg, Austria: View during festival time.

Istanbul, Turkey: Galata Tower.

THE WORLD CITY—liveliness of people, exciting things happening, night and day; theatre, music, crafts, restaurants, shops, bazaars, delightful streets, varied quarters, parks; convergence of innovative ideas, an international hinterland, and international influence.

New York.

Paris, France: Montmartre.

THE PERIPHERAL CITY—Desolate towns; declining or stagnating hinterlands; lack of vitality, interest, and meaningful opportunities.

Cripple Creek, Colorado, U.S.A.: View down Main Street.

The decadent areas even within our greatest cities—the seamy side—the dreary, the provincial, the callous.

Paris, France: Rue de Jardin.

Dreary or monotonous areas.

Manchester, England.

Somerville, Massachusetts: Mystic Housing Project.

THE OVERDEVELOPED CITY—Great cities concentrate power and markets. They have huge costs, congestion, and slums and stunt development in other regions.

Tokyo, Japan: View of central district.

THE CITY WITHOUT SIGNIFICANT ROOTS—Sterile and uninteresting.

Brasilia, Brazil: General view.

However, in a number of other countries, the studies show that disparities increased or were merely shifted from one spatial level to another (for example, from interregional to intraregional). Even more importantly, the qualitative and structural aspects of spatial disparities "have essentially remained unsatisfactory and . . . have even deteriorated." This is because the new activities in these areas were mainly modern industries "offering high productivity, high demand elasticity and export base demand."[20] In peripheral areas the consequences of this trend included the increased use of limited production facilities for exportable goods (as opposed to basic services) and an underutilization of the natural resources of these areas. The expansion of the production facilities led to increased dependence on the financial resources and the communications and transport networks of core regions (and also to an increased dependence on external demand and external, private decision making); these tendencies clearly ran counter to the objectives of regional self-reliance and sustained economic growth.

The net effect of these changes were leakages of the positive effects experienced in some quantitative indicators of economic development. Such leakages occurred

via organizational linkages of multinational firms or public agencies, leading to the transfer of employment and income effects to other regions through increases in the regional import propensity and a deterioration of the regional terms of trade through the closure of employment or service facilities by extraregional decisions, etc.[21]

What is more, the positive effects may have resulted from the spill-over of bottlenecks of productive factors in highly developed and congested core regions as well as from the explicit regional policies. Therefore, when conditions change, these effects could be reduced or might even lead to a negative spiral.

To count on increased investments makes no sense to Stöhr and Tödtling, because increased transfers are politically and economically difficult and may only be offset by greater leakage. To turn things around, leakages must be reduced. The new policies must veer in the direction of more autonomy and self-reliance.

They must be designed to utilize regional resources and to serve basic needs rather than external demand. They must also transform existing institutions to promote regional development in line with objectives and criteria which would take account of factors now systematically neglected. Items especially emphasized by Stöhr and Tödtling are diversity of employment opportunities and skills, regional-income and employment multipliers, more participatory organizational and decision-making arrangements, increased accessibility among peripheral areas, impact of measures on total spatial disparities, devolution of political powers, equity in the satisfaction of basic needs, and selection of appropriate technologies to serve these aims. In retrospect, Stöhr and Tödtling's study is an abbreviated "second generation" version of the dualism thesis based on two or three decades of experience with regional development.

Still another group of economists, representing the World Bank's Development Research Center and the Institute of Development Studies at the University of Sussex, have reached similar but somewhat more optimistic conclusions. Their data, again admittedly inadequate,[22] are drawn not only from the available information from some 66 developing countries in Latin America, Asia, and Africa, but are based also on case studies of the experience of countries where the inequalities were reduced. The data in general showed that

While in some growing economies the poor receive little or no benefit, in others the opposite is true; even the relative share of the poverty groups has increased in several notable cases. This diversity of experience provides a basis for identifying different approaches to policy.[23]

The economists emphasize that the poor have shared more equitably in Taiwan, South Korea, Sri Lanka, Costa Rica, and Tanzania, because these countries have taken positive action to achieve this end. The conclusion they draw is that it is possible to devise a mix of policies which other countries might employ if they so choose. The group even devised a variable index of economic and social performance (based on preferences of a given society) designed to evaluate various projects. The recommended policies and programs would be targeted for both the rural and the urban poor and in substance would increase their access to land, capital, and jobs. For example, the rural strategy would focus on increasing the productivity of the small farmer and the self-employed through better access to land, water, credit, markets, and other facilities, and the programs for the urban poor would be designed to achieve shifts toward more labor-intensive products and processes. The recommendations stress the feasibility and desirability of achieving growth and income redistribution, *but the great problem that is foreseen is the political issue, not the technical issue.* What will actually happen, it is claimed, will depend on "the determination of developing countries to redefine the objectives of development, to reorient their policies, and to implement them."[24] Others will surely question to what extent the less-developed countries really do have these options!

REALISM AND UTOPIANISM

This ends my story of regional planning over the past quarter of a century. Almost needless to say, others would tell it quite differently. I will go no further here than I already have in depicting, rather than (explicitly) evaluating, these different versions of "reality." However, I do want to draw attention to some additional inferences and observations that can be made about these versions.

Technical versus Political Approaches

There is a widespread belief—let us call it the technical bias—that whenever possible we should transform difficult political or policy questions into technical problems which can be handled with analytical tools. Yet there is an almost equally entrenched belief—let us call it the political bias—that when so-called technical issues involve significant values or change, they should be shifted to the broader political arena, since such issues are too important to be decided by narrow technical specialists.

The technical bias is reinforced when there are apparently successful or dominant paradigms and tools, such as the notions of comprehensive planning or of systems theory or price theory, which may channel the main ways of thinking about problems, sometimes for generations. The political bias is more likely to gain ascendancy if and when technical approaches turn out to be controversial or not particularly successful. It is revealing to examine the main trends in regional planning from this perspective. A quarter of a century ago the problems of regional planning were deemed to be largely technical. Today they are not. In the main, the shift has occurred because pressing the political issue has become a way of challenging or even discrediting what is considered a wrong or inadequate technical approach. The conviction has spread that the wrong groups and interests are benefiting or failing to benefit from technical programs and effective change can occur only in the political arena. This is how the situation is now viewed by the left, right, and center (albeit for different reasons), and there do not appear to be serious grounds for expecting these views to alter much in the near future.

Equality and Decentralization

There are, as we have implied, both a worldwide shift of emphasis in aims from growth to greater equality, and worldwide pressures for less centralization and more regional autonomy. How this came to be and how far it may yet go are not altogether clear; but. despite the increasing influence of these ideas, there are sharp differences of opinion on whether planned decentralization and autonomy are consistent with equalization and whether other alternatives may prove more feasible. Skeptics point to the case of Yugoslavia, where decentralization led to greater inequality by inhibiting the interregional transfers of capital and income. Others underscore the success of the strong central-government policies in South Korea and Taiwan in redistributing assets through land reform and in providing powerful incentives supporting a shift from import substitution to export markets for labor-intensive and small, entrepreneurial activities. These measures, designed primarily to spur growth, also had extraordinarily favorable equity effects by raising incomes for very small farmers and tenants as well as unskilled and semi-skilled labor in urban and rural areas. The measures also sustained or made feasible greater investment in education, and made a subsequent shift to capital-intensive activities less onerous for those least able to shoulder the burdens. The examples in the Chenery study[25] suggest that decentralization and greater autonomy are neither necessary nor sufficient conditions for moving toward income equalization. Also, important as decentralization and autonomy may be under some circumstances for spurring initiative and self-reliance, they may often benefit from and perhaps even require these other forms of assistance to achieve their intended effects.

Spatial Aspects of Inequality

The concern today about inequalities is quite different from the egalitarian ideals of the late seventeenth and eighteenth centuries, which depicted commerce and industry as beneficial counters to the arbitrary power of the state, to the privileged position of the aristocracy, and to the severely constricting effects of existing career patterns.[26] In turn, arbitrary economic power became the force to be controlled, and then in the early twentieth century, intellectuals began to examine the dual role of the state as the tool of the private sector and as a countervailing power against the same private sector. Simultaneously, inequality of income began to be viewed as a singularly geographic or regional phenomenon. Indeed, this view is essentially a twentieth-century development: it is only toward the end of this century that rural-urban, North-South, interregional and intra-regional inequalities receive worldwide notice and the attention of the planners. Also, it is only in this period that the issues of self-reliance and the decentralization of power begin to attract attention. They have done so on an international and a subnational scale and with specific reference to whether multinational activities and assistance programs aid or weaken efforts to cope with inequality and powerlessness.

Regional, National, and Autonomous Versions of Regional Planning

Over the past half-century there were some marked changes in the approach to regional planning. The planning of regions in the future is likely to incorporate the lessons of these experiences. The original aim was to dissect and comprehend: the focus, especially in the more-developed countries, was on the nature and character of the region, on a search for roots and identity, for those characteristics which would enable us to distinguish one socioeconomic spatial configuration of activities from another.[27] Still later, there were public-intervention strategies to solve specific regional problems. Eventually, this tendency led to the view that the most effective levers were at the national, not the subnational level. The national government had the funds, the power, the greater capability to deal with regional problems and to shift resources and attention from other areas. Also, many national problems could be tackled more effectively if the analysis and the implementation could, so to speak, be disaggregated. Small wonder, then, that there was a major shift in perspective favoring national policies and planning for regions.

These national strategies still left much to be desired. There were charges that they smothered local values and initiatives and strengthened the very groups and interests which drained the region of its resources, income, most creative leaders, and energies—hence, the mounting pressures to promote autonomy and self-reliance.

Viewed in retrospect, however, these approaches to regional development do not appear inherently inconsistent with each other. What matters is their combination and application. All three elements will undoubtedly be deployed differently in varying circumstances; but there are, as yet, no clear or persuasive examples of a successful application of all three approaches in less-developed countries.

Utopian Elements

Three dangers generally confront planners—insignificance (i.e., helping something to happen which will happen anyway); interference (i.e., messing up things which would work well or might work even better without the intervention of the planner); and utopianism (i.e., trying to make something happen which cannot happen, or at least not within some reasonable time horizon). By a process of elimination, one might claim that the third danger is the really critical one for regional planning in less-developed countries.

We can dismiss the first danger, for even if Williamson's thesis were correct or without serious qualifications, the job of regional planning might be deemed essential to achieve or to speed up convergence. We can reject the second danger on the grounds that the resort to regional planning arose from a dissatisfaction with the way things worked without such planning. For all the limitations of regional planning, there is at most a disposition to change the policies and to perfect the processes, but not to dispense with the instrument. The tough-minded cynic might argue, however, that all of the scripts promise substantial gains in human happiness by proposing aims that are presently unattainable and destined to remain largely unattainable for a long time to come. In an age of disenchantment, and taking reasonable account of the disappointed expectations over the past 25 years, this accusation is much harder to parry—even if one accepts the view that a quarter of a century is not an unreasonable period for learning processes to occur.

CHAPTER TEN

Changing Perspectives on Area Development Strategies

REGIONAL PLANNING: BLEAKNESS AND PROMISE

There is today in Third World countries little consensus on many crucial aspects of subnational as well as national development planning. This lack of consensus applies to the general aims of development and to technical issues such as the role of growth centers or policies for the handling of the informal sector. It applies also to the interpretation of institutional bottlenecks, to the differences among ecologists, urbanists, and partisans of rural development, and to questions of centralization and participation. The divergence on these matters, like the divergence between left and right, is anything but trivial; and it would be complacent to assume that there is much likelihood of simple resolution.

But conflict, when coupled with need, can stimulate creative responses, perhaps all the more so if the issues are significant and if there is pressure either to make the competing views more serviceable or to ultimately innovate a better version of the rival views. It is this challenge to recast the tools and the perspectives of the field which makes the period ahead potentially one of great promise—for programs in city and regional planning, and for practitioners in the field—especially the younger generation.

Suppose we were to view the main area-planning perspectives in Third World countries[1] (TWCs) through the prism of hopes rather than regrets. Suppose, in addition, we also try to do what T. S. Eliot suggested was so wise and so difficult, namely, "to draw insights from our limitations."[2] What can we say about some of the current changes in development- and area-planning perspectives? How are these views changing and in response to what forces and criticisms? In what ways are the roles of city and regional planners likely to be changed and what obstacles are likely to be encountered in trying to achieve the new aims?

Anticipating our conclusions, two main trends can be noted. The first is that the TWCs are in the process of getting rid of a narrow, conservative tradition of regional planning inherited from the more-developed countries (MDCs), which they are doing partly by drawing on more relevant contemporary ideas and partly through critiques of regional-planning experience made by analysts from TWCs as well as MDCs.

Second, the new development-planning perspectives which place more emphasis on providing employment, income, services, and improved environments for the poor pose four exceptionally difficult problems for regional planners: (1) the policy makers' frequent lack of understanding of the poor; (2) the institutional and managerial tendencies to tilt the benefits of reform programs in favor of those better able to protect their interests; (3) the lack of an effective political voice for the poor; and (4) the limited effectiveness of centralized administrations.

EVOLUTION OF AREA-DEVELOPMENT-PLANNING PERSPECTIVES

Despite the contributions of many scholars to our understanding of the experience of area-development planning in different parts of the world, many of the roles and functions of area-development planners are still quite obscure. It would be worthwhile to have a comparative analysis of these planners in Third World and other countries, indicating in particular the ways they are trained, their social and economic backgrounds and values, what they in fact do compared to what they say they do, and how their activities are changing and how they are likely to change in the future. In the absence of comparative studies providing such information, the remarks below can only be put forward as tentative impressions and hypotheses.

In the past, and this is probably still the case today in TWCs, most regional planners were trained as specialists in some ways of manipulating the physical environment. Mostly middle-class in background, with a few upper-class exceptions, their training for the most part has been in engineering (with jobs in public-works and resource-development programs), and in architecture, landscape architecture, and city planning (with jobs related to housing, industrial development, shopping centers, urban design, and urban and regional landscaping). Whether involved in the making of plans for the city, for regional or urban parks, or for resource development, the main emphasis was on either infrastructure or the physical environment. There was never a sustained central interest in administrative issues such as better city management or regional administration, or in basic policy or economic issues such as the right allocation of resources or the appropriate beneficiaries of the activities of planners.

This area-planning tradition was the one inherited by most of the TWCs. It was not an indigenous tradition. It came either from the administrators when the countries were still colonies or, later, from the foreign consultants when the new nations were still dependent on the more advanced countries for assistance in dealing with specific problems of cities and regions. The main concerns in this tradition were the protection and enhancement of the physical quality and economic value of property, as well as the efficient organization of the environment and exploitation of resources. The patrons of the architects, of the engineers, and of the city and regional planners were the men of wealth and the elite groups who managed the municipal and corporate enterprises.

It was only since the 1930s that regional planners in the MDCs significantly broadened their horizons.[3] They produced a challenging literature dealing with cities and regions. They broadened perspectives on the nature of the physical and social environment. They developed dramatic programs such as the Tennessee Valley Authority. They created independent training programs in city and regional planning and brought housers, legal specialists, land and regional economists, sociologists, and other social scientists into their faculties; they developed greater facility in modeling, policy analysis, and applied research.

One reason for the change was the widespread concern over the social and human costs of unemployment and low income coupled with the widespread dissatisfaction with the physical environment and the quality of life in cities. The other major reason was the conviction that an appropriate combination of public policies for cities and regions would produce viable economic activities and jobs and transform their physical and social environments. These perspectives spread in most of the more advanced countries. For example, in Great Britain and Western Europe there were policies to implement full-employment goals and to improve housing, welfare, and public services. New urban- and regional-development programs were also devised to cope with the problems of big cities and lagging regions.

There were, of course, dissenting views. There were those who felt the emphasis should be on encouraging growth and migration, not helping marginal economies; others felt there was undue emphasis on infrastructure and physical development rather than the needs of the local population; and still others felt the plans did not take adequate account of the economic realities and possibilities of the regions. But such objections were brushed aside—to be considered later if at all—in the fervor to move ahead.

The new perspectives in regional planning, it is worth emphasizing, added a national-policy dimension to regional planning. Better coordination between economic, social, and physical planning became necessary; a new, macroregional dimension to area-development planning, beyond resource development, was added; and significant income transfers from the better to the poorer regions were explored. Although there was some question as to the adequacy of these ideas in practice, most of them appeared to be strikingly relevant to the needs of TWCs and tended to be recommended to them by their foreign advisors or by their elite administrators, many of whom were trained abroad.

However, there were many circumstances that were radically different in the TWCs.

1. In the MDCs, the toughest regional problems affected only a small segment of the nation and of the economy; in the TWCs, lagging areas affected a large segment, sometimes even most of the regions of the nation.

2. In the MDCs, there was a relatively vigorous private sector as well as mature economic institutions; in the TWCs, these elements were often absent or underdeveloped.

3. In the MDCs, rural-land-reform and area-development strategies did not receive major attention because the proportion of the population and economy associated with subsistence agriculture was relatively small and their institutional problems less critical; whereas just the reverse was often true for many TWCs.

4. In the MDCs, it was relatively feasible to handle the administrative burdens of the new programs; but for many TWCs there was at least some question whether this was possible.

5. In the MDCs, there were shortages of trained regional planners and related specialists but these were not serious enough to undermine the programs; whereas in most TWCs there were and are shortages of trained professionals in general as well as few trained professionals in regional planning and related fields.

6. In the MDCs and the TWCs there was increasing interest on the part of the regional planners in developing more regional studies in the social sciences; but because the interests of these disciplines tend to be scholarly, rather than vocational and pragmatic, and because the central focus of these disciplines is on matters other than regional planning, work along these lines was very limited in both TWCs and MDCs; and the prospects for a change do not appear to be promising.

7. In the MDCs, there were often differences between the aims and values of the central-government officials and the local people; in the TWCs, the gulf in class and economic status was apt to be even wider and more difficult to bridge.

8. In the MDCs, the infrastructure investments were apt to benefit the more well-to-do groups in the region, who could profit from these investments, rather than the poorest segments

of the population who were less able to do so; this was probably even more the case in the TWCs.

9. In the MDCs, there were often some organizations or mechanisms to represent more or less the views of the poor and to press for policies that would be responsive to their needs; this was far less the case in the TWCs.

10. In the MDCs, the experience with comprehensive regional planning (which requires a great many things to be done at roughly the same time) was rarely successful; even more difficulties, longer time horizons, and greater patience were likely to be involved in the TWCs, and—given rising expectations—possibly even greater prospects of disillusionment.

ALTERATIONS IN DEVELOPMENT PERSPECTIVES

Let us turn now to some of the shifts in thinking about the problems of development in the TWCs which are likely to be relevant for future policies and programs in regional planning. Four of the most significant are the downgrading of growth as the dominant aim of development, the disenchantment with growth centers, the current popularity of rural development, and the ambivalent interest in the prospects of the informal sector.[4] Our aim is less to evaluate these shifts than to portray them in a way that will enable us to sharpen the issues of area-development strategy.

The Aims of Development

Whatever disagreement there may be about the appropriate aims of development, there is apt to be a consensus that the conventional aims are being reassessed and diversified.[5] The new views stress the political as well as the technical issues. The concern goes beyond growth to the incidence of benefits. The new aims are intended to ensure that the poor profit significantly from development and perhaps even participate more in decision-making processes, and that there be a greater concern for autonomy as well as environmental effects.

One of the consequences of the new aims will be to promote more area-development studies and programs, and to increase the demand for regional planners. These effects, which are especially likely if more attention is given to rural as well as "eco-" development, are not surprising. From the start, regional planning involved criticisms of three lines of thought: the excessive reliance on aggregative analysis of the economy; the identification of the growth of GNP and national income with national welfare; and the view that to achieve high growth and increased income, it would as a rule be best to invest in the most productive regions. There was no consensus that—save for financially attractive resource-development programs in the undeveloped, underdeveloped, or lagging regions—redundant or less productive labor or other resources should and would move to the growth regions. The full-employment, the "basic needs," the "unified," and the environmental approaches are all further expressions of lack of faith in those views.[6]

Pursuit of the new aims would require more varied professional skills. For in addition to much of the traditional knowledge about growth problems, there will be a need for (a) more understanding of environmental and ecological issues; (b) more familiarity with social and ethnic groups about which most planners know all too little; (c) more knowledge about how to make plans for resource-conserving cities as well as plans for rural centers and rural-urban linkages; (d) more skill in handling new, unknown subjects (e.g., analyzing and measuring the effects of alternative technologies or estimating environmental and ecological effects; and (e) more paraprofessional assistance because of the great shortage of trained regional planners.

It is likely, however, that some of these aims, when institutionalized, will prove inconsistent or costly or unworkable. For example, the unified approach, if taken too literally, would involve interdisciplinary, intersectoral, multilevel, and centrally directed relationships which could well involve administrative and other capabilities that may not exist in any society, including TWCs. Similarly, the feasibility of the "basic needs" approach depends on definitions and assumptions about standards, timing, and scale, about people's values and preferences, and about patterns of hierarchical decision making which are quite controversial. These assumptions may also be inconsistent with other aims and potentially explosive, especially if they end up being defined by central-government officials and are hierarchically implemented. Yet these are the ways most TWCs now function. Some of the new aims may also be used to block each other. If experience elsewhere is any guide, ecological considerations will be both used and neglected to serve special interests. For example, the rhetoric of ecology is sure to be mustered to get rid of tidewater, ravine, and hill settlements where the very poor might live, or to block necessary new developments in areas which have special qualities and attractions for others; on the other hand, in the name of development, nations tolerate rape by foreign and local interests of virgin tropical forests in areas like the Amazon and Kalimantan (not to mention the remorseless reduction of the number of primitive cultures in these areas).

In other words, although the new development aims are laudable and reflect some of our deepest social concerns, there is a possibility—and in some environments a probability—that the effects will be mixed and not necessarily positive.

Urban-Growth and Urban-Development Centers

Another major change is the disenchantment with the concept of urban-growth centers.[7] There are some familiar criticisms: the ambiguity of the concept; its faddish and its flexible application when subject to political pressures; its undue and unnecessary reliance on capital-intensive activities; the naïve assumption implicit in it that employment, income, and other salutary effects of growth, of backward and forward linkages, will spread through diffusion processes to the hinterland within a reasonable period and without significant backwash effects or leakages of income; and, last but not least important, the neglect of the relationships of such centers to national-, urban-, or area-development policy.

Nonetheless, the chances are that the concept will be modified (perhaps along the lines suggested by Higgins, by Lo and Salih, and others)[8] but not discarded—because influential ideas with a sensible, pragmatic core simply do not die or get discredited that easily. The fact that there are not enough resources, capital or human, to invest everywhere and hard choices must be made is likely to reinforce the notion that some centers are more appropriate for these investments than others; and that there is a need to distinguish urban centers (a) with different functions and economic activities; (b) with different potentials for propulsive and other kinds of growth within and outside the region; and (c) with different characteristics when serving different strategies (e.g., industrial development, decentralization, rural development, military considerations, etc.) But these notions are a far cry from the original notions about growth centers, and this fact needs to be explicitly acknowledged.

But let me also stress that support for a policy favoring urban-development centers—what I once called "concentrated decentralization"[9]—is likely, even if development policy in most countries tilts far more in favor of rural rather than urban development. This is because urban growth will continue in most of the larger cities, partly because of inertia and partly because even a massive rural-development strategy (as some simple calculations might show) is unlikely, in poor countries, to accommodate the current growth of rural population. The situation in Java, Indonesia, provides the most dramatic illustration (but similar considerations apply elsewhere, as Richardson and others have indicated).[10] In the case of Indonesia, the evidence is that close to two-thirds of the rural migration is now going to Djakarta and Surabaja, and despite the "involution" of the past, some specialists believe that the intense population pressure on the land will produce an even higher rural-urban migration rate in the next 25 years. After evaluating a number of best-guess alternatives, Alan Strout has projected a population for Djakarta of 27 million for the year 2000 (it was about 5 million in 1975), and 9 million, 4.8 million, and 3 million for Surabaja, Bandung, and Semarang, respectively.[11] If it makes sense to slow down this growth (it cannot be arrested) and to change its pattern, then there is a need for a national area-development policy to decide what the maximum proportion of the population is that could be directed to rural as well as various types of urban centers, and on what priority and what scale. The policy, if rural-oriented, would also have to examine densities of urban growth, since Java contains the most fertile soils in Indonesia and the agricultural potentials on the other islands turn out to be quite limited, partly because of the fragile ecological conditions and partly because the transmigration schemes are turning out to be extremely expensive operations.

In short, whatever one might think of urban-growth or urban-development centers in the context of subnational planning for TWCs, there will be pragmatic adaptations of the idea to serve a variety of different needs. Such centers constitute a tool which cannot be dispensed with; but the limitations and adaptations of the tool must be better understood. Several lines of research appear particularly promising in this connection, for example: (a) the examination of how urban centers might function to promote rural development; (b) the exploration of the differences in effects if priority in development is given first to rural and small centers; (c) studies on the nature of the functional and other linkages between urban centers and between urban centers and their hinterlands; and (d) inquiries into ways of reducing income leakages from the region.[12]

Rural- and Agropolitan-Development Alternatives

Rural-development alternatives now enjoy, partly in reaction to the disappointing experience with growth centers, a fairly high standing in most development circles.

There is a widespread acceptance of the view that the poorest, the most neglected, and possibly the most exploited groups are in the rural areas. Reinforcing these feelings is the conviction that national development is hobbled by a rural sector, dependent to a large extent on subsistence agriculture and characterized by marginal incomes, negligible infrastructure and services, poor health, and drastically limited opportunities for improvement. At the same time, there is only a limited consensus on what to do about these conditions. Many economists and agricultural specialists opt for efforts to remove urban bias, to increase demand and productivity through relative price changes (for food and industrial products), and for incremental improvements, for example, better services to improve production processes, technology, and marketing, as well as credit, tax, and tariff reform. Some persons would concentrate these efforts particularly in the areas with great growth potential;[13] others would especially emphasize the poorest regions.

Still other analysts favor, in addition, integrated area-development programs (development of roads, irrigation, rural marketing and servicing facilities, and a network of rural centers). For these programs, too, there is an issue of whether to put the emphasis in the areas where the poor are concentrated or in those with the most attractive growth potentials.

There are also structuralist (and what might be called "born again" agropolitan planners) who favor macro changes: rural-urban linkages, selective closure to avoid leakages of income, and territorial reorganization to facilitate local control and to avoid elite domination.[14] (Almost everyone, structuralists and nonstructuralists alike, favors land reform.) Moderate structuralists count on the help of the central government aided by pressure from below; the less optimistic structuralists put more faith in pressure and turbulence from below and even revolution.

From the vantage point of regional planning, critical constraints would be limited manpower resources and the likelihood of powerful and perhaps even intransigent opposition; hence, it would appear that a surer way of improving conditions would be to increase the demand and prices for products and labor, rather than resort to measures which require either intermediate or long-term adaptation of "culturally embedded resources, institutions and practices [through] participatory processes and strategic interventions," or even more difficult structural changes—essential as these may be in many environments.[15]

In circumstances where only structural change will work, there is little that the regional planner can do until the right combination of conditions makes structural change possible. But in the absence of such conditions, and in recognition of the kind of intractable and often bloody opposition structural change is likely to provoke, planners tend to favor incremental reformist policies which promise some relief (e.g., subsidies, price changes) and the building of organizations which might make it increasingly possible for the rural poor to coordinate their efforts and create effective pressures from below to ensure greater responsiveness to rural-sector views.

In the past, the contribution of the regional planner with regard to these matters has been very limited. This aspect of regional planning is not well developed and often is not taught in planning schools. Yet there is a growing need to learn more about subjects like rural ecosystems, rural population movements, the functions and organization of rural centers and regions, rural public services, regional area- and resource-development strategies, and rural-planning programs and processes. In these matters regional planners (as compared with regional economists, regional sociologists, etc.) ought to have a comparative advantage; but it would probably be prudent to recognize that much time may elapse before the typical regional-planning programs in TWCs will be able to demonstrate genuine capability rather than good intentions.

The Informal Sector

The belated effort to understand and interpret the informal sector is another distinguishing feature of current regional-planning perspectives of TWCs. There is still no agreement on how to define and explore that fuzzy complex of precarious, low-status employments ranging from casual labor and minuscule services to "the most proletarian forms of capital enterprise."[16] These activities, often characterized as small-scale, competitive, unstable, poorly paid, and lacking job and other forms of security, are also said to involve easy entry, the use of indigenous resources, family enterprise, and skills acquired outside the formal educational system. The term "informal sector" itself is loaded with values and implications which are anathema to revolutionaries and "realists." Both reject the notion of a two-, three-, or four-sector world (i.e., modern-informal; modern–rural informal and urban informal; or modern–urban and rural; and informal–urban and rural). There is little or no agreement on many of the activities which are encompassed in the informal sector, the nature of the interaction between formal and informal, and the significance of the functions in the economy performed by these activities. Hypotheses about the phenomena range from speculations about the industrial-labor reserve and marginality to hopes of revolutionary possibilities[17] or of unsuspected resource-development potentials. Recent empirical research is correcting some of the misconceptions about ease of entry, competitive characteristics, and range of income, but such research has not as yet shed much light on the future prospects of the informal sector, or on the significant differences—or at least the varying features—in different environments. The research and debate are sure to continue, but meanwhile, what about the area-development issues?

There appears to be a surprising match between the informal sector and the new aims of development. For better or worse, it is through the informal-sector employments that the poor—both urban and rural—are now obtaining income, services, a toehold in the system. Hence, all sorts of research is now under way seeking to pin down whether these ways of coping and living are really so unproductive and marginal, or whether they are far more labor-intensive, easier for the poor to manipulate, and perhaps likely to prove of great importance now and in the future, both for serving the needs of the poor and for the functioning and the growth of the economy.[18]

How should we interpret this gestaltlike shift in perspective? Only a short time ago the bleak existence eked out by small landholders or tenants on tiny plots of one acre or less—with occasional off-season jobs either on other farms or in rural villages and nearby towns—were deplored as examples of the misery bred by parcelization or involution of landholdings. And the peasants' as well as the local artisans' movements to the city (where they plied their crafts or scrounged at odd jobs or set up as petty traders, because, presumably, there were far too many of the migrants to be absorbed in the growing activities) were also deplored as disguised unemployment. Equally or even more deprecated were the shanties that mushroomed in the hills, the tidelands, the refuse areas, and the outer edges of the city: barely tolerated, frequently bulldozed, they now seem destined to be grudgingly accepted as the most authentic, indigenous, dynamic, and inescapable "new look" in international vernacular design.

Why are the current views so much more tolerant and positive? To begin with, there is recognition of the hitherto unappreciated, positive common denominators in the diverse expressions of this coping phenomenon associated with the informal sector. There is in these diverse activities a dynamism and innovativeness, an astonishing energy and enterprise. There are no rules, or they are made from below; in limited ways the people and the activities involved in the informal sector are a force to be reckoned with, especially when their numbers increase beyond certain thresholds. And these people are surprisingly (or depressingly) conservative.[19] Most of the persons in the informal economy, in rural and urban areas and in the settlements where they live, seek a stake in the system; and there is ample evidence that, despite steady opposition, policy makers everywhere are being forced to take some account of their needs.

Whatever one may think of the sites and services programs, they are the results of policies modeled on the lessons of the migrant settlements; so too are the many experiments now under way to find inexpensive ways of providing services and improving the existing shanty settlements. There is, in addition, increasing evidence of interaction between the formal and informal sectors: of movements from one to the other in terms of employment, income, services, materials, and even location of housing, and often on a scale which is anything but trivial in relation to the local and regional economy—indeed, on a scale which makes the term "dualism" suspect or less meaningful.[20] For many persons, also, there is a clear preference for work in the activities of the informal sector rather than in the industrial plants, despite the advantages of the latter in steadiness of employment and fringe benefits.[21] Not least in importance, there is persuasive evidence of the fairly high productivity of the small landholdings in comparison with the larger farms with expensive capital equipment.[22] Small wonder, then, that some planners are undoubtedly feeling, like Ghandi, that the people are moving and they ought to catch up with them.

But that is far from the whole story. The euphoria felt by many persons about some of these neglected possibilities tempts one to make the reminder that efforts, still groping and experimental, to promote the informal sector are, at best, ameliorative, involving for the most part very limited improvements of living and working conditions. Accepting this limited way of doing things may be an admission of the inadequacy of the economy just as rejection of the informal sector may be a failure to recognize the strength the sector brings to the economy. Even more worrisome is the question of whether enough is known about the informal sector to do more good than harm by intervening. Easy credit could well produce an inflationary impact and raise the rates for access to privileged niches within the informal part of the system. Another possibility is to strengthen the syndicates, which have sprung up to help owners of minuscule enterprises cope. (Lisa Peattie even reports that "Barranquilla, Colombia was recently the focus of the first International Congress of Latin American Shoeshiners.")[23] But efforts to strengthen the syndicates are likely to produce the same inflationary and quasi-monopolistic effects. And we know so little about how infrastructure investments or subcontracting requirements might be arranged so that the benefits reach the groups one intends to help. Perhaps the most paradoxical fact of all is that the absence of the institutional rules which govern the modern sector is one of the striking strengths (as well as weaknesses) of the informal sector. One cannot but wonder whether the introduction of incentives and programs for improvement (and other intervention strategies, no matter how well intentioned) might eventually change for the worse these essential preconditions for the survival of the activities in this sector.

So the exploration of these complex subsystems of TWCs must be part of the new thinking about area-development strategy; but how many people are there in regional-planning circles qualified to conduct the search and to interpret its meaning?

PROBLEMS OF FULFILLMENT

What is the likelihood that the refocused aims of development, especially the stress on employment, rural development, autonomy, and the informal sector, will produce an adequate response from regional planners? One might suppose that getting a shift of focus was the hardest thing to be done. But there are all sorts of handicaps which make an adequate response difficult, perhaps even impossible. Four problems, in particular, have to be taken into account: the pervasive lack of understanding of the activities and needs of the poor, the habitual ways in which systems function to strip the poor of the greater parts of the benefits, the anemic political mechanisms which exist for amplifying the demands and potential clout of the poor, and the frustrating inability of the centralized regional-planning bureaucracy to get jobs done.

Inadequate Understanding of the Poor

One of the recurrent lessons learned from programs around the world to help the poor is how badly these programs are often designed and how much this is due to the sheer ignorance of the needs of the groups to be served and the nonconsultative processes on the basis of which the decisions were made. There are many reasons for these failures including physical and social distance, hubris, and the customary differences in frames of reference. This latter problem obtains particularly in TWCs, where planners often operate out of a capital city or a provincial center viewing the poor (with feelings varying among affection, pity, distaste, hostility, fear, or indifference) always from the top down.

So far as I know, we have no adequate studies of the self-images of regional planners in TWCs. The odds are that they perceive themselves as enjoying a much higher class status than most of the groups they are serving, particularly when the groups they are serving are the poor in urban and rural sectors. Anthropologist Lisa Peattie suggests that

A member of a relatively high status group finds it difficult to see people below his class line with precision and clarity and even more difficult to interact with them as fellow humans with equally valid conceptions of and claims on social reality. His vision is as it were, refracted off the class barrier as off the surface of a pond.[24]

It may be possible but it is probably quite unlikely that sensible policies and programs can be worked out for groups or activities one does not understand. One can try, of course, and often does, and the policies and programs may move full speed ahead . . . until some day there is the sickening realization that they just do not work.

This limitation has been painfully evident in the past in the programs of planners everywhere, but especially in TWCs. Thus, planners' hostile attitudes and their efforts to discourage petty employment, tricycle transportation, and makeshift shelters reflect the incompatibility of these activities with their typical repertory of policies, land-use plans, and criteria for commercial and residential development. Their well-meaning and generally unworkable alternatives, such as the efforts to provide alternative sites for these activities in some remote or less accessible parts of the city, tend to encounter the same problem. What is still hard for the traditional planners to grasp is that their rules and programs are often apt to be the opposite of what may be needed, and may in fact ensure more expensive, time-consuming, and often less adequate solutions.

Florence Nightingale suggested that hospitals, whatever else they did, ought not to reduce the prospects of survival for the patients who entered them compared to those who did not. Many hospitals in the nineteenth century did not satisfy this modest criterion. It is at least worth pondering whether the current capabilities and training and programs of regional planners, in relation to the needs of the poor in TWCs, are likely to improve the lot of the poor. It is the discovery of this doubt which lends special poignancy to the testimony of John Turner that it was essential for him to stop working for people and to begin working with them to learn what was necessary to make the programs they worked on succeed, and to create a mutual learning situation so that he as a professional might learn what he needed to learn in order to do his job adequately.[25]

How the System Disadvantages the Poor

The second problem concerns the myriad ways in which social systems operate to the disadvantage of the poor. Planners generally assume that their intervention can make the system operate more effectively and equitably. This assumption presupposes that planners understand the systems they are manipulating and how the tools they employ actually work, so that when they try to do something they achieve the intended effects—more or less, or at any rate, sooner or later. What is being discovered all over the world—in socialist as well as market-oriented economies, and not least by area planners—is that this "ain't necessarily so!" It is hard to accept this perverse reality until one has actually wrestled with the ways institutions, interests, and individuals often operate so that programs for the poor end up benefiting other groups instead.[26]

A concrete example is the problem of trying to devise a mechanism in Bangladesh that would supply relatively inexpensive credit to small farmers, tenants, sharecroppers, and landless population. In Bangladesh as elsewhere, the poor are not served by institutional credit but by the informal sector (money lenders), affluent farmers, and various suppliers (of seed, fertilizer, etc.).

An experiment (backed by the Agency for International Development [AID], a technical-assistance agency), was undertaken by the central bank and nine different types of participating financial institutions. Funds were to be made available at varying interest rates for a wide range of purposes (seed, fertilizer, insecticides, farm equipment, rickshaws, etc.). There were also a variety of mechanisms for making credit available (use of local villagers or schoolteachers as bank representatives, setting up offices in nearby towns with a minimum of red tape, combining the credit efforts with area-development programs, etc.). The aims of the experiment were

to learn what kinds of problems particular programs were likely to experience, including indirect as well as direct effects, and how the programs are received by those who implement them, by those who participate in the programs and by those in the area who do not participate . . . with particular attention to the distributional consequences of variations in program design and interest rates.[27]

The program is still under way and the final results have yet to be assessed. But a review group noted at the early stages of the experiment that even this program might turn out, like others in the past, to favor the larger farmers and their allies because of the relationships among the different groups as well as the insitutional and other biases embedded in the program design.[28] A key problem, for example, was that many people were loath to take advantage of the programs for fear they might offend local officials, religious leaders, money lenders, or other influential persons whose help might be needed in case of trouble; and it was not easy for the public agencies to do much about these fears. Indeed, the attitudes of the financial institutions often contributed to this behavior, since they are often more inflexible than the local money lenders in their demands for repayments even when there are good reasons why repayment is impossible. In addition, the reliance in most of the credit arrangements on cosigners was likely to reinforce the local structures of patronage and dominance by the more substantial farmers.

Also revealing were the administrative and institutional

biases built into the program. Thus, the principal villages included in this experiment were close to branch offices, and so were likely to be the more prosperous villages. The rules of eligibility and the definition of the target group specified a line below which applicants would be deemed eligible, but there was nothing to prevent and much to encourage the clustering of loans at the upper end of the distribution. All of the experiments were also designed to be administered by agents of the bank—with no experiment in which landless or marginal farmers could control the management of the programs.

These factors were augmented in turn by other assumptions as to the purposes to be served by rural credit and the processes by which credit could generate additional rural income. For example, it was assumed that credit programs with project settings and villages in areas with roads, irrigation, and storage facilities would have more productive outcomes, but these villages are usually the more prosperous centers. The focus on agricultural investment also disadvantaged women and landless persons who might wish to finance productive enterprises of a nonagricultural character. And to the extent that many of the nonagricultual rural prospects required the building of collective institutions for success, the predominantly individual focus of the credit program would disadvantage them.

Finally, the programs assumed that savings by the rural poor in banks served their financial interests better than alternative investments of traditional forms of savings regardless of current or prospective rates of inflation, and that savings in the branch banks of the financial institutions would be used primarily to sustain or expand the rural credit programs among small farmers and that the funds would not be invested in the major city of the region or perhaps even outside the region.

The Bangladesh experiment is only one example, but we can be sure the problems extend to many other aspects of the system we seek to control; and this is why, to achieve the aims of development, we are obliged to make the confrontation with these realities key components of our education, our research, and our policy programs.

Political Clout

The third factor which hobbles the poor in most TWCs is the weakness of mechanisms which not only amplify discontent and ensure that attention will be paid to the opinions or grievances, but also influence priorities and resource allocation. "The effort an interested party makes to put its case before the decisionmaker," Edward Banfield observes, "will be in proportion to the advantage to be gained from a favorable outcome multiplied by the probability of influencing the decision."[29] Many, perhaps most, of the unorganized poor in TWCs are less demanding in part because they do not have (or perceive) effective ways of influencing the system, and in part because it is not always clear how significant the benefits would be in relation to the efforts made.

Wayne Cornelius has mustered much evidence to show that

the low income migrants should not be viewed as a "non-demanding" sector of the population, even though the demand making in which they engage is considerably less frequent than has often been assumed. However, the demands which they make upon the political system remain highly parochial and limited in scope. They are the kinds of demands which can be satisfied most easily by incumbent authorities without fundamental changes in government priorities or patterns of resource allocation. A political system in which most participation by the urban poor is confined to contacting officials about community-related needs is one which tends toward preservation of the basic sociopolitical order.[30]

Put differently, many, perhaps most, of the political parties in the TWCs do not depend for their support on the rural or unorganized urban poor, and neglect of the interests of the poor involves relatively modest risk to the parties' ability to stay in power. It has been observed that, in Venezuela,

Even an unemployment rate averaging 17% of the non-agricultural active population is not a "national problem" unless it is so defined; without such a social definition it is the problem of the people who are unemployed. If their individual discontents and maladjustments are never aggregated and organized in political institutions, they may demand to be coped with by society merely as they emerge indirectly in other recognized problem areas. . . . Although the "problem of unemployment" figures in the rhetoric of politics, and the reduction of unemployment is stated as a major objective of national planning, none of the political parties has yet developed the kind of mass base among the unemployed or marginally employed which would use their situation as a lever for change.[31]

Where there is no serious political penalty, it is unlikely that the ministers or staffs of the key public agencies will be pressed to come up with far-reaching ideas or programs to deal with the needs of the poor.

Albert Hirschman has suggested that the main ways to bring pressure on an organization to improve its performance are either through exit (to leave) or voice (to protest). The poor are poor in part because their exits and their voice are so constrained. Most of us in the United States know that those who can complain to decision makers and can impose high penalties on them for failing to respond effectively are not likely to have their interests neglected. One inference Hirschman draws from all of this is that

The role of voice in fending off deterioration is particularly important for a number of essential services largely defining what has come to be called the "quality of life" [and] since, in the case of these services, resistance to deterioration requires voice and since voice will be forthcoming more readily at the upper than at the lower quality ranges, the cleavage between the quality of life at the top and the middle or lower levels will tend to become more marked.[32]

One of the questions for training in regional planning in the future in TWCs is whether the regional planners can and should do more than they have in the past to help the poor acquire significant ways of exercising both voice and exit, both in community- and work-related organizations: voice, in part through participatory processes and local control of programs, and also through mobilization around issues, monitoring of the bureaucracy, and (where feasible and appropriate) even dramatic confrontations—all designed to give pressure, group solidarity, and organized expression of demands more of an educational role and greater legitimacy; and exit, by making other alternatives, including migration, more visible and meaningful as ways of improving local conditions.

Centralization

The fourth problem is the frustrating inability of the centralized bureaucracies to make many programs work. There may be a few exceptions—Singapore, Hong Kong, South Korea, Taiwan, possibly even Botswana, Mexico, and Brazil—but by and large the national bureaucracies of most TWCs suffer from tremendous inadequacies and overload.

In most of these countries the national ministries concerned with regional planning are also ministries of housing and public works, and are also preparing plans for local and provincial organizations. There are often not more than a handful of professionally trained staff within these ministries who are reasonably knowledgeable about urban- and regional-program development or about major policy issues. Even if they were on the whole more knowledgeable, these professionals are burdened with the responsibilities of preparing or supervising the preparation of land-use plans, urban-development programs, and area-development projects for most of the major cities, not to mention land-use standards and regulations and ad hoc chores ranging from emergency assignments to reports needed by the ministers or international agencies or by some legislative or interministerial groups. It does not take much probing to learn, if one is privileged to talk frankly with these high officials, that they are skeptical: dissatisfied with the duplications, disproportions, and sheer inefficiency in programming, and worried about the fact that they may be making wrong or badly informed decisions and that they are neglecting the more significant policy planning, evaluation, and local technical assistance which constitute their more appropriate responsibilities.

Major changes are needed; but they will not come easily. Budgets are inadequate; the number of professional staff is small; and their quality is uneven. Many persons do not work seriously—and for understandable reasons. Poorly paid, they need two or three jobs to earn enough to support a family. What is suprising is how devoted many of them are and how hard they often work. Outside consultants who have been called in with funds obtained from technical- or bilateral-assistance programs are sometimes very helpful; but their number is limited and the quality of the expatriate staff is quite varied: some are capable and devoted; others would have difficulty finding equivalent positions in their own countries.

Information, reporting, and research systems are poor. Top staff often lack reliable data needed to manage their own operations or to guide key policies. They are frequently embarrassed to learn about major new developments (private and public) of which they were not aware and which will create serious problems for services they should be providing (water, roads, housing, even commercial and industrial development). They are sometimes stunned by shocking errors—like zooming ahead with agricultural settlements in areas with fragile environments which will produce "green deserts" in just a few years, sometimes before and sometimes, alas, even after appropriate studies are made.

That too much is being attempted in the central office is quickly conceded, but then extenuating circumstances are always cited: the weak offices in the regions; the unwillingness of most well-trained people to go to the regions which lack the services, the schools, the friends, the family ties, or the opportunities to move ahead; the limits to the premiums and adjustments of salaries which can be arranged to provide more tangible incentives for the shift. What is more, some of the regions are dominated by separatist elements; hence, the people on top deem it too risky to give the regions greater power to run things.

Coordination, too, is often a morass. Some ministries, because of negative experiences, will not even seriously consider proposals or programs if they require the cooperation of or implementation by other sectoral agencies. There are many reasons. In come cases, these other agencies may be run by different and hostile political parties. In other cases, these agencies may not agree with the policy or they may feel threatened if they view the programs as invasions of their turf; or they may not have the funds or the staff to do the job; or quite often they may simply be unable to do what is needed, and a change in management and staff may not be in the offing for some time to come.

Often what appear to be reasonable policies bog down when it comes to implementation. This is one of the classic quandaries of centralized planning. Implementation always turns out to be far more of a problem than anticipated. Take, for example, the policies of discouraging or reorganizing further growth in the big cities and of encouraging new activities in the hinterlands. The tasks of making the firms in crowded areas pay full costs and of providing sweeteners to get firms to areas that need jobs are not easily achieved. The subsidies are inadequate. They rarely provide meaningful incentives to go to the less attractive areas; they are often not used, or they are taken up by firms which are planning to move to these locations anyhow. Even public enterprises go their own laissez-faire way. Planners in about every TWC could probably produce quite a list of important activities—from integrated steel plants on down—which went not only to untargeted areas but often to precisely those locations where they were not supposed to go.

Administrative controls, too do not work, or work badly. There are always exceptions—and bribes. Enough illegal building is going on to make a mockery of the efforts at land-use control. Some wrong kinds of development are being discouraged; but there are also thousands of houses and plants that have been built or are now being built in areas which have been interdicted. The odds of getting caught are small; and the penalties are insignificant compared to the rewards.

These difficulties sum up a lot of situations we know or suspect are occurring and which require radical changes in the way we plan, manage, and teach. To be sure, many of these same problems will be found in MDCs, but the failures are often not quite as disastrous, and usually are easier to remedy. In any case, it would be imprudent to ignore these realities, especially for those people who are critical of the way the market functions, of the way private wealth concentrates power, and of the way large segments of the poor tend to get the short end of the stick. But if government is to rely less on the market, it must understand better what it can and cannot do. It will not suffice to argue that many things are better than before; that a dent has been made in the birthrate; that public services are being improved; that there are more jobs, schools, clinics, roads, extension services; that there are many new initiatives, some even coming from below, and that a lot of them may even take root. Even if it is not true that *"plus ça change, plus c'est la même chose,"* expectations are higher and current performance in most TWCs is not good enough. This must be clear even if it is understood that there are no quick, easy panaceas—not from the government and not from the market.

PART FOUR

Educational Dilemmas in City Planning

CHAPTER ELEVEN

Four Approaches to Urban Studies

THE MAIN EDUCATIONAL PROGRAMS

Formal instruction in the urban-regional field is proceeding today under four different kinds of banners: city planning, regional science, area-policy analysis (or applied disciplinary studies), and urban and regional studies. From a historical perspective each has emphasized a neglected terrain: city planning has dealt with the interrelationships between land uses, regional science has stressed the disciplinary aspects, area-policy analysis (or applied disciplinary studies) has analyzed urban and regional problems and pragmatic policy issues, and urban and regional studies has sought a balance between these components.

The differences in assumptions and styles in each of these fields are not trivial. Nonetheless, those who attach great importance to political economy or to the market economy may well dismiss this range of educational approaches to urban studies as minor technical differences. The radical would argue that these approaches assume the market economy works or could be made to work with appropriate policy and planning, and that this assumption is precisely what must be challenged. The conservative would raise equally strong objections to the presumed capabilities of planning. Both the radical and conservative would probably argue that the more significant alternatives are quite different: the former emphasizing how to produce structural change in the economic, social, and political systems; the latter emphasizing how to curb the bureaucracy, reduce the role of government, and strengthen the market. From our perspective, however, these critiques would miss the main issue under consideration, namely the kinds of skills considered necessary in the more- as well as less-developed countries—socialist and nonsocialist—to guide area development; and it is for this reason that we shall focus our attention on the formal educational approaches touched on above.

City Planning

Most area- or physical-planning programs throughout the world operate under the labels of "city," "regional," "environmental," or "town and country" planning. Their emphasis is generally on land-use planning.[1] In the past, land-use planning involved aspects of city engineering, surveying, landscape architecture, or urban design. Today it generally embraces concern for the ways our behavior and decisions affect land use and the built environment, and the ways land use and the built environment can be shaped to serve our ends. The base for these programs is generally in schools or departments of architecture, landscape architecture, city planning, environmental design, or civil engineering; and the principal specialists come from these fields. If resources permit, these programs will often include on their faculty an urban or regional economist, a transportation specialist, a sociologist, a geographer, and an attorney—part- or full-time. These programs also try to establish close collaborative relationships with allied fields, particularly architecture, engineering, and the social sciences, but these relationships do not always develop easily or evenly.

Many, perhaps most, of the staff specialists in the planning offices in local and central government, and in the present consulting firms in regional or area planning, are likely to have been trained in these programs. The demand for these specialist skills, especially in environmental design, site and land-use planning, and civil engineering is apt to continue; and if these specialists show any leadership qualities, they will obtain a fair share of the top policy positions.

On the whole, city planners believe that city or land-use planning is a profession, not a discipline: it is a field like law or medicine which emphasizes practice—that is, the application of theory, doctrine, and techniques to recurring or new cases—in contrast to fields emphasizing the quest for systematic knowledge, such as economics or one of the other social sciences. There may be differences of opinion whether architecture or civil engineering or city planning constitutes the best training for the purpose. In part, this question may depend on whether the handling of facilities, urban design, or land-use policy and development requires the most attention. The services of other specialists (economists, urban sociologists, and geographers) are important but their contribution is tangential. And although occasional individuals 'from these fields may be versatile and capable enough to develop leadership roles, they are clearly exceptions that can be accommodated. Certainly the existence of such exceptions should not change the main training or career development channels.

Regional Science

Regional science, on the other hand, puts its emphasis on the "disciplinary" side. To date, however, it has won more success as a professional organization than as a formal field of study. As of December 1979, there were 2,100 members in the Regional Science Association, and 2,300 subscribers to the *Journal of Regional Science* and 2,700 subscribers to the *International Regional Science Review*.[2] (There are 800 members in the Regional Science Association in North America [compared to approximately 16,000 members in the American Planning Association], 850 members of the European Branch [Germany, France, Scandinavia, Britain, etc.], 300 members in Japan, 100 in Australia, and 50 in Latin America, Africa, and elsewhere.) But there are only two "active" programs in regional science offering the Ph.D. in the United States (the Department of Regional Science in the University of Pennsylvania and the Program in Regional Science

at Cornell); one offering a Master's degree (Syracuse); one allow-
ing a concentration in regional science at both the Master's and
Ph.D. levels but no degree program *per se* (State University of
New York at Binghamton); two undergraduate programs
(Pennsylvania and Cornell); and four overseas programs
(Karlsruhe, Liverpool, Louvain, and Queensland). None of the
postdoctoral programs is now active.

Regional scientists would undoubtedly like to see many
more independent educational programs in universities throughout the world. They may possibly develop in the future, even
though the current prospects do not appear too promising.
Meanwhile, in the absence of such programs, the Regional Science Association draws its membership from specialists (associated either with programs of urban planning or with various
branches of the social sciences) who want to advance or to keep
abreast of the application of various models and quantitative
studies in urban fields. In this respect it has been more successful, for whatever one may think of regional science as a formal
field of study, there can be no doubt that the association has
attracted some of the ablest minds in urban and regional studies.

The very term "regional science" indicates the main aspiration of this approach, which is to establish the scientific character
of work in area studies. The way to do this, regional scientists
believe, is to extend the application of models and quantitative
analysis to area problems. The fact is, however, that most of the
basic concepts, models, and tools were innovated elsewhere:
they come from economic theory, decision theory, game theory,
linear programming, operations research, ecology, and the like.
In any case, most regional scientists place their faith in the re-
finement of analytical techniques as *the* way, or as the most important way, in which significant progress will occur.

The essence of the Regional Science view is that area studies,
like any other scientific field of study, must be tackled with mathematical and other rigorous quantitative methods if it is to escape
from the hazy, discursive, anecdotal approach of the past. Work
along these lines must be pursued as a separate field of study,
or it will be neglected. However close regional science may be

to geography, urban and regional economics, and urban and regional planning, it involves tools and perspectives which are not common to these fields or go far beyond them; and this work, if entrusted to any of the traditional disciplines, would not progress effectively. Set up as an independent field, however, with an active professional association, journals, and the like, regional scientists can provide a critical professional audience for their own community and for specialists in related disciplines who are interested in their approaches and whose work would otherwise languish or receive insufficient encouragement. Nor is there any need to be concerned about future prospects, for sooner or later the ability and the accomplishments of regional scientists will spur recognition of the importance of setting up independent educational programs in regional science in many universities.

Area-Policy Analysis or Applied Disciplinary Studies

There are no good data on the number of urban or regional specialists in each of the social sciences. Most, perhaps as many as two-thirds or more, have degrees in geography, economics, or political science. Many of them probably acquired their urban and regional skills in area programs or field studies. Others supplemented their formal disciplinary training with some urban and regional courses in their disciplines (e.g., urban and regional economics for economists, urban and regional geography for geographers, and so on), and doubtless they included some urban and regional subjects outside their disciplines—if suitable courses were available. Nonetheless, the principal aperçus and methods of these specialists come from their disciplines.

There are, to be sure, too many variations to consider each category separately or in detail. But we need to consider at least the case of area-policy analysis, one of the more recent competitors in the urban-regional field. Not surprisingly, it is not even viewed as a competitor in some quarters, whereas others consider it the approach with the most potential for the immediate future. Its orientation—like city planning—is problem-oriented rather than disciplinary. It seeks to provide diagnostic skills for the development and implementation of policy, and for policy analysis in the public or private sector with some formal training and field work in a specialized area. These programs have acquired quite a vogue in the United States, partly because of the disillusionment with the outcome of previous policies (public, not simply urban). The view in many quarters is that some of these failures could have been either foreseen and avoided, or at least made less serious, if there were more effective policy analysis and more sophisticated application of pragmatic, evaluative techniques. The individual programs vary, of course, but in general they rely on an assortment of modeling and quantitative-analytical tools. The practitioner is expected to become adept in employing operations research, decision and game theory, welfare theory, cost benefit and effectiveness concepts, and the like when dealing with evaluation problems—whether of goals, programs, or projects. This is the core methodology, which is then supplemented with relevant backgound courses in economics, political science, organization behavior, and so on. The Kennedy School at Harvard is one example of such a program, but there are several other policy programs in institutions such as the University of California at Berkeley, not to mention potential variants on this theme represented by the Universities of Pennsylvania, Stanford, and Carnegie-Mellon, or by the Political Science Department of MIT.

The proponents of this approach hold the following general beliefs: More and more tasks are being thrust on the public sector and large organizations; hence we need to make things work much better. Policy analysis is the general professional skill needed to improve the performance of the public sector and, for that matter, large areas of the private sector as well. The tools and habits of mind provided by these programs can help the decision maker and the manager diagnose and attack his problems with more sophistication. Since these techniques apply "across-the-board," there is no reason why specialists in the policy sciences should not work in the urban field (and vice versa), for the skills of these specialists can respond to need, opportunity, and interest.

Urban and Regional Studies

Although, because it has evolved gradually within departments of city planning, it is not generally heralded as such, urban and regional studies represents still another approach—now based at centers such as MIT and, to a lesser extent, the University of California at Berkeley. The main features of the MIT program warrant examination, because at this time they probably constitute the most important expression of this experiment.

Until the end of the 1960s, MIT was one of the leading institutions emphasizing, in the main, the professional approach to land-use planning. Today, MIT still emphasizes professional training in urban and regional studies but has a Ph.D. program which stresses research capabilities, joint-degree programs with economics, political science, architecture, and engineering, an undergraduate urban-studies program, and two special one-year, nondegree programs, one on the problems of developing countries and the other on the problems of minorities in American cities. The current program in urban and regional studies involves many generic as well as disciplinary research and analytical skills, associated particularly with applied social science. Although the main focus is still on community and regional development, environmental policy, urban design, and resource management, the scope of the field is much broader, for it encompasses the socioeconomic, institutional, and political problems within cities and regions as well as the problems of city and regional growth and development.

The kinds of faculty associated with the teaching programs include specialists in the related aspects of the social sciences (urban and regional economics, sociology, psychology, anthropology, social policy, political science, and history); specialists in substantive areas (land law, housing, legislation and the legislative process, criminal-justice systems, social services, community development, urban and regional problems of developing countries, organization behavior, and decision theory); specialists in policy, institutional, and comparative analysis, and political economy; and, finally, land-use planners, architects, and specialists with exceptional methodological skills; for example, computer programming, operations research, modeling techniques, and quantitative as well as qualitative research tools.

Summing up, proponents of this program say that urban studies is an effective way of providing not only professional training, but also disciplinary skills and a general education. What is more, such a convergence of functions may prove indispensable for coming to grips with basic urban and regional problems. Perhaps in no other way is it likely that this field can develop the sustained, multidisciplinary attention necessary to develop the intellectual capital and capabilities of the field. This does not mean that specialists from architecture, engineering, law, public health, or the social sciences will not (or should not) work on urban problems, too—quite the contrary. However, the central interests of these other professions and of the social sciences are not in this area; and marginal or even intensive sectoral contributions will not suffice to produce the intensity, range, and continuity of effort necessary to advance the capabilities of this field.

THE CASE FOR URBAN AND REGIONAL STUDIES

It is easy to resonate sympathetically with each of the views just presented. We do not have here a situation where only one is "right." What we have are a variety of programs with quite different heritages and capabilities trying to be responsive to increasingly visible and complex area-development problems. It can hardly be surprising that those who are responsible for guiding programs in architecture, engineering, and the various social sciences should look with more or less sympathy on urban extensions of their work, and with all the more sympathy if these extensions bid fair to provide a new market for their products.

One need only scan the subject matter to observe that the different programs are at least complementary, if not overlapping. Nonetheless, the current differences in emphasis between the programs are of considerable consequence for urban and regional specialists. For example, city planning in the past underemphasized disciplinary considerations (modeling and theory) as well as institutional, social, and policy aspects. On the other hand, with rare exceptions, social-science programs in general, and policy-analysis programs in particular, treat urban and regional issues as one of many examples of social-science and policy problems, and therefore somewhat superficially—unless these programs are effectively allied to a professional program of urban and regional studies. Regional science has neglected political economy as well as institutional and policy issues; and urban studies, which presumes to cut across the professional and disciplinary aspects of urban and regional issues, requires extraordinary resources to do so. In the process urban studies has run into great difficulty in establishing a focus and in pursuing particular topics in depth. Nonetheless, there are five advantages in the urban-and-regional-studies approach compared to the rival views outlined above.

One of the most important advantages is that if there is a strong core of urban and regional specialists in a program of urban studies, urban and regional specialists in particular disciplines in the university can receive more wide-ranging conceptual and professional support and can therefore operate with more effectiveness at the margins between their disciplines and urban studies. The reverse is also true: that is, urbanists need help from colleagues in the different disciplines, and since they are most likely to receive this help if there are such disciplinary specialists, they will encourage such activities. In other words, an urban-studies program need not and probably will not come at the expense of disciplinary efforts along these lines. What is more likely is that a broad program in urban studies can furnish critical support and reinforcement for more specialists as well as more comprehensive efforts.

A second consideration—already noted—is that urban and regional problems are far less likely to be effectively attacked in any sustained fashion by disciplinary programs. This is because the central focus of these programs is not on the urban and regional aspects. The main focus of economists and management specialists, of political scientists, sociologists, psychologists, and anthropologists, is not—and doubtless ought not to be—on urban issues. Some work, sometimes even a good deal of work, may be done on these problems for several reasons: because they can provide a convenient testing ground for ideas; because on occasion some specialist takes a fancy to the field; or because certain urban questions have become important or fashionable public issues. But the focus is often short-lived, since the urban issue is not the central concern, or one of the more significant growth frontiers of the field, and so the interest and concentration of energies wane with time. This decline is all the more likely if the men working at these margins fail to find support and peer approval among other colleagues with sufficient reputation and clout to offset the lack of interest of the more orthodox members of their own discipline.

Third, many analysts of urban and regional problems (such as racial conflict; changes in the economy and social characteristics [actual or needed]; strategies for housing, land use, transportation, and area development; etc.) have much to gain from having closer access to specialists with different skills and points of view. They benefit from exposure to holistic and multidisciplinary as well as reductionist and disciplinary perspectives. These opportunities are not excluded for those working within conventional disciplinary boundaries; but they are more difficult to exploit in departments where the rewards are largely for those working within the discipline. It is usually easier to collaborate with colleagues who are nearby than with those who are in different departments and often in different and often distant buildings. Just as friendship formation has been shown to occur with much greater frequency among people who have been brought into more frequent interaction by the accident or the deliberate design of the arrangement of buildings and of points of entry and exit, so too joint efforts can be nourished by programs which bring together in a single facility (or in closely adjoining facilities) different professionals interested in common problems.[3] This is one way of aiding common efforts—not, to be sure, the sole or even the main approach; but an important factor and often a neglected one.

Fourth, separation of environmental-design, policy-analysis, modeling, and quantitative studies is procrustean from the standpoint either of furthering the disciplinary aspects of urbanism, or of providing an effective professional education. Whether one is interested in analysis or professional practice, it is vital to have adequate exposure to the different component elements of the field and to know the power and perhaps even the weakness of their interrelationships and of their applications. For example, just as professionals should see urban design as an exercise in policy analysis, modeling, and applied social science, as well as a problem of the efficient or visually appealing physical organization and form, so too the insights of analysts might often be wiser and more realistic if they better understood the creative possibilities of design and social process.

Fifth, a reasonably endowed program in urban and regional studies makes feasible, for those who are interested in such experiments, an additional option for undergraduate education. Such an option may be very attractive to some undergraduates who are not sure of their plans for the future and who want a general education, one which might equip them with tools and points of view enabling them to do something fairly specific if they should leave the university. In the United States at least, an undergraduate program in urban studies might well be of value for some students who want a good foundation for subsequent specialization either in the professions or the social sciences as well as urban planning and design. Work in urban and regional studies provides skills in social-problem diagnosis, modeling and analytical methods, and data handling; a broad view of the approaches and concepts of the applied social sciences, as well as possibilities for some specialization in a particular field. There are several ways of providing a general education; urban studies is one of the new alternatives. What is more, studies along these lines would require (and justify) additional resources which would extend the range of staff and opportunities for specializa-

tion which could be afforded by the general program in urban
and regional studies.

THE EXPERIENCE OF THE MIT URBAN STUDIES
PROGRAM

By way of example, consider some of the experiences behind
the transformations of the Department of City and Regional
Planning at MIT. This program in the School of Architecture
and Planning is the second oldest of its kind in the United States.
(The first was the Department of City and Regional Planning
at Harvard set up in 1929.) In about 1950, it was one of the two
or three most influential professional programs in the country
in city and regional planning. This was attributable at least as
much to the general reputation of MIT as to the relatively high
quality of the department's staff and the important positions held
by its graduates. However, some of the key faculty were at that
time profoundly skeptical about the future, for the program was
weak and marginal at MIT and lacked the minimum critical size
to offer either a good undergraduate education, solid professional
training, or good prospects for the development of the disciplinary aspects or the extension of the intellectual capital of the
field. Nor was it easy to change the situation, since the critical
variables were exogenous. Although interest in the problems of
housing and of cities, and then in urban development and renewal, had mounted in the late thirties and early postwar period,
there was really no intense concern about cities in the United
States at that time; nor were there any major foundations com-
mitting significant resources to transform attitudes or to accelerate change. Under the circumstances, it was virtually impossible
either to increase more than marginally the resources of departments in universities concerned with urban problems, to upgrade the quality of entrants to the field, or to deepen or broaden
the range of study.

About the most that could be done was to develop a slightly
more varied staff and program. These efforts led, in the first
decade or so after World War II, to more work in urban politics,

housing and land economics, site planning and urban design. This was in addition to the regular subjects of "planning principles," land-use regulations, urban sociology, and elementary research and survey techniques—all of which supplemented the principal activity: the studio or drafting-room courses in physical land-use planning. (The latter took approximately half the time of the students.)

During the early 1950s, however, interest in urban problems mounted steadily and, after a half-decade or more of resistance, there was eventually agreement on the need for a research program to increase our understanding of these problems. Strange as it may now seem, this modest innovation was once considered as unnecessary and marginal in planning as it was deemed to be in architecture and law. Two additional reasons for the change in attitude were the hopes that such a research program might tap some new resources (including foundation funds), and might improve the quality of the student recruits relative to the quality of students in more prestigious fields. These considerations probably contributed as much to the interest in urban research as the prospect of strengthening, not to mention transforming, the intellectual foundations of the field. In any case, the crossing of this threshold led to the creation at MIT, in 1958, of a departmental urban-research center and a Ph.D. program.

However, a similar center had been established at Harvard at the same time, and it seemed impractical to have two neighboring urban centers chasing the same funds and persons, especially in light of the fact that both sought a "minimum critical size." Joint efforts appeared to be desirable, especially since the two centers had similar aims and since their directors happened to be friends; and, eventually the initially skeptical colleagues and university administrators went along with the recommendations of the directors to combine the two centers. This decision was facilitated by the preference of the Ford Foundation staff for such a joint center for the "Cambridge community." The Ford Foundation also sought to encourage the active participation in the new center of as large a number as possible of the other schools and departments of both universities. This desire was shared by the two directors, and by the other key figures in and outside the two departments of city planning involved in the decision.

The avowed aims of the Joint Center (which eventually received financial support from the Ford Foundation) went far beyond the confines of land-use planning. The intent was not only to study problems of housing, transportation, land use, and urban design, but to encourage the comparative analyses of cities, particularly their history, growth, and structure; to examine the functioning of urban government and institutions, including the influence of politics and the mechanisms of policy formation and decision making; and to investigate the major urban and regional problems of developing countries. To facilitate a multidisciplinary approach, distinguished social scientists from the fields of economics, sociology, political science, and engineering, as well as from city planning, were appointed to the governing faculty policy committee. There were even efforts to enlist some leading scientists in the program, but, save for one or two exceptions, the scientists approached found little in the way of relevant problems that they could identify with as scientists.

The initiation of the Guayana project in Venezuela extended further the vistas of the Joint Center. This was an enterprise designed to assist the *Corporación Venezolana de Guayana* to transform the economy of Venezuela (from one based on oil to one based on heavy industry) via a national-, regional-, and local-development strategy for the Guayana region. The project involved making regional plans for rural, industrial, and commercial development (which were included in the national plan of Venezuela); the working out of a land-use strategy for a new city of perhaps half a million people; and the planning of the basic infrastructure (transportation, land use, utilities, housing, and community facilities) and of the public services (including health, education, and local government).

The aims and activities of the Joint Center were in part a response to the mood of the times, especially the euphoria of the "New Frontier" of the Kennedy administration. Similarly, the hoped for interplay between basic and applied research and between scholars and practitioners reflected the quest to broaden the vistas of urban planning and increase the field-research and learning opportunities for faculty, professionals, and students. But the experience also foreshadowed some of the serious problems in the future development of urban studies.

One lesson, not altogether surprising, was the limited interest of the social-science departments. Only a few key individuals, who had either a genuine, long-term or a temporary interest in urban studies, participated in the program. These persons were attracted by the aims of the Joint Center, by the quality of the associates, by the challenge of some of its projects, and by the funds and services available to the Joint Center's "research associates." The Joint Center could facilitate some urban study, short- or long-term, that individual social-science faculty members wished to pursue, and perhaps even improve the quality of this study; but research into problems of cities and regions, no matter how generously defined, proved, not surprisingly, to be marginal to the central interests of most departments. There were some understandable reasons for hesitancy, beyond the fact that a department might have quite different priorities: in some cases there were no really first-rate candidates; in other cases scholars in other areas of specialization within the discipline were clearly superior and the tenure decision often rested on the stature and promise of the person as well as on the field. This experience made it clear that, even at a time when urban problems had become highly visible issues, it would be naïve to expect traditional departments to allocate more than a tiny portion of their resources and energies in these directions.

Another critical issue concerned the time horizon for results. The aims of the Joint Center were deliberately defined broadly, so as not to exclude able scholars who might be interested in and capable of making even an indirect contribution to the program. The emphasis was on brilliance and range, not a "narrow" urban-research program. And the Joint Center did in fact produce some notable books, monographs, and articles.[4] But those persons interested in pragmatic solutions were not at all satisfied with "great books": they wanted answers to real and pressing problems, or at the very least more research to be focused on them. There is no question that more concrete and immediately useful (but perhaps not such prestigious) studies might have been produced by hiring staff and developing a specific and perhaps even cumulative set of research studies. But this approach would have involved far less of the high-quality (as well as high-prestige) faculty of the different departments of the two institutions, and would thus have forfeited much of the support of these departments.

Third, the spin-off effects for the departments of city and regional planning at both universities turned out to be real, but limited. This was all the more so for the ten or more other departments from both universities participating in the program. The reason was simple. A million dollars[5] is a lot of money: but deduct even as little as a quarter of the total for overhead; then divide the remainder by 4 (to cover the term of the grant); and then by 8 to 10 (to provide for the various participating departments), and the average amount of money available for each department is less than $20,000 per department. So—even if some departments received somewhat higher allocations—the amount of money available for research for faculty and students turned out to be a very small sum. And this in turn made it clear that no department or program which had to build up the very foundations of its field could afford to rely *only* on these resources.

Of course, the Joint Center was not dependent on foundation funds alone. It performed contract research for government agencies; it had the Guayana project (which exceeded the Ford grant in scale of financing). It also had smaller grants from other foundations. However, most of the contract research and the smaller grants only added to the spread of interests and visible lack of focus of the Joint Center. And although the departments of city and regional planning at both universities benefited from these resources, the additional funds could make only a modest contribution to the development of either department's research goals.

Later, when the renewal of the Ford Foundation grant came up for consideration, the president of the Foundation invited

MIT and Harvard University to review the problems of the city and region in relation to the capabilities of both institutions and to consider the possibility "of a whole new level of activity." This led to a major reevaluation by the two universities of their efforts in this field. The net result was the decision to strengthen and to extend—while continuing the Joint Center on a standby basis— the urban resources of both universities. Harvard opted for several chairs (i.e., professorships), since it was less interested in program- or problem-oriented research. MIT embarked on a major new effort involving the creation of an interdepartmental Urban Systems Laboratory and the setting up of an Urban Fellows Program run by the School of Management. The former placed special emphasis on research dealing with building, transportation, environmental, and information systems; the latter was an effort to encourage advanced graduate students and younger members of the MIT faculty to join the staffs for a limited period of exposure to significant urban programs in the field.

The School of Architecture and Planning, and in particular the key faculty of the Department of City and Regional Planning, were not sympathetic to the new programs. They were persuaded that these efforts, however well intentioned and ably staffed, would disperse resources and fail to achieve any significant impact, because the central focus of the major schools and departments (other than the Department of City and Regional Planning) was not in urban studies and would not remain there any longer than the funds held out. Nonetheless, resistance proved futile. The key representatives of the MIT administration and of the other departments—people who had almost no personal interest in urban studies—were convinced they could muster the necessary brains for the job and achieve a real breakthrough. The polite criticisms and desultory opposition from the Department of City and Regional Planning, some of whose members wanted the resources invested in their "backyard," sounded very much like sour grapes. The Ford Foundation staff, which felt urban problems were too important to be left only in the hands of city planners, ardently sought the active involvement of engineers and scientists. What is more, it was just possible—given the generally distinguished record of MIT in

setting up successful task forces on other matters in the past—
that the urban planners were wrong. Why, under these circumstances, should the urban planners stubbornly resist an "involvement" that in principle they welcomed, especially since
they were unable either to sway or to veto the decision?

So the MIT program moved ahead under a grant which for
MIT use alone was almost five times the size of the original grant
to the Joint Center, and the Joint Center remained in a state of
limbo (until the changes which occurred toward the end of the
1960s).[6] Unfortunately, despite some diverse research efforts,
little of real consequence either in urban literature or intellectual
breakthrough resulted from the activities of the Urban Systems
Laboratory or the Urban Fellows Program; so that finally the
responsible leaders of MIT were persuaded that this was not the
way either to tackle urban problems or to ensure long-term,
comprehensive MIT involvement.

The fizzling out of these efforts, as well as further reflection
and changes in the MIT administration, and mounting concern
over urban issues led, toward the end of the 1960s, to the adop-
tion of a new strategy, one which still looks promising a decade
later.

The key change was the acceptance of the view that it was
essential to establish a strong program in the Department of City
and Regional Planning (the name of which, incidentally, was
changed to the Department of Urban Studies and Planning).
Linkage to this strong core, it was believed, would provide the
foundation for the strengthening of related programs which
existed or might be developed in architecture, civil engineering,
the social sciences, humanities, and other schools and departments at MIT. At long last, the notion of developing active urban
programs in other schools and departments was abandoned;
however, other schools and departments were encouraged to
develop such ties and linkages to the urban core as was consistent
with their own interests and priorities.

During the next five years, a broad urban-studies program
was vigorously supported. Financial resources and staff of the
department almost tripled. As noted, the new faculty included

social scientists, as well as a wide range of specialists in substantive areas of urban studies, various modeling and analytical techniques, and computer programming. An undergraduate program was reestablished. New areas of specialization were set up in policy analysis and urban management, environmental policy and problems of developing nations. There was also a considerable deepening of resources bearing on urban social policy, law, history, housing, urban and manpower economics, organization learning, urban decision making, and urban design. New or sturdier bridges were built between the urban-studies program and other branches of MIT largely via collaborative research and teaching efforts, joint degrees (involving architecture, economics, civil engineering, political science, and education), and joint appointments (involving the same fields). By the end of 1973, and continuing until at least the end of the decade, this program, in terms of university general funds invested in urban studies, turned out to be perhaps the most ambitious of its kind in the United States.[7]

This summary has not included most of the details that were involved—especially the uncertainties, conflicts, setbacks, and personal confrontations, all of which have no place here. What ᴊould be underlined, however, is that the program did move forward, and still remains at the forefront even in the current period of great financial adversity for universities in general; this despite the fact that MIT was no exception in the need and pressure for retrenchment, although MIT may have fared somewhat better financially than the average university.

CONCLUDING OBSERVATIONS

Despite the progress that has been made in the urban-regional field, quite difficult problems lie ahead. Maintaining, if not increasing, resources in a period of inflation is one; continuing to attract highly talented staff and students at a time when urban problems are no longer privileged issues on the national agenda is another; achieving an effective focus and integration of the professional, the disciplinary, and the general education goals of the field is a third. The latter problem is now of exceptional importance; and for this reason two cautionary observations on the issue of area focus and integration may be appropriate.

First, as observed in Chapter 10, the shift from physical or land-use planning to urban studies was in part a reaction to an earlier tradition which assumed that the shaping of the physical or three-dimensional environment, or of "built form," was an effective way of solving some of the problems that afflict our cities and regions. However important some of these physical trans-formations may be, many of the expectations associated with them have been naïve and often wrong. We now see the training of such planners in the past—especially on the socioeconomic-institutional side—as having been sadly inadequate. But it is probably equally misleading to take for granted—as most of us still do almost inadvertently—that if the urban planners had had more training in the social sciences (of the time) they would have had clearer or sounder views. Considering the state of the social sciences then and also now, perhaps one can be pardoned for being somewhat skeptical on this score. Nonetheless, the hope is that such knowledge might prove increasingly helpful in the future. To the extent that this assumption turns out to be correct, the urban-studies approach is advantageous, for it has embarked on explicit efforts to create, within a single program, not only ties between the theoretical and the empirical and between the positive and the normative, but also between the physical and the social (in the broad sense that encompasses all of the social sciences) and between the disciplinary—which seeks to advance systematic knowledge, and the professional—which teaches practitioners how to apply existing concepts and techniques.

This is but a description of an aspiration, to be sure. We do not yet know how to achieve such ends. It may take a decade, a generation, or more before we learn. There are, however, many advantages in maintaining the "urban-regional" label during this learning period. One is that the label in no way implies the hackneyed physical, social, economic, or other disciplinary perspectives. Nor does it imply a predisposition for a particular method or emphasis—be it modeling, quantitative, qualitative, institutional, normative, or positive. The focus need not even be limited to a particular kind of area—a neighborhood, city, metropolis, region, nation, or world region—because the boundaries depend on the nature of the problem. But anything so flexible, it might be argued, is not apt to have much content, and, therefore, is not likely to be very useful. Others will strongly disagree: for although the only touchstone emphasized is a concern for an interrelated approach to different kinds and levels of area problems and their implications, these are precisely the considerations which are systematically neglected by most policy makers, social scientists, engineers, and so on. It is this neglect which is difficult to correct—in general or professional education—if there is no break with the conventional disciplinary, sectoral, and macro approaches.

CHAPTER TWELVE

Training City Planners in Third World Countries

OVERVIEW

Aside from a few very poor countries where there are no city-planning or urban-studies educational programs, such programs as there are in most of the Third World countries (TWCs) are generally weak, inefficient, class dominated—and irrelevant. They are weak because resources are limited, entrants into the field do not rank among the ablest students, and the range and quality of the subject matter and teaching are often poor; inefficient because it takes too much time to get even inadequate training; class dominated because the system of education makes it difficult and unlikely for poor and middle-income persons to participate in such programs; and often irrelevant because they focus on the wrong skills and subject matter. Radical change is necessary; but it is not easy to achieve because the possibilities for effective, long-term change are constrained and the capabilities for carrying out and sustaining such change are limited.

What can be done about this situation? Much less than is needed, no doubt, but nonetheless more than one might suppose. Specifically, the length of training could be cut, the focus altered, the resources modestly increased, and the quality improved. No doubt these changes will not come easily, for the field of urban and regional studies does not rank high in the hierarchy of educational programs. The chances are that the urban situations in these countries may have to get a lot worse before key leaders rivet attention on these problems. Nonetheless, changes are feasible and a discussion of the issues is long overdue.

CURRENT STATUS OF EDUCATIONAL PROGRAMS IN URBAN AND REGIONAL PLANNING IN THIRD WORLD COUNTRIES

There is very limited information on the current trends of education in urban and regional studies in these countries. The brief account of the state of existing education given here is based on (a) impressions from scattered articles, conferences, and other reports; (b) information gleaned from discussions with professionals in different TWCs; and (c) impressions gathered while working with a number of education and related programs in TWCs in all of the major regions of the world.

Although there are no comprehensive studies providing reliable information on the need or demand for urban and regional planners in TWCs, there are ad hoc estimates of the manpower requirements of relevant planning programs in specific countries. These estimates tend to reinforce the impression of most knowledgeable persons that the shortages (which, of course, exist for other skilled urban specialists as well) are serious enough in many, perhaps most TWCs to hobble programs for urban and regional development.[1] Aside from the shortages, our knowledge about the specific roles and functions of urban planners is still quite obscure, despite many studies for different regions of the world of urban- and regional-planning programs in TWCs by the United Nations Research Institute for Social Development, the Ford Foundation, and various scholars.[2] We do not have good comparative analyses for TWCs indicating the ways urban planners are trained, their social and economic backgrounds and values, what they in fact do compared to what they say they do, how their activities are changing and how they are likely to change in the future. This information would be of considerable value in appraising the performance requirements of training programs.

We do have a little more information—but not very much—about the programs for training urban and regional planners in the TWCs. To date, about 30 educational programs have been identified which deal more or less with regional-development problems in developing countries; the programs are distributed about equally among Western Europe, North America, and the countries of the Third World.[3] Most of the programs have not been in existence more than a decade or two, and there are doubtless other programs which have not yet been identified. The average number of students in the regional-planning programs ranges around 15; and the total annual output has been estimated to approximate 100 in more-developed countries (MDCs) and 120 in TWCs. The programs generally involve postgraduate training, often combining regional planning with another discipline.[4]

More specifically, in many of the TWCs there are no independent educational programs in urban and regional studies and at best only two or three courses dealing with these matters in undergraduate or graduate schools of architecture and engineering. Let us call this Level 1—the lowest level of training. There are very few trained professionals, only a small number of development programs in the cities and regions, and there is substantial dependence on outside specialists to implement these programs.

At Level 2, which typifies a large number of countries, there are urban-planning areas of specialization in architecture and engineering curricula and even departments with professional-degree (Master's) programs in the urban and regional field. In some cases there are also modest research institutes. But the emphasis is mostly on urban physical planning. There is limited or negligible association with the social sciences and there is still much dependence on the training and ideas of the MDCs.

Level 3, or higher-level programs will be found only in a very few places. These programs embrace the social sciences and broad environmental issues (rural as well as urban), and the principal participants are fully informed of and can critically evaluate the ideas, technical and political, in MDCs as well as TWCs.[5]

One point, a familiar one, but still worth noting, is that many of the graduates of these programs, even those at Level 3, conscious of the limitations of their training and of the prestige and stimulation of foreign study, seek experience or additional training abroad. Agencies or universities for which they work generally share these attitudes and often sponsor foreign training—despite the risk that such additional training might lead to more attractive job opportunities in expatriate countries or with international agencies. This attraction persists even though it is well known that the educational programs of the MDCs, save for a very few exceptions, are geared to their own needs—that is, their own economic circumstances, institutional requirements, technology, and values. Small wonder, then, that there is increasing dissatisfaction with things as they are, and an increasing number of corrosive evaluations of these educational offerings.

CHANGING EDUCATIONAL REQUIREMENTS FOR URBAN AND REGIONAL DEVELOPMENT

Our earlier chapters have emphasized that in the past, urban planners in the MDCs were trained as specialists in ways of manipulating the form of the city. Mostly middle-class in background, their training in the main has been in engineering, architecture, landscape architecture, and city planning. Whether in the making of plans for the city, for regional or urban parks, or for resource development, the emphasis was on infrastructure or the built environment.

However, the area-development problems of the TWCs, as in the case of the MDCs, have turned out to involve much more than traditional land-use planning. Concern about the costs and the problems of management of big cities has persistently been voiced in almost all TWCs by the more articulate interest groups, and by the directors of the development as well as the technical-assistance programs in the TWCs. In part, this concern reflects efforts to counter the mounting cost of the infrastructure investments, and to find adequate staff to cope with the socioeconomic and physical problems of managing a big city. The concern also reflects the desire to encourage economic growth and jobs in lagging or resource-development regions. Recognition of the potential relationships between the problems of curbing the rate of growth of the big cities and of encouraging rural and urban development in the poorest regions reinforces these views.

Several other trends have also been influential. There is currently a worldwide upsurge of interest in such matters as the maldistribution of income and of opportunities (between groups as well as regions); job-creation strategies; ways of coping with migration and social change; and the avoidance of urban bias through the promotion of rural economic activities, service and marketing centers for agriculture, and other complementary linkages between urban and rural areas. The convergence of these concerns has created new agendas for change in many institutions including programs of education. This makes the present situation opportune for those who can provide a sense of direction, and tempts one to ask: What do we now know about urban and regional development which educational reformers in TWCs ought to take into account in redesigning their curricula in urban planning? One way to answer this question is to review the changing perspectives on urban and regional development with regard to four items: aims, planning style, analytic methods, and scope.

Aims

The most fundamental but elusive aspects of area studies and planning in all countries are its aims: not simply what they are and how they have changed, but how they are weighted and how these weightings might change over time.

Three kinds of aims—status, developmental, and social—have been influential in the history of area studies and planning.

In almost all fields with professional aspirations there are strong social pressures (on the field and the practitioner) to acquire greater technical capability and to enjoy higher social status. In the absence of adequate studies, one can only surmise that these impulses, which have been fairly influential in the past, are today as influential as ever.

However, there have been significant changes in the relative importance attached to the developmental and social aims. Roughly until two decades ago, the main concerns were with ways of encouraging or coping with development. The avowed aims were to promote growth, efficiency, health, and amenity by improving the accommodation and location of human activities and by preparing land-use plans to realize these ends. Understandable as the aims have been, the fact is that the emphasis was not on the poor regions, the poor in general, or the minorities in particular—or on the social costs of growth.

The current social emphasis emerged in the 1960s, as the practitioners and analysts in the field and the relevant interest groups became increasingly dissatisfied with the results of planning policies and programs. This discontent spurred studies of planning behavior and the nature of the planning process and led to a reexamination of the aims of planning, the participants in these processes, their values, how decisions were reached, who benefited, how effectiveness was evaluated, and how policies were improved by feedback and learning. The concern with "process" and the incidence of costs and benefits led also to the exploration of political—as well as planning—processes including the handicaps and limited influence of some groups and regions. These studies reinforced the growing concern about inequality and problems of equity as well as questions about the ecological and social limits to growth and development.

What the future emphasis is likely to be is hazardous to say. Fashions will surely shift; advances in learning will occur; circumstances will change; and new ideas will develop. In the 1950s, there was a great burst of enthusiasm in the United States for developing allocational and optimizing models of the metropolis to promote more efficient use of land and of transportation systems. Eventually, this enthusiasm—intensified by the development of computers—was extended to comprehensive information systems. In the 1960s there was a shift of interest to methods of evaluation, especially when various policies and programs, including the efforts to help the poor in the early 1960s, did not achieve the intended effects. Because our past failures reflected lack of sophistication about such matters (as well as lack of political willingness), we have become more wary about our aims and about the costs and problems of planning. Policy analysis and evaluation techniques are, as a consequence, enjoying a great vogue; there is likewise an increasing focus on implementation, management, and learning mechanisms, partly to increase the likelihood that things will happen the way we intend and partly to avoid in the future the errors of the past.

In the 1970s there has also been an increasing interest—in contrast to the attitudes of the 1950s and the 1960s—in the views of the dissenters and radicals concerning the role and the importance of institutional constraints and of the political realm in determining the outcomes of urban and regional planning. We are now conceding, grudgingly or otherwise, that many problems betray not simply human and technical inadequacies: they are deeply embedded in the nature of the socioeconomic-political system and its institutions, and many of these problems cannot be corrected simply by finer adjustment of procedures, policies, implementation, management, or evaluation mechanisms.

How we resolve some of these differences in views is less important for our purposes than realizing that all of these matters are important under certain circumstances and that the reality as well as the perception of their relative importance is likely to vary in accordance with the historical context, changing conditions, and the individual's values. But whatever the balance of these factors may be in particular situations, one can hardly question the need to provide a sensitive understanding and assessment of most of these perspectives in any effective training program for urban and regional studies.

Planning Style

There is, today, fairly rapid interchange and convergence of ideas and policies between nations. But our educational programs in urban studies rarely provide adequate comparative analyses of experiences with planning methods and programs in different social, institutional, and physical settings. For example, although there are great disputes between the advocates of incremental and comprehensive (or systems) approaches, it is more important to understand the pros and cons of both approaches rather than to ally oneself with one or the other. Systems analysis is popular today partly because it is identified with effective ways of dealing with interacting complexes of activities. Effectiveness in systems analysis, however, depends on the ability to identify the aims as well as the critical operations, components, and environments of the complex systems. But this latter ability is just what we lack in confronting many critical problems—for it requires more knowledge, experience, and resources than we now have. Often, from a behavioral perspective, if prompt action is necessary, the only option open may be to tackle problems with ad hoc improvisations and approximations. No doubt such efforts produce side effects and unanticipated consequences that exacerbate the problems or frustrate the achievement of the desired objectives: hence the oscillation of views in favor of systems or incremental approaches, each, or both, of which may be appropriate *depending on the circumstances.* This is why it appears fruitful to emphasize comparative analysis—especially to serve the needs of TWCs, where there are compelling reasons to profit from relevant case studies of successes and failures elsewhere.

There are, of course, many other examples which could be cited of actual (or proposed) solutions (or rejections of solutions) which might be unacceptable or simply ill-advised for the circumstances to which they might be applied. Thus, neither regional nor national integration of physical and economic planning will amount to much if the civil service is weak or corrupt. Similarly, the French and the British planning systems appear inappropriate for cultures with less—or more—of a tradition of, or a respect for, administrative centralization. And the Soviet Union's cultural and institutional traditions and policies are regarded with increasing skepticism by many European and Asian nations (and political parties) with communist leanings. Turning to specific programs, the Guayana, Venezuela regional-planning model is not feasible for more than one or two regions in a country with very limited resources, especially skilled human resources. Similarly, "new towns" may be irrelevant and even economically absurd in poor countries or countries with relative "slack" in the infrastructure capacity of their existing cities. And the building of high-rise public housing projects for very poor families has turned out to be ill-advised or infeasible in most TWCs, but not, so far, in others such as Singapore and Hong Kong. It would also be presumptuous to make recommendations regarding the use of regional boards or public corporations or the recourse to tax, credit, and other incentives—regardless of context.

In short, to facilitate this critical understanding and learning, there is a need to analyze devices or approaches which have worked in different circumstances, for different cultures and economic activities, and for different types of countries (e.g., large and small, hierarchical and egalitarian, with mixed or socialist economies, with or without a minimum number of educated and capable professionals and administrators, with or without massive population problems, etc.). But the concern must be with the circumstances under which one set of policies would be more appropriate than another for different countries to follow, rather than with which set of policies is correct or superior in all cases.

Analytic Methods

Analytic tools now available to urban and regional specialists (i.e., modeling techniques, quantitative methods, survey instruments, information systems, field research, and a variety of qualitative methods for guiding analysis and data evaluation) have extended the land-use planners' traditional kit of graphic, analytical, and land-use planning techniques. Understanding of the potential uses and abuses of these tools is essential for most planners in developing countries simply because they are increasingly confronted with the need to participate in, evaluate, or supervise analyses or proposals which require such knowledge and skills. It is no longer a novelty in many, if not most, TWCs to encounter (a) surveys reporting on public attitudes and values as expressed in consumption and activity patterns: (b) anthropological or sociological field research regarding the values and responses of people to the changes going on about them; (c) policy recommendations (based on operations and other research) for the reorganization of specific public services; (d) models and programs for setting up systems of villages and towns to serve as marketing and service centers for key rural regions; or (e) even proposals for simulation models of subnational regions to report on the impact for output, employment, income, migration, and growth of various policy options (e.g., patterns of infrastructure investment, location of industries, and various fiscal measures).

There is great promise in the availablility of these tools. But they are often expensive, and indeed unnecessary if simpler tools can suffice. There is also great danger of misuse by technical specialists lacking common sense, not to mention a sense of plural values. Difficult as the mastery of these skills might be, their right use is even more difficult because it requires experience, shrewd judgment, and the absence of those serious blind spots concerning the culture with which foreign (or foreign-trained) specialists are often afflicted. It is for these reasons that developing sensitivity to the problems of misuse has now become an indispensable part of the training of planners.

Scope

Over the last three decades, as we have already noted, there has been a shift of emphasis from the local-, land-use-, physical-, and practitioner-oriented approach to the problems of cities and regions. The new emphasis requires more familiarity with values and interpersonal and intergroup behavior; greater knowledge of how organizations, institutions, interest groups, and social systems function; and a more sensitive grasp of the art (and the limitations) of modeling, of policy formulation, and of the handling of the administrative and political systems at all levels of government. These changes are reflected in three trends: (a) the increasing dominance of the applied-social-science components of the programs; (b) a widening scope which encompasses rural, national, and international aspects of urban- and regional-development strategies; and (c) both a deep questioning and a strong reemphasis of the importance of the urban and regional focus.

Sooner or later, one consequence of these changes is likely to be the creation of more training programs outside the tra-

ditional schools of architecture and engineering—as in the case of
the Center for Development Studies (CENDES) in Venezuela
and the urban- and regional-studies program in the Kennedy
School at Harvard, as well as other programs elsewhere.

Still another consequence of the extension in the range of
the subject matter of urban studies and planning has been the
sharpening of the controversy over what should be taught in such
programs and in what depth. In the past, for example, it was
deemed essential to understand the characteristics and the behavior of the principal economic activities and population groups
of the city and region and to develop techniques for accommodating their requirements for space, utilities, community facilities,
and public services. For several decades, this basic doctrine appeared to be sensible, pragmatic, serviceable. But in fact, it has
turned out to be far more difficult to implement than anticipated.
Perceptive analyses of the economy require sophisticated applied
economists, not land-use planners functioning as pragmatic
amateurs. The same holds for analyses of the social topography,
or of the land-use planning problems of the industrial, commercial, residential, recreational, and rural-urban-fringe areas. The
beleaguered generalists, with their rough judgments and tools,
found themselves, especially in the United States, increasingly
on the defensive in confronting both the onslaughts of the interest groups affected by their plans as well as the critiques of the
disciplinary and other specialists who had of a sudden been attracted to the field when the problems of cities and regions
loomed as a major issue in the 1960s.

The need for expansion and increased specialization was
conceded and even welcomed, of course. But adequate support
of the new, burgeoning specializations has turned out to be a
huge and very expensive, if not unmanageable, problem. The
most advanced university programs of urban studies and planning in the MDCs have staffs (full-time equivalents) ranging from
30 to 35 persons, yet these programs are still not able to cover in
adequate depth the main topics in the field.

Meanwhile, budget and program imperatives are sharpening two conflicting views. On the one hand, in many quarters in

the MDCs, as we noted earlier in this chapter, the urban and regional lens is not considered the significant one for viewing many problems. One reason for this is that it is not at these levels that the critical financial and human resources are concentrated. Also, for many purposes, these urban and regional designations are deemed too macro to get at the critical variables, which are either sectoral or micro, or otherwise different in character. These considerations have led many analysts to rely more on other approaches—on nonarea-oriented ideas, concepts, models, and policies as well as studies of the behavior of individuals, groups, or organizations—in addressing issues of development.

But there have also been increasing pressures in the MDCs to decentralize policy making and management. One reason to do so is to respond to the demand for more effective local participation in policy and decision making; another is to provide greater financial autonomy to reinforce these combined administrative and area changes. There are similar pressures in the TWCs, where there are generally centralized administrations which are often at odds with strong local traditions and loyalties. In many of the TWCs, although the area-development programs are shaped by explicit as well as implicit national policies and managed by bureaucracies operating out of the capital city, there are increasingly obdurate efforts to promote effective subnational planning, legislative, taxing, and decision-making agencies. For TWCs as well as for MDCs, the handling of these problems is likely to intensify the interest in area-organization problems, in ways of dealing with them that take account of the conflicting ethnic, economic, and other interests within and between regions as well as in appropriate guidelines to help identify or reconstitute these regions.

CONCLUDING OBSERVATIONS

So much for this sketch of those elements of urban and regional studies which need to become, or are now in the process of becoming, part of the curricula of the most advanced professional programs in the TWCs as well as the MDCs. The new requirements are anything but simple; but they are more likely to be challenging rather than frustrating if capable people can be gotten into the field. A major issue, however, is how that might be achieved.

There are four main incentives for entering the field: high returns, power, prestige, and the allure of challenging, visible, potentially solvable problems. In TWCs (and in many MDCs) the field of urban and regional studies lacks money and power, and even relative prestige; and although the problems are real and plentiful and significant, there may well be controversy as to their relative tractability and priority in comparison with a great many other urgent and possibly more tractable problems facing these countries.

A further complication is that the lack of trained urban specialists makes it necessary to get appropriate staff at the earliest opportunity—probably at the undergraduate or technical-college level; and this necessity makes it all the more difficult to ensure the prestige associated with the professional credential.

In addition, the weaknesses of the educational systems in most TWCs further inhibits change. One example is the need to reorganize, transform, or otherwise strengthen the elementary- and secondary-school systems; another is the need to develop the social sciences. These obstacles would frustrate countries with relatively adequate resources; they are far more crippling for countries that are less well endowed, and that are struggling to cope with inexperience, weak administration, overcentralization, corruption, and unstable government. Because of these constraints, there are no simple solutions. However, there are some modest measures which appear sensible, and which are being pursued in one form or another in TWCs in different regions of the world.

To begin with, very poor countries need to break radically with the tradition of the overvalued, long-term, expensive credential programs of the MDCs. One way to achieve this break is to rely more on paraprofessionals—trained in vocational- or specialized training institutes—for drafting, mapping, statistical, monitoring, and other necessary functions. In addition, it is still quite feasible to learn the essential requirements of urban and regional studies in a polytechnic school, or in the last two years of undergraduate education. It may also make sense to abandon for two or three decades the Ph.D. degree. To ensure relatively high quality, the number of graduate programs at the Master's level might also be limited for a generation or two—perhaps to no more than a very few universities. The policy could be reinforced by the educational-grants programs (if one exists) of provincial and national governments.

To the extent that it may be feasible, the core of an undergraduate specialization in urban and regional studies might include work in substantive areas, such as how people live and work; the nature and history of cities and regions; problems of housing; land-use policy and planning; transportation; environmental policy; national and regional strategies for urban and rural development; and workshops on applied problems including such issues as the informal sector and appropriate technology. The student requires, too, competence in quantitative and qualitative analytical techniques, in survey and case methods, in project evaluation and policy analysis; as well as some facility in comparative analysis and modeling and in various presentation and communication techniques. There could also be some optional background courses in the planning, behavioral, and institutional processes of different economic and social systems; and, in addition, courses in institution building and political economy as well as in organization and decision theory.

The list of courses is only illustrative. It should also be pointed out that only the equivalent of one year of academic studies ought to be required for core subjects, so that the student can have some choice in selecting subjects within the area of specialization and in other fields; and even within the required core there might be some possibility of choice.

Almost needless to say, all of these possibilities must be adapted to different environments and climates of opinion. We have noted in Chapter 10 that there are growing pressures today in several directions: to understand better the behavior of organizations and institutions; to downgrade growth as the dominant aim of development; to emphasize the importance of rural programs; to explore the possibilities of the so-called informal sector; to encourage genuine and effective participation; to adapt technology and local materials to "basic" needs and constraints; and to evaluate the impact of various policy measures on equity, welfare, and development.

The primary aim of the graduate programs must be to produce a greater number of more skilled professional practitioners. They might also provide specialized professional training (along the lines noted above) for those who have completed undergraduate or polytechnic programs in some other field of study. If, in addition, more rapid increase in manpower is essential, another possibility may be to attract highly qualified graduates from other fields (architecture, engineering, humanities, and the social sciences) for an intensive one-year training program at one of the leading educational institutions within the country. This policy would be all the more feasible if formal degree prerequisites for the future government or university positions are relaxed. For a limited period it may also be appropriate to send the ablest candidates abroad, preferably to nondegree programs, until there are enough capable professionals to staff the training programs. Those candidates selected should be sent to a variety of different programs in Europe and North America in order to encourage a healthy range of views.

It is also essential to build up some research capabilities. Although doctoral degrees are the traditional vehicle for such efforts, undergraduate and graduate students can participate in field-research programs, some of which might be financed by and serve the needs of key planning organizations. Research topics might include evaluations of government programs; analyses of neglected problems or subregions; the design of new, simpler, and more feasible urban-planning procedures; ways of encouraging the informal sector; and so on.

If desired, some additional financial and advisory assistance can be gotten from friendly governments, international agencies, foundations, and other universities. But since the quality and relevance of the assistance obtained can vary substantially, it must be carefully evaluated, perhaps with the aid of a trusted advisor.

Most of the suggestions made above are based on elements of programs already in existence in different countries. They are deliberately cautious rather than ambitious, and are designed to reduce expectations and disappointments. Nonetheless, putting even such modest programs into effect will not be easy. In many quarters there will be concern that such paraprofessional, undergraduate, and polytechnic programs will create an inferior system of education; and policy, it will be argued, should strengthen existing programs, not produce inferior competitors. There will be concern, too, arising from the fact that universities enjoy considerable autonomy in most countries. How, then, can the new programs come into being without government dictation or undue strife?

The advocates of modest but potentially effective change are not apt to persuade those who benefit from the traditional system. Almost inescapably, the main approach must be to use the governments' power of the purse. Funds could be made available to support innovative programs subject to certain conditions. The incentives ought to be attractive; and if the charge is made that universities are being tempted to do what they prefer not to do, then the response to the charges must be that the universities need not be tempted. There is no assurance that the universities will choose to meet the conditions; and no university ought to carry out such a program unless it is disposed to do so.

Another solution is the creation of special institutes or new universities. These would be expensive. However, new universities and institutes are often created in developing countries; and if such institutions become necessary on other grounds, the need for such urban programs might be taken into account in the terms of reference of these new institutions.

Finally, it will be argued by some persons that the proposed reform does not change the basic system of education or of influence and power. The charge is correct; but just how serious is it?

"Radical changes" are not likely to be inconsistent with this reform. For example, changes involving more responsiveness to low-income and underprivileged groups and regions, more egalitarian and participatory programs, and more (or less) public ownership and direction of the economy may well be desired or justified in particular countries; but such changes in power, in beneficiaries, or in substantive ideas might still take place and yet advantage may be taken of this framework.

PART FIVE

City Planning:
Promise and Reality

CHAPTER THIRTEEN

On the Illusions of City Planners

Urban specialists, asked to explain the need for intervention in the growth and management of cities, would doubtless point an accusing finger at the market mechanism and the need to correct its inadequacies or to substitute new mechanisms which would function more adequately. So familiar and plausible are the critiques of the market that many planners find it hard to grasp any grounds for opposition save those understandably held by interests which would be hurt in the process. What is often ignored, however, are the limited capabilities of urban planners. In the past, it has been all too easy for them to assume that they could correct the inadequacies of the market or that they could create new mechanisms that would function more adequately. It is this assumption that makes the period when urban planners get significant status and power such a risky one for the profession. For then city planners must show that they can make matters better, or at least not worse; which is precisely what they all too often may not be able to ensure, and for all sorts of reasons, some good, some bad. The situation today is critical because the failings are becoming embarrassingly obvious. A few familiar examples are subsidy programs serving the wrong firms or failing to produce the intended effects; land-use regulations inhibiting development or increasing its cost; public housing serving the wrong families or demeaning the groups served; and inflexible or poorly designed rent controls accelerating the deterioration of the existing stock of housing. There are, on occasion, special or extenuating circumstances—pressures from certain special interests, limited resources, the novelty of some of the efforts and the need for patience and a reasonable period for learning how to carry out some of the tasks. Nonetheless, one has only to study

229

the backgrounds of the staffs of most planning programs, or to compare the number of specialists needed and now being trained in most Third World countries (TWCs),[1] or to examine what is taught in most schools of planning to realize how few well-trained planners there are and how limited the intellectual capital of planning is. The situation is all the worse where the pay is low and the general quality of the Civil Service is poor—and that is the case for most TWCs.

In short, it does not take great insight today to see that, however inadequate the market may be, there is no reason to suppose that urban planners will necessarily do a better job, at least in the short or intermediate term. This reality of the inadequacy of planners and their tools offsets the other reality of the inadequacies of the market and the price mechanism. For purposes of promoting deliberate change, both realities ought to be taken into account; yet they rarely are. The failure to do so constitutes one of the major weaknesses of the efforts of the past. If urban planners, especially in TWCs, are to cope more effectively with the growth and management of metropolitan areas in the 1980s, they need to examine candidly some of the illusions which still haunt them from the past as well as some of those which might yet betray them in the future.

SOME OLD ILLUSIONS

Illusion 1: Comprehensive Planning

One of the proudest claims of the urban-planning profession has been its special kind of comprehensiveness—its unique professional concern with the nature and ties between the different activities of the city and region: with the requirements for linking the places where people worked and lived; with the relationships among schools, residences, and recreational and shopping areas; with the accessibility and other requirements of the industrial and commercial as well as rural and "rurban" areas; and with the factors which affect the efficiency of these activities and how they would change over time, and the ways of serving—more adequately than the market or the market alone—the varying needs of the firms and families and users of the areas. Among planners this emphasis on comprehensiveness produced a substantial consensus during the four decades following World War I.[2]

The charge frequently made in recent years that this was all a romantic illusion—that the notion of comprehensive planning was neither accurate as description, nor feasible in practice, and perhaps not even desirable as a way of getting things done—came as a rude shock. But study after study of planning practice showed that the so-called comprehensive plans were no more than pious aspirations. The constraints imposed by limited budgets, manpower, information, and professional skills made it impossible to do what was needed to make adequate comprehensive plans for the entire metropolitan area, to keep them up-to-date and to monitor how they were carried out. As a consequence, the ideas of Lindblom and Hirschman and others on incremental and "disjunctive" planning acquired great vogue. A growing number of planners came to believe that these alternative views interpreted planning behavior better—especially the incessant pressures to improvise, to negotiate and compromise, and to be content with solutions which "satisficed" rather than "optimized."[3]

But it was no accident that the dream of comprehensive planning dominated the field for some 40 years. Most planners were all too familiar with the tragicomic experiences of clogged transportation, housing crises, cities running out of water or power, and long, dismal, and costly journeys to work. True, there were corrections—but often slow and at great cost; and sometimes there were no corrections: the mess grew worse and many activities were simply stunted.

Other kinds of ad hoc pragmatic approaches led to shifts of emphasis, with the most limited effects. In the field of housing in the United States, for example, attention kept shifting from one aspect of the problem to another: a concern for middle- as well as low-income families; for rural as well as urban housing; for remodeling the existing stock as well as building new housing; for rebuilding central areas as well as providing areawide programs for the entire metropolitan region. The impulsions to make these shifts were less the successes than the failures: the neglected groups, the pressures to use resources more equitably, and the need to cope less superficially with the visible problems and policies.

The view that the failings could be counted on to spur the corrective measures explains, in fact, the resort to comprehensive planning. Indeed, the high prestige now associated with systems analysis (a more sophisticated version of comprehensive planning) derives partly from the need to identify and to pay more attention to all the critical subsystems, and their components and interrelationships, which may shape the understanding and solution of a problem. But systems analysis, in turn, has proved far more successful with physical and biological (rather than social) systems where the critical variables are limited, relatively precise, easy to define, and manipulable.

Since the limitations of each approach generate proponents for the other, perhaps the views of both sides may be worth heeding—but more of one or the other at some times and in some circumstances. Certainly this was the way the strategy evolved in Ciudad Guayana, Venezuela.[4] At the outset, to deal with the mushrooming developments, those in charge improvised ad hoc responses to cope with the myriad infrastructure, programming, organizational, and human problems. But the tangle of difficulties soon led to a search for a more effective basis for making decisions. Those in charge sought two things in particular: a broad, long-term perspective on how development might proceed for the region as part of a development strategy for the country; and a broad, long-term perspective on the character of likely developments within the region which might provide clues as to the scale of the city, the factors which would influence its location, and the layout of the main activity areas within the city, including the housing, the commercial centers, the transportation, and the other infrastructure investments.

The planners chafed at the fact that they had to live with the ad hoc improvisations for a year or two while the basic studies and plans were being made, studies which were necessary to gauge and test the various alternatives. On the other hand, they found that even after this work was completed, they were beset with different pressures for incrementalism. This time the need was to adapt the broad policies as well as the particular programs and projects agreed on by the planners and decision makers: to fit them to the realities and constraints at the center and at the site, and to the varying capabilities of the planners; to pay attention to the small but no less critical adjustments required in the process of coordinating and linking the diverse activities; and to reckon with other changing circumstances. What the planners also found was that quite different scripts were being improvised by many other actors besides the planners. They acknowledged this fact somewhat grudgingly, and they had to rewrite their own script many times—partly to take account of the actual situation, as well as to influence it.

There was a need to be not only comprehensive and ad hoc but very adaptable, for neither doctrine was altogether feasible or likely to work in all circumstances. Given limited resources, the basic concerns were which factors were the most important at different stages and at different levels of analysis and policy making: which had to be taken into account if the program was to thrive and which could be safely neglected at least for the time being. On these critical matters, there was only the most modest lead from systems or incremental analyses. It would be easy to exaggerate the help one might get from research on these matters; but surely it can provide more adequate evidence concerning the policies and behavior that have proved effective in different circumstances and those which have not, and why; and that would be no mean contribution.

Illusion 2: The Planning Process

Another key idea of urban planners, one which still grips most minds in the field, is the concept of planning process.[5] It involves at least two basic notions. One is the need to cope on a continuing basis with many problems which will recur or change and which cannot be dealt with by "once and for all" solutions: substantive problems, such as transportation, housing, or industrial development, or methodological problems, such as ways of planning or criteria to guide strategies or programs to put them into effect and to judge their effectiveness. In addition, there is the view that how problems are approached and decisions are made is often as important—or perhaps even more important— than any particular decision or solution. This conviction is the other basic element in the notion of process.

Some planners would add, however, that the legitimacy and ultimate viability of these processes depend on the significance of the roles played by the persons and groups affected by the processes. Whatever one may think of this view, it is now challenging the way planners are serving different groups in most countries, socialist and nonsocialist alike. The challenge is sensed even in quarters where little can be done to meet it. I recall the skepticism of a group of participants in a United Nations meeting when the chief planner of the capital city of a totalitarian regime stressed that the plans for his city were formulated with maximum citizens' participation; and I especially recall the roar of laughter when, in response to a request to identify the changes in the plan attributable to this participation, there was an awkward pause followed by the observation—with an amused smile—that since the plans were so well worked out no vital changes were indeed required.

On the other hand, processes may be sophisticated and ingenious as well as flexible and democratic—and still not particularly impressive. I suspect most people would regard well-honed but ineffective planning processes with the same wry disappointment with which one might view a basketball team which excels in passing, "cutting," ballhandling, and teamwork, but not in scoring.

Nonetheless, to most planners today, a willingness to stress planning process is a sign of progress—a great leap forward in relation to past practice and even a good deal of current practice. With flexible planning processes, planners can presumably ensure feedback, correct errors, and adjust to changing circumstances. This is the faith planners now accept; and sometimes, perhaps often, planning even happens this way. But we have limited evidence on this score, and especially about the circumstances when such success might be more or less likely.

We do have much evidence, however, that the characteristic behavior of the groups who wield power and the ways their political and administrative systems function reinforce centralized decision making and hobble effective participatory processes. But this view, too, may be somewhat distorted. Many groups devise means of making their views felt—some more effectively than others, depending on the circumstances. We know all too little about these processes, not to mention the ways they are changing. It is not simply these possibilities and their potentials, but the way planning processes actually function in MDCs and TWCs and the problems encountered in trying to appear—as well as to be—equitable which may be one of the more promising areas for research concerning the management of metropolitan areas in TWCs in the 1980s and beyond.

Illusion 3: Limiting the Size of Cities

To limit the growth of cities to some optimum size has been one of the recurrent dreams of utopians over the ages. The benefits sought were less congestion, lower costs, more amenity, a more "human scale." But wherever tried, the efforts left much to be desired. One reason is that the dreams occur when growth is getting out of hand, and it is precisely then that it is least feasible to do much about it.

There were several other reasons for the failure. There was never a consensus (nor, for that matter, any clear criteria) on the optimum size of cities. Nor did policy makers always grasp what made cities grow at certain periods, where economic activities needed to be, and how strong these two forces actually were. When they tried to lure firms to preferred locations such as lagging regions, it turned out that the policy makers knew all too little about the kinds of activities which might go there and about the inducements which would produce the desired outcomes.

When industrial growth was restricted in inner areas, it took place elsewhere in the region; and in those cases where the restrictions proved effective, it was often because many of the firms were already leaving the areas. The rules and administrative mechanisms also did not—perhaps could not—cope with the small firms or with the secular increases in the service activities in which the principal increases of employment were taking place.

The arguments, too, proved elusive. There were, to be sure, many higher costs in very large cities, especially for services like water, roads, police, education, and sanitation; but the higher costs were not decisive since other critical advantages had to be weighed in the analyses of the net benefits. For business activities, there were the large markets and the array of labor and business services; for principal and secondary wage earners, there were the opportunities afforded by the variety and quality of jobs; and for both firms and households, there was the quality of the urban services.

Even the British New Towns policy—the most innovative effort to do something about these matters in the MDCs—was not able to change the character and relative size of the components of the urban system of Great Britain. No doubt these new towns provided a little more choice in physical environment; but even if the number and scale of these towns had been doubled or tripled, they still would have served only a minuscule proportion of the total number of families and firms within the London region or the other regions they served.

What is especially disconcerting today, however, is the drop in population and economic activities and the resulting financial crises now taking place in many of the large metropolitan areas of the United States and Europe. These downward trends, so sought and valued by some writers and some leaders of the planning fraternity, were neither understood nor anticipated by them, nor by most of the other urban policy makers and administrators. The decline is being stubbornly resisted, of course, by the interests associated with large, "mature" metropolitan regions, but so far not very successfully. This is the case because the decline reflects many deep-seated, long-term changes in technology and markets as well as in migration, patterns of living, and of growth of economic activities which can resist even massive intervention strategies.[6]

On these matters, urban planners are still only able to influence the details—perhaps not unimportant details—of what will happen. They may alter rates of growth or decline and influence the places where they might take place, but even these modest aims, to be achieved, must be developed and backed at the national as well as regional level. Only national governments have the resources, the power, and the effective jurisdiction.

National policies, however, involve more than explicit policies affecting infrastructure investment, tax incentives, and other inducements to redirect the location of economic activity. They must take account, too, of the secondary effects of other policies, such as the criteria for awarding government contracts, for setting transportation rates, or for designing export and exchange policies. Such efforts are anything but easy to ensure; and the difficulties are compounded because they take at least a decade or two to produce results, and because more or less sustained as well as consistent national government policies are other essential prerequisites.

But a new and relevant question is whether the massive shifts in the location of population and economic activity now taking place in the MDCs are likely to occur in the TWCs, and if so, approximately when? As yet, there are few, if any, thorough analyses of whether the main factors responsible for these trends are likely to become important in the future in the TWCs. Such comparative evaluations should rank high in any research agenda focusing on the growth and management of the metropolitan areas of the TWCs.

Illusion 4: The Importance of the Physical Environment

There has been a widely shared notion among many reformers—health specialists, attorneys, social workers, and economists, as well as city planners, architects, and engineers—

that by upgrading the built environment, they could fulfill the aspirations of many low- and middle-income families and significantly advance human welfare. For over a century this faith inspired efforts to secure building and land-use regulations, the expansion of public services, higher standards for new housing in the inner and outer areas of the city, and the building of public housing. These ideas, once so persuasive, now increasingly appear not simply banal but downright misguided.

On these matters, imposing the priorities of the rule makers makes little sense to the critics. Jobs, food, access to certain services, information, and contacts, they emphasize, are far more important for most families at certain income levels than some of the proposed housing or physical improvements. Economists reinforce this view with evidence that cash subsidies are more efficient, more favored by families, and more useful to them than subsidies in kind.[7] A spate of studies also scores the typical large-scale, high-rise housing built to serve low-income families. These expensive units serve only a small fraction of the population, mostly middle-income families; and much of the housing targeted to serve the poor often ends up getting built in inaccessible areas utterly inappropriate for their needs.[8] "Doing good," some cynics are also inclined to add, turns out to be not altogether disinterested—for it does offer attractive jobs, often with solid financial rewards to the professional "caretakers" and planners of the programs, not to mention the customary returns to the economic interests which benefit from investments in housing, roads, infrastructure, and other physical services.

The ironic result is that the programs for which reformers had fought for generations are now very much on the defensive. So devastating have the critiques been that strong reminders are required that the housing and city reformers of the past were far less naïve or self-regarding than they seem to have been. That higher real income was the more effective—and eventual—solution, they would have readily agreed to; but there was no prospect of such a solution within a reasonable period. There were, at the time, no full-employment nor redistributive-income policies—indeed, even such policies as we now have are of limited effectiveness. Social security, too, did not exist or was still in its infancy. There was also the overweening pressure to get away from "relief" payments—limited in scale, profitable to "slum landlords," degrading to the recipients. Later, the Depression of the 1930s riveted attention on employment; and then when Keynesian ideas took hold, housing and public-works programs were embraced by economists and administrators because of the employment possibilities and the anticipated "multiplier" effects. Another feature at that time of the programs advocated for housing, transportation, schools, and area development was their identification (as today in many TWCs) with "basic needs," not just "make-work" programs. Above all, there was the expectation in the past that there would be the will and the wealth to divert enough resources to raise the standards of housing for all groups in society.[9]

Bitter experience, however, now compels recognition of the justification for some of the warnings and skepticism about environmental investments, including the tendency of their aims and programs to be perverted in the process of implementation. Almost everywhere, evidence is accumulating that the wrong type of infrastructure is being provided for the low-income families: wrong in terms of costs, functional adequacy, and relevance in serving the actual needs and preferences of these families.

For TWCs with limited resources, a critical social question today is whether it is indeed possible to avoid subsidizing the well-to-do more than the poor; and if so, what kinds of programs might be developed which could reach a significant portion of the low-income population within one or two decades. Two additional lines of research, especially helpful for policy, might be to document the dubious ways of developing infrastructure programs, and far more important—to identify the more promising alternatives, together with the circumstances and tools which may make these possibilities replicable elsewhere.

Illusion 5: Planning, Management, and Politics

Most of us are familiar with the fervent prayer of technocrats that someday planning and management might be liberated from

the thralldom of politics. Persons in the grip of this illusion associate politics with the spoils system, vested interests, and sordid deals, and associate planning and management with technical
skills, the weighing of evidence, and objective decisions on the
merits of the case. It is because these notions are so inadequate
that it would be prudent to underscore the naïveté of a narrow
interpretation of the growth and management of metropolitan
areas which would only buttress the technocratic bias. Two
examples may be helpful on this point.

In the British civil service, still one of the best in the world,
a sharp distinction is made between politics and administration.
Civil servants—up to the very top levels—are supposed to work
for the minister and must keep out of "politics." The doctrine is
probably carried out as well—or even better—in Britain than in
most other countries; but even there it does not always work.
Lord Silkin, the former Minister of Town and Country Planning
in Britain, once observed that on some issues (one of those he
had in mind was the legislation on the "purchase" of the development rights to land) he was not sure he could count on his
civil service to carry out the ideas and programs he and his government wanted.[10] Almost a generation later, another labor
minister, R. H. S. Crossman, spelled out in his diary with some
exasperation some of the difficulties he had in coping with high-
level civil servants with strong reputations and convictions.[11] In
both cases the circumstances may have been exceptional;
nonetheless, the British experience is revealing because it might
be supposed that there, if anywhere, the tradition of technical
subordination to political leaders might well hold firm even when
dealing with inflammatory issues.

In other environments, such as the United States, there is a
long history of high-level civil servants—through leaks of
information—"building fires" under their political chiefs, or de-
flecting action in particular directions with the kinds of information gathered and the way reports are written.

Even more important, however, than the occasional dissonance or even intermittent conflicts between the political leaders
and their civil servants are the subtle, underlying considerations

which tend to produce consonant patterns of thinking. Often dissonance and conflict are kept within bounds because high-level civil servants come from similar backgrounds and share many of the same values of the political leaders; but it is a fact that, consciously or otherwise, they tend to be finely attuned to the kinds of conduct that might affect the course of their careers.

To be sure, if it is possible to transform difficult political issues into "technical" questions, to do so can reduce the range and intensity of controversy and help to achieve more of a consensus in making and implementing decisions. But the technical label can—and often does—serve other, less edifying purposes. For one thing, it can be a convenient ploy to prevent, or at least to reduce, the participation of other groups in the making of decisions. In the development of the Guayana region by the Venezuelan Development Corporation of Guayana, the high visibility given to the role of the Joint Center for Urban Studies of MIT and Harvard University was deliberately designed to underline the image that the Guayana program was the heritage of the entire country and that the decisions by the corporation were being made only after taking due account of the studies and recommendations of a competent, disinterested, outside group. Much as that may have been the case, it is also true that many of the questions under consideration involved highly controversial political issues: for example, whether in the decisions made there should be participation by local groups—and which local groups; or what the right mix was of capital- versus labor-intensive investments; or what priorities and groups should be served by the investments in housing, education, and community and recreational facilities. The collaboration of the Joint Center helped to screen the political significance of the decisions being made by men with certain values and class backgrounds and political points of view, and the fact that quite different and responsible decisions might well have been made by men with different values, backgrounds, and points of view. These observations hold despite the extraordinary competence and dedication of the people who made these decisions.[12]

In thinking about these relationships, the critical problem

turns out to be not how to minimize political issues or how to maximize the technical approach. It is which issues ought to receive more political emphasis and which ought to receive more technical emphasis. The criteria for making these judgments— including the relevance of such factors as the adequacy of the information and the technical tools, the nature of the decision-making process, the probable outcomes, the groups affected, and the time constraints—warrant much close scrutiny.

At present there are few TWCs in which the metropolitan management and growth issues are not regarded as technical issues. One reason may be the frequent absence of accepted or responsible opposition parties. No doubt this circumstance reinforces the view in many quarters that there are only a limited number of persons and social groups who can or should have a decisive role in shaping these decisions. But sooner or later this assumption is likely to be challenged, for there is no denying the nontechnical and often controversial character of the issues relating both to metropolitan management as well as the grossly uneven incidence of the costs and benefits of the metropolitan development programs. When this challenge occurs, however, the technical approach will still be indispensable to deal with the complex problems which have to be tackled even when the political implications and issues are faced. Working out an appropriate balance in these relationships will be anything but easy—which is all the more reason for studies of the ways and means, the examples and contexts in which such efforts have been tried and have worked or failed to work, and why.

SOME CURRENT ILLUSIONS

In contrast to the traditional illusions associated with the physical and technical methods of planning, there are some which relate to what urban planners know and can do and to the groups most likely to benefit from their services. Perhaps taking the measure of these illusions may be helpful in gauging some of the additional tasks that lie ahead.

Illusion 6: Goals and Planning Behavior

Almost all planners take for granted that getting some agreement on the ends of planning is a high priority, and one of the first tasks of planners. But with rare exceptions, aims set in the early phases of any planning activity are at best crude first approximations. One has only to examine the history of any innovative efforts to deal with housing, transportation, industrial development, new towns, community services, and, of course, urban growth and management to see how general, how ambiguous, and often how wrong the declared aims were at the outset, and how often redefinition and changes in approach became inescapable as the program evolved and learning occurred. In retrospect, a most critical task for planners is how to design deliberate learning processes to discover worthwhile aims which might be able to achieve a consensus.

Viewed from this perspective, the most serious and really effective goal setting would occur later, rather than earlier, in the evolution of particular planning efforts. The irony, however, of this more realistic version of goal setting is that, more often than not, it would prove embarrassing or worse for top executives and policy makers to tell legislators, finance committees, or other monitoring organizations that they need some latitude to experiment a bit—or a great deal: for whereas they do not doubt for a moment that they have a few plausible ideas on the subject, they must in all candor concede that they do not really know what to do or quite how to do it, and they need the equivalent of a hunting license, and a reasonable amount of spending money— perhaps thousands or millions of dollars to get started; and then—maybe, for there are no guarantees—they will come back with more knowledgeable proposals about what they should be doing. Surely such a confession would be hard medicine for most monitoring organizations to swallow.

There are, however, many behavioral studies which in different ways are reinforcing these views. The evidence is not simply that time, cost, information, and other constraints oblige us to "satisfice" rather than "optimize" on these matters; and that to do so is all the more necessary when a welter of unclearly weighted goals are being sought.[13] The studies also show that it is not always, or even often, the case that persons on top prefer frank exposition of goals. Leaders and organizations are change oriented only in certain limited ways. For good and substantial reasons their basic aims include system maintenance and maintenance of personal power, but it is as a rule prudent to pass over these details just as it is to pass over the considerable advantage that ambiguity and conflicting goals may offer administrators, as well as the rest of us, when we do not want to be tied down to precise or easily identified criteria by which our work might be judged.[14]

Extending these disenchanting insights in still another direction, Hirschman has advanced what might be dubbed the blunder theory of planning: in substance, the view that there may well be unsuspected advantages in the persistent inclination of planners and managers to underestimate difficulties or to overestimate benefits, thus trapping themselves into getting things done which might not be done, and which Hirschman—generously—assumes often ought to be done and could be done without undue costs.[15]

One inference which might be drawn from these current perceptions of the goals and behavior of planners is mildly exhilarating. By disclosing what has been left out of the statement of formal aims, we do get rid of much intellectual cant. But the net effect is likely to be disquieting for those who prefer more positive contributions. What has been gained from these insights is more realism, but what has been lost (at least as yet) is a sense of direction.

The problems of managing urban growth provide as convenient an illustration as any we might pick. Maximizing growth, or maximizing efficient growth of metropolitan regions is today less acceptable or even credible as a goal for development. To add the concept of equity or of ecological soundness or both is supposed to improve matters, and might even do so if we knew how to measure or weight or reach a rough consensus on the combined criteria. But it might take a generation or more of wrestling with these problems before we even think we know what it is we should be seeking and whether and how we might be able to attain it. Meanwhile, gambling on some crude hypotheses about what it is we should be doing, the hope is that our research might disclose what, in fact, is actually happening and whether any of it has any ascribable relationship to what we now think we want to have happen.

Illusion 7: The Influence of Planners

Fewer urban planners write or behave today as though their main job is to scan their domains and to decide what needs to be done, where and when, and to build a consensus along these lines—although sometimes in certain environments and for some planners it still happens this way. What troubles planners far more often is how little they really do influence the public agenda. The big issues of metropolitan planning—whether of jobs and housing, or of decentralization and participation, or of transportation and other public services—do not become public issues simply because of the initiatives of planners.

The main explanation is that the leading interest groups, the communication agencies, and the powerful personalities and organizations play, as a rule, the pivotal roles. And so they do; but they do so in an environment constrained in several respects: in part by basic secular trends as well as the conflicts in interest between groups; in part by the bearing of particular issues on matters of concern to these persons and groups; and in part by the immediate situation, such as a crisis which may inhibit or precipitate the action. So, powerful as these groups may be, their influence is limited, nonetheless, in significant ways.[16]

For urban planners, however, there are still other constraints. As a rule they lack not only the necessary power and funds, but—partly as a consequence—the charismatic personalities and followings. When circumstances are propitious, and sometimes even when they are not, planners can overcome some of these limitations. They often do so when they have made shrewd assessments of what might be done in a particular environment, or of the changes in opportunity and strategy which might be feasible as the environment changes, and they have managed to exploit the situation to the hilt and make things happen—often things which others did not think feasible.

Although the opportunities are far more limited than they would like, there are ways in which planners do manage to exert influence. One is by working with different groups and organizations, learning about their needs, and helping the leaders to develop effective methods of promoting them, thereby generating claims to offset the pressures of particular groups. Another mode of influence has come through the procedures for handling the conflicts and complementarities of the different group activities. When successful, these efforts earn respect, buttress coalitions, and otherwise help to determine what may get done. Still another important pattern of influence is wielded by planners who have worked closely with top executives, ministers, or others who have formal power. Often, outside of a few main concerns which shape the thinking or catch the attention of these officials, their ideas may have no particular orientation. Ready and eager to do things which make sense, they are not sure what they might be. Buffeted by conflicting pressures, they welcome and sometimes desperately seek guidance. When these conditions prevail, planners with strong personalities, ideas, and personal contacts with these leaders have a disproportionate impact on the public agenda.

These brief observations, of course, oversimplify. They point to some of the constraints and opportunities—there are doubtless others—which may be important at different times and in different environments in shaping policies on the growth and management of the metropolitan areas.[17] What we know about these matters, however, is drawn largely from perceptive surmises and what is now popularly referred to as "casual empiricism." We do not have adequate studies of how these problems have been handled in different environments. For the next decade or so, it may be especially helpful to produce some reliable case studies—of successes as well as failures, partly because the literature is now replete with failures and partly because the payoff may be higher to verify a success than to document a failure. "More is learned from a single success," Robert Merton has reminded us, "than from the multiple failures,"[18] because the success teaches us what can be done if we can replicate some of the requisite conditions.

Illusion 8: Jobs and Metropolitan Development

One of the disquieting aspects of city planning, especially in TWCs in the past has been the ways in which planners have ignored or misjudged the elementary importance of jobs for the migrant and unemployed population of these areas. Of course, there have been efforts to make the economy grow—mainly by arranging for different areas to accommodate various types of economic activities (light and heavy industries, commercial activities, offices, and the like) and by furnishing, as soon as feasible, the water, sewerage, power, roads, and other public services needed by these activities. But the tendency has been to adapt to the kinds of jobs that became available on a "catch as catch can" basis, and to cater, in particular, to the larger, established, and more influential firms and activities, especially those associated with modernization and development. The responsiveness to the executives and managers of the firms which provide the jobs is easy to understand. But in the process, the very pressing but inchoate requirements of those who need the jobs and the requisites of those jobs have been slighted or played down.

The importance of the issue is well illustrated by an analysis that was made of the appropriate mix of capital investments in the Guayana region of Venezuela.[19] The study examined the implications of using a fixed amount of capital either for some additional industrial projects, such as an expanded or more integrated steel mill or an iron-ore-processing plant, or for the promotion of rural development by encouraging large or small dry farms or dairy farms. The calculations showed that for equivalent funds the investors could obtain one steel mill, or 19 ore-reduction plants, or 3,525 larger farms, or 70,500 small farms. Assuming that markets proved stable for all of the activities examined, the investors could count on getting 60,000 more jobs from the investment in small farms; in addition, it was shown that the value-added of the farm projects would go to a larger number of relatively lower-paid workers as well as more workers on the whole. As a consequence,

the demand would be greater for basic consumer goods such as clothes, small appliances and housing which are themselves made by labor intensive processes [so that] the overall net employment advantage of the agricultural projects could be as high as 120,000 jobs.[20]

These effects are certainly important in an economy characterized by high unemployment—even for policy makers who associate industrialization with economic independence and progress, and who equate agriculture with conservatism and dependence on elastic demand and fluctuating international prices for agricultural products and high-priced foreign goods.

Still another example in most TWCs of the importance of jobs involves the policies for the so-called informal sector. No doubt official attitudes on this score are now definitely changing. But as we have noted in an earlier chapter, the assumption that these employments will wither away as economic development proceeds is now seriously questioned in many quarters. There is even more of a consensus that the length of the period it may take for this dwindling to occur and the very substantial groups dependent in the interim on these activities for survival (often the majority of the population and the labor force) justify a policy of aid rather than neglect or harassment on the part of the state.[21] One danger, however, is that given our ignorance and very limited studies of these activities, even well-intentioned efforts to correct the neglect or bias of the past may produce inflationary, quasi-monopolistic, or other untoward effects which may do more harm than good.[22]

An illustration of the sheer lack of understanding of the elementary need of poor families for jobs in order to survive is the way efforts have been made to provide better housing for families living in shanties. Again and again, one encounters public-housing or sites-and-service programs banished to remote or inaccessible areas badly served with transportation. The net effect has often been a heritage of bitterness and dissatisfaction in recompense for the energy and resources expended on these efforts. The harsh truth is that many, if not most, of these very poor families need jobs more than housing, and, if forced to choose between one or the other, will opt for the location that will help them get the jobs they need, however miserable the housing conditions may be.

Each of the cases cited underscore how risky it is for planners to substitute their criteria and their judgments for those of the families concerned—without adequate information or research, without respect for the groups concerned, and without arranging for them to participate effectively in making the decisions and in monitoring the ways they are carried out.

Illusion 9: The Ecological Frontier

Environmentalists have amassed evidence indicating that some very grave problems—perhaps even global disasters—may lie ahead once the growth of population crosses some critical thresholds. Their warnings about the depletion of exhaustible resources or the pollution and degradation of the environment are sobering; others—relating to the increase of carbon dioxide in the atmosphere, the loss of oxygen in the upper atmosphere, or the increase of heat in the biosphere, with the possibility of the melting of the polar ice caps, tidal waves, or even a new ice age—are, to say the least, dramatic, if not mind-boggling. The net effect has been a heightened sensitivity to environmental issues.[23] So it is not surprising that many planners assume that ecological considerations must receive top priority in the management and growth of cities.

However, the credibility of many of the dire forecasts about available resources has been challenged in a number of quarters. Possibly the most skeptical reactions come from the economists who think the problems of scarcity are not only greatly exaggerated but are exacerbated by underpricing. Most of them believe that the shortages are likely to be offset by the resort to substitutes, the tapping of new and more abundant, albeit more costly, resources, and the effects of increased incentives in spurring more effective conservation measures.[24]

The reactions of the TWCs have been mordant, hostile, or both. Some have emphasized their greater concern with the pollution of poverty; others have anticipated a deplorable shift of emphasis away from the problems of the poor and disadvantaged; still others have seen in environmentalism a devious new means by which the MDCs could justify slowing up the development of the TWCs and keep them poor and subservient. Nor is the skepticism of the TWCs too surprising, however distorted their characterizations of the motivations behind the environmentalist movement may have been. TWCs could see scant reason for serious concern, given the lavish, and in some respects irresponsible consumption in the MDCs, especially the United States, Europe, and Japan. As long as none of the MDCs shows a serious disposition to cut consumption or to adopt significant conservation measures, the TWCs are are not likely to do so.[25]

True, the sharp differences in views between the MDCs and the TWCs obscure some important common denominators. Both the MDCs and the TWCs are seeking certain "basic" levels of health and living conditions. Despite the disclaimers, there is, in fact, growing concern in many TWCs as well as the MDCs about the loss of their resources as well as the perils involved in the rape of the environment. There are, too, in both TWCs and MDCs the disappointed expectations associated with development. Modernization, viewed in the past as desirable, even if somewhat painful, now appears risky and often cruelly disappointing. Material development may assure some real satisfactions, and may be inescapable; but in its train one must reckon with formidable problems of inequality, erosion of values, anomie, environmental degradation, and social and political turbulence.

The ecologists, however, are quite divided about the implications for metropolitan development. There is, for example, the ecosystem perspective of Sachs and others with its concern for appropriate technology and the enhancement of existing traditions coupled with an emphasis on rural development and the encouragement of small and intermediate-size cities.[26] There is also the contrary vision of the future-oriented ecological techno-crats like Richard Meier with their faith in applied science and its capacity to devise resource-conserving technologies and to en-hance the versatility, resources, managerial capabilities, and other advantages of the great metropolitan complexes.[27]

At present, there is no consensus on how these issues will be resolved. All that is certain is that metropolitan areas are sure to grow even if the moderately successful efforts to slow the general growth of world population should continue. The declining size of households is one reason. The prevailing tendency for urbani-zation to proceed at approximately twice the rate of population growth is another. By the year 2000 world population[28] is ex-pected to range between 5.8 and 6.6 billion people, an increase of approximately 2.3 billion or about 38% from the estimated 3.9 billion population estimate for 1975. About half of the total popu-lation in the year 2000, some 3.1 billion people, is expected to be in urban areas. This would amount to an increase of 1.6 billion people, which would represent an increase of 2% per annum in the past 25 years or a total increase of 56%. From 1950 to 1970, Africa, East and South Asia, and Latin America gained 58 new cities in the size category of one million or more, most of them in Asia. So, regardless of the policies which may be considered appropriate in particular countries, there will be a massive growth of metropolitan areas for at least another two generations and probably much longer.

The net effect of these trends will be to intensify the pres-sures to create or to adapt "intelligence" mechanisms (nationally and within regions) to identify the new environmental aims; and to formulate policies and programs plus incentive and control systems to back them up in effective ways; as well as research and evaluative mechanisms to monitor what occurs and analyze the results, including an evaluation of the environmental effects of other major policies. These efforts will have all the characteristic advantages of national urban-growth strategies: that is, central direction, the possibility of tapping available knowledge, and the prospect of more effective utilization of scarce resources and personnel. But there will also be some formidable limitations. These include limited knowledge, the uncertain effectiveness of centralized, underpaid bureaucracies operating in environments where there is a high premium for practicing or conniving at corruption, and the ever real and present danger that the new programs may impose further burdens on the poor because of the likely uneven incidence of benefits and costs.

Illusion 10: The Public Interest

The planner takes for granted the obligation to serve equitably the interests of the local public agencies and of the different groups within the community, accommodating their needs and reconciling or helping to compromise them when they conflict. For this reason, urban planners, when asked whom they represent, are likely to say "the community" or "the public interest." If one suggests that by working for the government or by proving as a rule responsive to the more powerful organizations or groups or well-to-do elements of the population planners are wittingly or unwittingly serving the "establishment," they are apt to take umbrage or simply dismiss the observations as radical cant.

But what is the evidence on this score? There is no denying that urban planners do work for governments—national, provincial, or local—or for private firms which depend for their survival on contracts with the public authorities. They have enough of a stake in the system not to want to uproot it, although they may know enough about the malfunctions of the system not to want to keep things as they are. The social backgrounds of planners do provide some additional clues but not very much, because there is only sketchy information on these matters available about planners in MDCs, and even less, of course, in TWCs. Such information as we do have suggests that most city and regional planners have middle-class or professional or quasiprofessional family backgrounds. They have had enough resources to obtain a university education. Their occupation tends to reinforce the liberal reformist, middle-of-the-road inclinations of their background. Their concern is to make the system work better—with wide disagreements among themselves as to ways and means and degrees. Actually, the self-image of the planner and the radical's image of the planner appear to be consistent.

Until recently, planners tended to revel in their progressive stance, convinced of the need to make the system work and balance the insights of the left and right while rejecting the less palatable extremist views of both. But that easy, almost complacent, assurance has been sorely tried and even shaken in some quarters by the critiques and the failings of the past decade, both in the MDCs and the LDCs. There is a growing awareness on the part of the urban planners that their solutions are often not reliable, adequate, or persuasive, not to mention efficient. To appreciate the growing unease, one has only to recall the controversies surrounding the policies for transportation or for programming commercial and industrial needs; or the conflicts in judgment and criteria between the clients and the planner on zoning and building regulations, on the character or layouts for residential precincts, or on the standards and other requirements for new developments at the periphery of cities or in the center. Ecologists, too, have been less than enthusiastic about the planners neglect of the ecological effects of private and public development policies; they have waged persistent battles to ensure that these considerations are seriously taken into account.

The limitations might be dismissed as understandable frailties reflecting the state of the art, likely to be overcome over time with greater knowledge and proficiency. One of the most serious charges, however, concerns not simply the characteristic neglect—or the failure—to protect the interests of the disadvantaged, but the sheer unlikelihood that they could be effectively protected by ongoing planning processes, as evidenced by the lack of effective participation by these groups in the making of policies and the implementation of the programs. This failing appears to be the most difficult one to correct, at least in the short or intermediate term, even if there were the disposition on the part of planners to do something about these matters. One reason is that the poor in most countries, and especially in TWCs, cannot easily organize to protect their interests. There are rarely powerful institutions providing support for the lowest income groups; and most TWCs lack other effective ways of helping them. Power, centralized in capital cities or provincial centers, is not too responsive to these matters. As already noted, what is remote—or below us—is less visible and, with rare exceptions, of less concern to those whose actions might be influential. The consequences are fairly inexorable. Interest groups and individuals with more resources, energy, and effective leadership can make their needs felt: they know how to exert pressure and are adept in exploiting all sorts of programs—even those designed to serve the poor—in ways that will ultimately serve their concerns.

Two questions over the next few decades will be whether this pattern can be changed within the system and the extent to which policies for the growth and management of metropolitan areas, especially in TWCs, will contribute to this transformation. There are already some indications of how these issues might find expression. Variations on evaluation criteria are sure to be applied. For whatever policies or programs are proposed, there will be pressures to identify the incidence of the costs and benefits. One can envision metropolitan development strategies being examined on the basis of weighted indices which consider not only the implications for health, efficiency, ecological effects and amenity but who pays for the outcomes and who derives the most significant benefits, direct and indirect. One can also envision examinations of metropolitan-development strategies focusing on the needs of the rural as well as the urban poor and how the policies for particular patterns of growth, for the location of new development, and for the location and character of the infrastructure investments and public services compare with other ways of serving these needs.

It would be premature, however, to draw much comfort from these prospects even though they are likely to be explored ardently or experimented with in some countries. For possibility is one thing, and probability another; and the odds are that even policies and programs designed to redress the balance in favor of the disadvantaged may still not do so, at least not in the short or intermediate term, because the mechanisms of the system and those manipulating these mechanisms remain tilted in favor of the more well-to-do.

CONCLUDING OBSERVATIONS

This evaluation of the limitations in what planners know and do and the problems associated with the groups they serve is anything but encouraging. But there is no denying today the great discrepancies between the formal descriptions of city planning and the actual practice of city planning; between the presumed and the actual knowledge and power of city planners; and between the claims made and the actual benefits which result from their activities. Although the profession may flinch from a realistic mirror of what it does, sooner or later it must recognize that many earnest planners, like some scientists in the field of molecular biology, are debating whether it is morally responsible to practice the professional activity in the customary ways when the consequences may be so ill understood, or so unfair, especially for the more disadvantaged groups in our society.

CHAPTER FOURTEEN

The Profession of City Planning

"TRUE" PROFESSIONS

As shrewd a participant observer as Nathan Glazer maintains that city planning—like divinity, social work, teaching, and other "minor" professions—is really not a "true" profession, for it has failed to develop a system of education comparable in quality to the "established" social-science disciplines (economics, political science, and sociology) or to the "major" professions (medicine and law);[1] and he attributes this failure to the repeated shifts in aims and curriculum content, which hobble progress and manifest themselves in characteristic *status conflicts*—between practitioners and academics and between faculty and faculty—which eventually break out also as conflicts between students, and between students and faculty.[2]

Glazer takes a baleful view of these conflicts and strains, but he does not explore whether some of them may be worth the anguish. This is surprising, for the benefits are surely not irrelevant. Agnes de Mille tells of a German ballet dancer exclaiming in the process of limbering up, "Ach, what a wonderful pain! Ach, what a wonderful pain!" because it makes for a better performance. The same holds for the strains of transformation and growth[3]—such as, for instance, those experienced during periods of adolescence.

City planning has been practiced since the dawn of urban culture; but as an independent field of study in Europe and North America it is less than a century old. It has had neither the intellectual traditions, the earnings, the prestige, nor perhaps even the daily impact on people's lives of either law or medicine. There are other things, however, which also affect the status and appeal of an occupation: the challenge of highly visible problems, potential social influence, long-term growth prospects, responsiveness to a wide range of talents. This combination of features distinguishes city planning from the so-called minor professions of teaching, social work, business, and divinity, and even from the "major" professions of law and medicine. These features help to explain the upsurge in the number of extremely able students, as well as the wide range of disciplinary and professional specialists who want to enter, or to develop some association with, the field. Nonetheless, because city planning is a young field in the midst of transforming its relatively old shibboleths, it is beset with nagging desires to identify vital directions of change and development. These considerations, rather than status conflict, are the clues for understanding the identity and thematic issues now causing strains and challenge in city-planning schools. To see why, let us first examine Glazer's views in a little more detail before turning our attention to these alternative perspectives.

ISSUES OF STATUS OR TRANSFORMATION

By "minor" professions, Glazer means those that do not

possess knowledge of the same level of technical difficulty and of the same importance to people's lives as that possessed by the classic major professions [law and medicine] [and] their claims to professional status and the privilege of maintaining secrecy concerning their professional services do not possess the same authority we grant to doctors and lawyers.[4]

Such professions, he says, draw in scholars from academic disciplines to bring students who will become practitioners "more sophisticated knowledge [and] to add to the prestige of the profession."[5] In a field such as planning, this practice results in a student knowing more about "economic, political and social trends in urban development [than] the practical details of his work 'on the job'."[6] The discrepancy, however, between the roles they expect to play and the subjects they are taught often prompt the students to teach themselves what they think they need to know, but what their faculty is not, it appears, organized to teach them. . . .

Since the teaching staff is in large measure trained in academic disciplines, and since teaching in the disciplines is considered most satisfactory when one reproduces in one's pupils the kind of scholar one is oneself, there is an attempt at seduction on the one hand and tendencies to disparage the majority of the students who will not be or cannot be attracted to academic study of their subjects.[7]

There are different reactions to these tendencies. Some students and faculty are persuaded that the academic emphases will strengthen the program. Others, Glazer observes, think these emphases divert attention from the things professionals need to know, especially since the academic staff outranks the professional staff. Thus, the program is tilted toward research rather than professional training. Understandably enough, both sides feel threatened when critical tenure and curriculum decisions have to be made. Many practitioners on the faculty feel divisive if they resist academic intrusion, and obsolete or irresponsible if they do not. Academics in the school fear that if they identify with the professional faculty they may become second-rate practitioners and lose status within their academic disciplines, but if they identify with the discipline, they risk neglecting the essential needs of the city-planning professionals.

These conflicts might be solved, Glazer suggests, if the professional degree could be made competitive with the disciplinary degree. But he questions whether this will occur because of the sweeping changes in the content of the curriculum "every decade or so."[8] As a case in point he cites the shift in emphasis in city planning to a curriculum featuring the social sciences instead of design, site planning, and local codes, with the result that the "design based faculty found itself redundant—all this in a very few years."[9] Contrast this situation, he adds, with the relatively stable training in medicine and law over the past 60 years (and more recently in business schools), despite major changes and advances in these two professions. The main reasons for these differences, he thinks, is that the fundamental ends of medicine (health) and law (success in litigation) are fixed and unambiguous whereas there are no clear ends in city planning. Although stability in educational programs might be achieved by adhering closely to existing practice, Glazer does not regard this as a promising approach because such practice is not respected in city planning; and were the schools to stress instead a more ideal exercise of these functions, the results, he thinks, would be unsettling because "there are so many different ways of reaching the good society."[10] There really is no solution, according to Glazer. "There are only choices and it is impossible to prevent schools and whole professions from swinging from one to the other." All of which leads him to a view which might be called "Glazer's dilemma": that is, that "we are face to face with a tension to be lived with rather than a problem to be resolved."[11]

Before examining Glazer's dilemma, let us first note in passing that he makes a number of very questionable assumptions about the advantages of esoteric (secret) knowledge as well as the stability and consensus of aims and educational programs of the legal and medical profession, assumptions which will not be dealt with here. As for Glazer's dilemma, it appears less unsolvable when note is taken of his nonhistorical perspectives[12] and of facts which do not fit his thesis. Take, for example, the aim of tying "academic" teaching more closely to professional practice. In law, medicine, and other fields, and in academic disciplines as well, students end up learning more about general concepts, theory, and methodology than about the details of the jobs in the world outside. But this is as it should be, since the jobs will change substantially over the lifetime of the practitioner. There were, and still are, differences of opinion in city planning on the right balance between "how to do it" courses[13] and the other courses drawn largely from the social-science disciplines. On this issue, there are substantial differences in views in most professional fields; city planning is no exception. What Glazer ignores, however, are the pressures of the outside world (not to mention the erratic and passing influence of fads, foundations, and the media); as well as the additional responsibilities in policy making, analysis, negotiation, communication, program management, and research which are incessantly influencing and sometimes transforming the roles of the city planner and the perceptions of practitioners, disciplinary specialists, and professionals in planning schools about what the city planner needs to know. Glazer says that

Science and higher education have become indispensable to the *dignity* of these new occupations [because the practitioners want] to elevate their status to equal that of the learned professions.

This replacement of experienced members of the profession for which students are training by members of academic disciplines undoubtedly brings into the school and into the training of students more sophisticated knowledge. It is rather more questionable whether this is the most useful knowledge for the intended occupation. It is certainly unquestionable, however, that it will add to the prestige of the profession if scholars from established disciplines can be induced to join the staff and participate in the training.[14]

Plausible as it may seem, this view is misleading in several respects. First, by putting the stress only on the quest for scientific status and dignity, it overlooks (a) the pressures on city planners to do their jobs *better;* (b) the perception of leading city-planning professionals (arrived at much earlier than the leading social scientists and architects) that grappling with the problems of cities and regions required a far more solid foundation in applied social science (as well as radical changes in the approach to urban design); and (c) the fact that city planners—despite more than a generation of neglect by social scientists, whose central interests were focused on other questions—not only managed to attract some social scientists to join their ranks but tried to get the social-science departments to devote more of their attention and resources to urban questions.[15]

Second, there is little evidence that the design-based faculty found itself redundant, or that the disciplinary specialists initially brought into the city-planning departments either outranked the city planners or were regarded by themselves or by the city planners as superior in status. The situation is the same today (at least for the MIT Department of Urban Studies and Planning, which probably has a higher ratio of social scientists on its staff than any other program in the country). Indeed, a contrary view is more plausible, for many of the applied social scientists were employed by the professionals. Very often the question was, and to some extent still is: Given the fuzzy state of the social sciences, how much could they contribute to the analysis of the professionals (who compared themselves to architects, doctors, or lawyers and not to "mere" applied social scientists)?[16]

Third, the critical conflicts that subsequently developed between the social scientists and the professionals were somewhat different from those formulated by Glazer. The big issues were not so much whether the social scientists were responding to the criteria and values of their disciplinary peers and failing to teach the planner what he needed to know in practice (although peer approval and relevance are problems whenever disciplinary specialists teach professionals). The conflicts involved more challenging matters because the applied social scientists did what it was altogether appropriate for them to do: that is, they questioned and often discredited some basic ideas of city planners. They documented, for example, the often erroneous assumptions concerning the needs of the groups the city planners believed they served; the wrong judgments concerning the nature and significance of the effects produced by the manipulation of the environment by the city planners; the questionable premises concerning the feasibility and the desirability of comprehensive planning; the appropriateness of the profession being dominated by specialists in physical planning; and the class interests of the groups which the planner actually served. These challenges, reinforced also by some physical planners, produced strains within the profession and forced a deep and painful reappraisal of theory and practice in city planning.[17]

As for the sweeping changes in the curriculum every decade, once again Glazer's view is misleading. The ruling theme or paradigm of comprehensive land-use planning has dominated the field for almost four decades.[18] And the main problem which practitioners face is not so much the radical swing from one extreme to another, but the confusion and uncertainty resulting from the erosion of faith in the traditional thematic position and the search for a new one which will encompass both old and new. No doubt such changes are messy and discouraging, but city planning is hardly unique in this regard. There is a world of difference, however, between the pessimism created by a vicious circle (Glazer's dilemma) from which there is little prospect of escaping, and the excitement and challenge of problems associated with growth and transformation.

IDENTITY ISSUES

There is another way of interpreting the current conflicts and moods in city planning. This alternative is to recall the kinds of highs and lows, of exaltation and depression associated with identity issues in adolescent human development, and to relate those experiences to one of the most difficult tasks of a practitioner in a relatively new field of study: understanding what his field is, has been, and might yet be, and how his role might change in the future.[19]

Although no literal comparison is intended between the behavior of an individual and the behavior of a field, some of the clinical findings relating to the periods of childhood and adolescence do provide an intriguing metaphor. For example, according to Erik Erikson,[20] three major early periods in human development are, first, emergence from the womb to begin life as a separate personality; second, the semiautonomous phase of early childhood—with great dreams of glory and achievement; and third, the shift to the socially and goal-directed adolescent phase. During this period there is a complex sequence which involves discovery of new and deeper realities and of more formidable constraints, interests, and demands which challenge and may frustrate the adolescent's dreams.

Although the sequences for city planning can be no more than suggestive, it is possible to show a rough correspondence with Erikson's epigenesis of ego development. For example, pursuing the metaphor (again with no literal comparison intended), it can be said that city planning first developed its independent "personality" when the various progeny emerged from the wombs of public health, civil engineering, architecture, land-scape architecture, and surveying; and in the semiautonomous phase that followed, city planners certainly prided themselves on their great dreams and potential for grandiose achievements. The subsequent shift of emphasis from master plans to the planning process then introduced the "socially and goal-directed phase"—adolescence. During this period, the profession's societal encounters disclosed a far more complicated reality than it had at first imagined. Time-honored ideas appeared superficial and inadequate. Cherished concepts like the neighborhood and the region turned out to oversimplify the mélange of micro and macro areas relevant for planning and development. Faith in the capacity of planners to organize the physical environment was shaken by the discovery of complex economic, social, and political terrains they knew little about. Employment of city planners by local governments and the well-to-do client evidenced ties with the established interests. There were great pressures to be more rigorous in thinking, more knowledgeable about research, more concerned with the underprivileged, more sophisticated about the realities of group bargaining, power politics, and participatory democracy. It would be surprising if the convergence of such challenges and criticisms did not generate anxieties.

In the case of human development, Erikson characterizes such a situation as "a crisis of wholeness" because of the need to achieve at this time "a sense of inner identity."[21]

The young person, in order to experience wholeness must feel a progressive continuity between that which he has come to be during the long years of childhood and that which he promises to become in the anticipated future; between that which he conceives himself to be and that which he perceives others to see in him and to expect of him. Individually speaking, identity includes, but is more than, the earlier years when the child wanted to be, and often was forced to become, like the people he depended on. . . . The search for a new and yet reliable identity can perhaps best be seen in the persistent adolescent endeavour to define, overdefine and redefine themselves and each other.[22]

The young city-planning field experienced comparable identity problems. Its initial dream of comprehensive land-use planning turned out to be inadequate. It then sought to transform itself in line with its new perceptions, and the perceptions and expectations of others. It tried to establish continuity between its old identity and its new needs and even to become like the people on which it depended. And so it was that funds were requested and became available for education and research programs which emphasized modeling, quantitative methods, the urban and regional applications of the social sciences, and the human and managerial as well as the ecological concerns of city planning. Foundations, particularly the Ford Foundation, and university administrations monitored and tried to reinforce these trends in the universities.

The new horizons led to at least three identity problems. The first involved new skills and roles. City planners learned modeling and the uses of the computer and applied the techniques with gusto to problems of transportation, land use, housing, urban systems, and the management of these systems. Soon their bulky plans, spruced up in the past with photographs, sketches, designs, and land-use maps, became even bulkier "scientific" studies replete with statistical and mathematical appendices and technocratic jargon. Other planners, however, rejected the emphasis on "scientism," efficiency, and rationality. Some mastered the art of bureaucratic gamesmanship and of political manipulation. Still others served as frank partisans of the poor and the minorities or outright rebels dedicated to the transformation of the capitalist system and its urban subsystem—calling attention to the historic contingency of the latter, that is, the special forms urbanism assumed during this stage of capitalist development. Before long it had become respectable to say that the planner could serve not only as a designer and a coordinator, but as an advocate, a negotiator, or a coalition builder. It was equally respectable to characterize him as knowledgeable not only about the problems of urban land use and environmental policy but also as someone with generic skills in policy design and analysis, in the processes of communication and negotiation, and in implementation and public management. He could also be a change agent and a social reformer (liberal and radical), not just a corrector of market imperfections. Increasingly, these multiple skills and roles were looked upon as significant dimensions and ways of functioning within the field, either as a versatile generalist or as a specialist.[23]

A second problem involved the dualism implicit in the term "city planning." Were city planners essentially planners or urbanists? Since both of these alternatives shifted the physical and design aspects of planning to the background, it was an easy next step to ask why one should hold fast to an urban (or regional) label if that is not the important modifier.[24] Why not be as free as possible to deal with all planning problems? This point of view was pressed especially by policy and planning specialists and by modelers, none of whom considered the physical environment, the city, or region as the critical variables in their own work. For them the terms "urban" and "regional" had become a "null or a negative identity," whereas to many of the practitioners these views only illustrated how serious role confusion had become. To still others the issue appeared ephemeral because some focus is essential as long as resources are limited. One response—to emphasize policy analysis—reflects a current wave of thought. But this emphasis offers no escape from identity problems. For if the profession is centrally concerned with the problems of cities and regions, why not say so; and if not, what is the emphasis to be? It is worth recalling that because the "Chicago School of Planning" (under the leadership of Rexford Guy Tugwell in the late 1940s and early 1950s) focused only on planning theory and lacked an area of substantive specialization and comparative advantage, this general approach failed to take root anywhere, and so most of the able members of this "school" sought and eventually found a haven in city planning and urban studies.

The third identity issue concerned the integration of the professional and the disciplinary elements. The early city planners emphasized the shaping of the built environment. This emphasis resulted in neglect of the societal aspects of cities and regions, in limited research, and in too great a reliance on multidisciplinary, collaborative efforts. But over time city planners discovered that the social scientists had a limited interest in urban and regional problems and that the architects, landscape architects, and engineers had very limited interest in macro-design (as well as urban and regional) problems. This situation was not only unlikely to change; but as leading specialists in the field, city planners were being accused by the "attentive"[25] as well as the general public of being too narrow. The recognition of the inadequacy of their traditional role as land-use planners and of the inadequacy of the assistance likely to come from the social sciences may well force—indeed, *is* forcing key planning schools to grasp the nettle, and to accept responsibility for building the applied social-science and macro-design foundations of the field.[26]

THEMATIC OR PARADIGM CHANGE

To compare city planning with phases of human development is at best suggestive; but the comparisons are not likely to be persuasive to persons skeptical of analogies in general and wary, in particular, of the oversimplifications and of the determinism implicit in the concept of stages. However, the same questions can be examined from another perspective—that of *thematic* or *paradigm change*. There are several studies of how the inadequacies of a ruling theme or paradigm[27] have generated challenge and crisis, and how the absence of a clear successor often exacerbates alternating attitudes of confrontation, confusion, frustration, and even despair.[28] We know too that an inadequate—and sometimes even a wrong—hypothesis is often better for research and policy than no hypothesis at all. The same holds true for thematic positions or paradigms; and this is why Gerald Holton has wryly observed that the attitude of past scientists has often been: "Let us not be misled by the evidence."[29]

But if problems persist, the normal approaches and values may become even more blurred and controversial and the problems will be cited again and again as the key issue.[30] Their resolution may take a variety of forms. For example, Kuhn suggests three of the more obvious possibilities: to adapt the old paradigm; to set the problems aside as currently unsolvable; or to achieve a combined conceptual and "gestalt" switch which will make it possible to attack all of the problems afresh within a different framework.[31]

Although city planning is not a science and the ruling ideas command less consensus than in the sciences, the process of adaptation to change has taken a similar course. Until the end of the 1950s, the basic paradigm of the profession was that the most important job of city planning was the comprehensive organization of the physical environment in the form of a master or general urban-land-use plan.[32] Urban designers, landscape architects, civil engineers, and land developers were regarded as specialists, whereas city planners were expected to have a much broader concern for the urban physical environment. To produce this expertise, half to two-thirds of the training of city planners at leading programs was spent in courses and workshops on land-use-planning principles and practice.[33] To the extent that resources were available, additional instruction was offered in survey and research techniques, statistics, and applied social science (land economics, housing, urban sociology, and urban government and politics). These courses along with some field work were expected to give the students the necessary knowledge to enter the field; the rest was learned through practice. It was taken for granted that some planners would become specialists in particular fields such as urban design, housing, or transportation; and still others—with degrees in law, engineering, architecture, economics, political science, sociology, or one of the other applied social sciences—might also focus on special aspects of city planning and administration. Since the scope of city planning was broad, the generalist, like the general practitioner in medicine, was expected to rely on others to deal with more specialized matters. Not all city planners were happy with the way their roles were defined. But in general these were the ruling beliefs and approaches in city planning in this country and abroad.

Over time, an increasing number of difficulties emerged which began to play havoc with these views. For one thing, the technical studies, especially the economic and social analyses for the land-use plan, were often superficial. Furthermore, master plans were inflexible or too flexible, a fault that was not corrected by comparing them to "impermanent constitutions."[34] There were discrepancies between the aims and expectations of the comprehensive plans and the results of crucial decision-making processes which were generally political. Conflicts broke out between the city planners and other specialists: for example, between the planners and the housers concerning the city planners' emphasis on economic development and physical renewal, and their frequent neglect of human requirements, not to mention their sheer lack of understanding and often callous treatment of the poor and the disadvantaged. Empirical studies of planning activities by social scientists made it clear that the doctrine of comprehensive planning was difficult to justify on the basis of descriptive or normative criteria. These studies showed most planning to be ad hoc rather than comprehensive, and that most decisions involved the short run rather than the long run, multiple rather than single goals, and "satisficing" rather than optimizing. Planning behavior seemed to be interpreted better by organization and game theory than by rational-decision models. In brief, the basic premises of comprehensive land-use planning simply did not take adequate account of the pluralistic features of society, and in particular of the bargaining and pressure groups and politics involved in influencing or making important public decisions.[35]

There were at least two responses from city planners. The first was to push for a broader and more direct involvement on the part of the social sciences in urban and regional studies. (This was one reason, as indicated earlier in this volume, for the organization in 1959 of the Joint Center for Urban Studies of MIT and Harvard University outside of the city-planning departments in both universities.) But even in the mid-sixties, when the interest in urban affairs reached its crest, urban and regional questions appeared to have only a minor bearing on the central problems of the different social sciences as well as law and civil engineering.[36] At best, social-science departments might arrange for faculty appointments, and perhaps even disciplinary specializations, in urban economics, urban sociology, and urban politics. And from time to time, one could expect cities and regions to serve as the occasional laboratory for illustrating or testing general problems of interest to these social scientists. This situation was much better than the egregious neglect of these questions in the past; but it was most unlikely that the problems of the city and region would receive sustained careful attention except from programs which had a *central, long-term* concern with these matters.[37]

These experiences led to a second response. It involved a more realistic view as to what the city planners could expect from the social-science disciplines and a raising of sights as to what they had to do themselves. More specifically, the aims at MIT, Harvard, Berkeley, and elsewhere were to develop research, modeling, and applied-social-science capabilities; to improve their abilities to handle the problems of policy making and implementation; and to expand the scope of city planning so that it might address problems not only *of* cities (e.g., urban land use, urban renewal, urban design, and urban-growth strategies—at the urban as well as micro and neighborhood scale), but related problems *within* cities (e.g., race, poverty, crime, welfare, health, and education).[38] The expansion in these directions, and especially the willingness to confront the major problems within cities, was a response to the times, perhaps inescapable, and in any case temporary; for the expansion was bound to raise questions of focus and of resource allocation, as it was not possible to achieve competence and depth in all of these directions.

The current drive for a focus constitutes the third response. What the focus will be and how it might change over time is not yet agreed on; nor is this puzzlement characteristic only of the minor professions. Indeed, Alfred North Whitehead once suggested that

The last thing we learn in a science is what it is all about. Men go on groping, sometimes for centuries, guided by a dim instinct and a puzzled curiosity until at last some great truth is unloosened.[39]

The odds are that city planners will not lose sight of their profession's comparative advantage. This is because the fate of a profession hinges on whether it has knowledge and skills and therefore services which people need, want, and will pay for, and which no other profession can (or wishes to) develop. In the past, the unique skills and services of city planners involved making land-use plans and organizing land-use-planning processes. In the future, city planners' unique skills will most likely involve a richer approach to land-use planning and design, including some combination of social-science and traditional professional skills for dealing with the spatial and environmental problems of society—for it is in these domains that the profession now has and can probably extend its comparative advantage. But increasingly city planners will have to function independently—leaning somewhat less not only on architecture but on the social sciences. In the process, they must correct two main weaknesses. One is their limited understanding of the people and of the physical as well as the economic, social, and political systems which they presume to serve; the other is their limited training in doing the essential basic and applied research. Future advances of the city-planning profession will depend on the success of the efforts to build on these strengths and to correct these weaknesses.

CONCLUDING OBSERVATIONS

The issues that confront the city-planning field are difficult, but they are identity and thematic problems, not status conflicts. They reflect the adolescence of the field, the extraordinary learning experiences and the pangs of transformation, not the tensions of unsolvable problems.

The identity problems are apt to change. There are, after all, diverse roles—radical, reformist, and managerial as well as professional—in all significant activities; and the quality of the performance of planners in these other roles, like that of doctors and lawyers, may have less to do with their formal training than some of their other abilities. It is quite likely, too, that whether one is an urbanist or a planner will depend less on one's inclinations than on the development of one's substantive skills as well as the demand for them. As for the question of profession as opposed to discipline, it is really less significant than it appears to be, for no activity will be greatly valued without great skill in practice and great intellectual capital.

The upshot of the change in thematic position or paradigm is likely to be increased efforts to integrate disciplinary and professional skills. Other perceptive leaders in the field share these expectations. Thus, William Alonso has astutely observed that in the future the demand will not be for multi-disciplinary approaches, but increasingly for

professionals who are first and foremost scholars in the urban and regional problems and secondarily members of traditional disciplines, [who] will bring to any particular situation a better sense of which problems can be tackled profitably and which cannot, and [who] will be versed in the relevant academic and non-academic literature, the problems of government and the social realities and [will] have developed a sense of the possible and of the manner in which risks are taken.[40]

From this perspective, puncturing the illusions of comprehensive land-use planning was wholesome, albeit painful; and for this achievement, the profession owes the social scientists a great debt. No doubt, many planners are still uncertain what their main job is, if it is not to make comprehensive land-use plans. But the fact is that a whole generation of young city planners are in the process of developing skills—diagnostic, analytical, design, policy making, research, implementation, and radical or liberal reformist—along the lines sketched out above.

The views expressed here exude restrained optimism on the grounds that a profession, like an individual, is in an essentially healthy condition when it increases its ability to deal with felt needs; when it achieves more realistic integration of its aims, subject matter, and tools; and when it perceives itself and the world more accurately. If the evidence and the interpretations developed here are correct, this is what is happening in city planning.

Acknowledgments

Of the chapters in this book, ten were commissioned articles and five were written independently.

Part of Chapter 1 was prepared in response to a request from the Cambridge Forum in March, 1976, to contemplate the future metropolis and whether it could be made more humane. It was subsequently published in *Harvard Magazine* (78 [1976], 59–61).

An early version of Chapter 2, "Great and Terrible Cities," was initially delivered as a Lowell Lecture in Boston in April, 1978. It is scheduled for publication in a United Nations Festschrift honoring Masahiko Honjo, the Director of the United Nations Center for Regional Development, Nagoya, Japan.

Chapter 3 grew out of an idea I hit upon while exploring the national parks and forests by car with my family. Written with Michael Southworth, it was published originally under the title "Needed: A National Urban Service," first in *Educational Technology Magazine* (10 [1970], 54–57), then in D. I. Roberts II, *Planning Urban Education: New Ideas and Techniques to Transform Learning in the City* (Englewood Cliffs, N.J.: Educational Technology Publications, 1972), pp. 328–337.

Chapter 4, a slightly revised version of an article written more than 20 years ago with Kevin Lynch, was published under the title "The Theory of Urban Form" in the *Journal of the American Institute of Planners* (24 [1958]). Unlike the other jointly prepared chapters, Lynch was the main author of this article, which incorporates ideas worked out when we taught a course on the theory of urban form.

Chapter 5, which sums up the results of some research and of a special seminar which I conducted in the spring of 1978 together with Professor Robert Hollister, deals with images of the city as they have evolved and are now viewed in the social sciences. This chapter is a revised version of the article published in the Charles Abrams Festschrift in *Habitat International* (5 [1980], 141–152.

Chapter 6 was commissioned by the National Institute for Research Advancement of Japan. I was invited to prepare a paper on some of the inner and regional area-development problems of the mature metropolis for the International Forum on The Metropolis of the World of Tomorrow which was sponsored by the Institute in February, 1979.

The two papers which eventually became Chapters 7 and 8 were written because I was asked on two not altogether fortuitous occasions to evaluate the New Communities Program in the United States. The first request, from the American Institute of Architects, was to consider the prospects for the success of the program, which had been enacted by the United States Congress in 1970 and was about to get underway. The result was an article, now Chapter 7, which was written together with Lawrence Susskind. Originally entitled "New Communities and Urban Growth Strategies," it was printed in the *Congressional Record* (July 21, 1972, pp. S-11461–S-11464) at the request of Senator Hubert Humphrey. Subsequently, it was published under the title "The Next Generation of New Towns" in The American Institute of Architects, *New Towns in America*, ed. J. Bailey (New York: Wiley, 1973).

The second request came eight years later from the International Federation of Housing and Planning (IFHP). The Federation was sponsoring a book that would evaluate new-towns policies in different parts of the world. I was asked to contribute a chapter explaining why the New Communities Program had failed. This request led to a paper (Chapter 8), prepared together with Hugh Evans, subsequently published by *The Public Interest* (56 [1979], 90–107). A slightly different version was also published by IFHP under the title "The Lessons of Failure—an Evaluation of the U.S. New Communities" in Working Party—New Towns, *New Towns in National Development* (Milton Keynes, United

Kingdom, IFHP Working Party with the assistance of the Open University of Milton Keynes, 1980).

Chapter 9 was a response to a request from Professor Walter Isard to prepare a review paper for the 25th Anniversary Meeting of the Regional Science Association. This paper, which was subsequently published in the *International Regional Science Review* (3 [1978], 113–132), dealt with regional planning in developing countries over the past quarter of a century.

As for Chapter 10, it was a response to an invitation to give the lead paper for a United Nations Consultative Meeting of Experts on Training for Regional Development, Nagoya, Japan, January 29 to February 4, 1980. The papers for this meeting, including an unabridged version of Chapter 10, are in process of being published by the United Nations Center for Regional Development, Nagoya, Japan.

Chapters 11 and 14 record my views on the different approaches to urban and regional studies and the profession of city planning. My main ideas on the subject were first drafted during a sabbatical year in England in 1974. An early version of Chapter 11 was delivered as the Norma Wilkinson Memorial Lecture at the University of Reading (England) in 1975.

A request from UNESCO to serve as an advisor to an international colloquium in Algeria in January, 1980, on the education of planners led me to write the paper which is now Chapter 12.

Subsequently, an invitation from the Center for Human Settlements of the University of British Columbia, Canada to give some lectures during March, 1980, on the profession of city planning led me to cast Chapters 11, 12, and 14 in their present form.

Early in 1980 the United Nations Center for Regional Development invited me to prepare a paper for a Seminar on Urbanization and National Development that took place in October, 1980. This invitation led to my reflections "On the Illusions of Planners" (Chapter 13), which, together with the other papers of the seminar, will be published by the United Nations Center for Research and Development.

I am indebted to my colleagues and students—especially

those from Third World countries—for their stimulation of many of the ideas in this volume. I wish to record my thanks to the journals and colleagues mentioned above for permission to print or reprint these papers. I am grateful to Farokh Afshar and Hugh Evans for help in obtaining and organizing the photographs, and to Gerry Levinson and Uma Roy-Chowdhury for their patient assistance in the typing and retyping of this manuscript. As in the past, however, I owe most in the way of ideas and assistance to Nadine Rodwin.

CREDITS

1—*top*, Editorial Photocolor Archives, Inc.; *bottom*, Kevin Lynch. 2—*top*, M.I.T. Rotch Visual Collections; *bottom*, Myron Wood, Photo Researchers, Inc. 3—*top*, E. Popko, from "Transitions"; *bottom*, United Nations. 4—*top*, Foto Schikola, Vienna, Austria; *bottom*, Marietta Millet. 5—*top*, Environmental Communications; *bottom*, French Embassy Press & Information Division. 6—*top*, Myron Wood, Photo Researchers, Inc.; *bottom*, Stanford Anderson, 7—*top*, Thomas Hollywan, Photo Researchers, Inc.; *bottom*, Alan Doksansky. 8—*top*, Environmental Communications; *bottom*, M.I.T. Rotch Library Visual Collections.

Notes

CHAPTER ONE

[1]L. Rodwin, ed. *The Future Metropolis* (New York: Braziller, 1961), p. 12.
[2]Ibid, p. 13.
[3]Ibid, p. 16.

CHAPTER TWO

[1]See, for example, R. Venturi, *Learning from Las Vegas: Forgotten Symbolism of Architectural Form* (Cambridge: MIT Press, 1977).
[2]O. W. Holmes, *Collected Legal Papers* (New York: Harcourt, Brace, 1920) pp. 267–268.
[3]We have yet to see this occur in the cases of Budapest, Prague, Peking, Shanghai, Havana, or even the great Russian cities; but in the case of the latter, it has been argued that the burgeoning of cities in Siberia and other regions in the Soviet Union illustrates the release of energy that occurs in underdeveloped regions when growth is motivated by the desire for internal transformation.

CHAPTER THREE

[1]S. Carr and K. Lynch, "Where Learning Happens," *Daedalus* 97 (1968): 1277–1291.
[2]The Park Service has also monitored an innovative urban ranger service for the parks of New York City. Initiated in 1979, it was financed by a small sum of $50,000 raised by private corporations. Under the program, 20 rangers were assigned to one park in each borough. They worked in pairs and patrolled on foot, reporting to a supervisor over a two-way radio. The 10 supervisors worked on an annual basis, but the rangers were hired for the season only. As preparation, the rangers were given training in first aid and self-defense. They learn the history of each park and undergo about 30 hours in "mediation of conflict." (*New York Times*, 19 August 1979.)

CHAPTER FIVE

[1]K. Lynch, *The Image of the City* (Cambridge: The Technology Press and Harvard University Press, 1960). For a comprehensive review of research on urban images in this tradition, see A. Rapoport, *Human Aspects of Urban Form* (New York: Pergamon Press, 1977).

[2]Clifford Geertz, "Ideology as a Cultural System," in *Ideology and Discontent*, ed. D. E. Apter (New York: Free Press, 1964), p. 57.

[3]The forerunner of this concept appears to have been A. Malraux's notion of a "museum without walls." A. Malraux, *The Voices of Silence* (New York: Doubleday, 1954). The idea was later extended to the city by many persons. For one interesting example, see S. Carr and K. Lynch, "Where Learning Happens," *Daedalus* 97 (1968): 1277–1291.

[4]K. Deutsch, "On Social Communication and the Metropolis," in *The Future Metropolis*, ed. L. Rodwin (New York: Braziller, 1961).

[5]G. Sternlieb, "The City as Sandbox," *Public Interest* 25 (1971), 14–21.

[6]N. Long, "The City as Reservation," *Public Interest* 25 (1971), 22–28.

[7]B. F. Hoselitz, "Generative and Parasitic Cities," *Economic Development and Cultural Change* (1955), 278–294.

[8]A. G. Frank, *Latin American Development: Underdevelopment or Revolution* (New York: Monthly Review Press, 1969); M. Castells, *The Urban Question* (Cambridge: MIT Press, 1977), pp. 437–471; M. Harloe, *Captive Cities: Studies in the Political Economy of Cities and Regions* (New York: Wiley, 1977), pp. 1–47; T. G. McGee, *The Urbanization Process in the Third World* (London: G. Bell, 1971), Chapters 1–3.

[9]J. Jacobs, *The Death and Life of Great American Cities* (New York: Random House, 1961); W. Baer, "On the Death of Cities," *Public Interest* 45 (1967), 3–19.

[10]See R. Alcaly and D. Mermelstein, eds., *The Fiscal Crisis of American Cities* (New York: Vintage, 1977).

[11]Ibid.

[12]See M. Webber, "The Post City Age," *Daedalus* 97 (1968), 1091–1110; C. L. Leven, ed. *The Mature Metropolis* (Lexington, Mass.: D. C. Heath, 1978).

[13]T. Allman, "The Urban Crisis Leaves Town and Moves to the Suburbs," *Harper's* 257 (1978), 41–56.

[14]Office of Community Planning and Development, U.S. Department of Housing and Urban Development, "Whither or Whether Urban Distress: A Response to the Article 'The Urban Crisis Leaves Town'," Working paper, 1979.

[15]We are indebted to the following guest lecturers in the seminar: Nathan Glazer, Leo Marx, Richard Sennett, Gary Hack, Robert Shefter, Paolo Ceccerelli, and Sam Bass Warner.

16Therefore, except for occasional allusions, we do not go into detail on these matters. This is not to say that we consider these fields, especially the arts, history, and the humanities, less important. If anything, they are perhaps more fruitful, but more complicated or difficult to incorporate in our analysis at this time.

17G. K. Zipf, *Human Behavior and the Principle of Least Effort* (Reading, Mass.: Addison-Wesley, 1949); J. Q. Stewart, "Demographic Gravitation: Evidence and Applications," *Sociometry* ll (1948); J. Q. Stewart, "Empirical Mathematical Rules Concerning the Distribution and Equilibrium of Population," *Geographical Review* 37 (1947); B. J. L. Berry, "Recent Developments of Central Place Theory," *Papers and Proceedings of the Regional Science Association*, vol. 4, 1958, pp. 107-20.

18H. S. Perloff *et al.*, *Regions, Resources and Economic Growth* (Baltimore: Resources for the Future, 1961); Part II. W. R. Thompson, A *Preface to Urban Economics* (Baltimore: Johns Hopkins University Press, 1965), Chapter 1.

19E. W. Burgess, "The Growth of the City," in *The City*, ed. R. E. Park and E. W. Burgess (Chicago: University of Chicago Press, 1925).

20L. Wirth, "Urbanism as a Way of Life," *Classic Essays on the Culture of Cities*, ed. R. Sennett (New York: Appleton-Century-Crofts, 1969), pp. 143-164; T. Parsons, *The Social System* (New York: The Free Press of Glencoe, 1951); N. Glazer and D. P. Moynihan, *Beyond the Melting Pot* (Cambridge: MIT Press, 1963); H. Gans, "Urbanism and Suburbanism as Ways of Life: A Re-evaluation of Definitions," in *Human Behavior and Social Processes*, ed. A. Rose (Boston: Houghton Mifflin, 1962), pp. 625-648.

21R. Shefter, presentation at MIT Seminar on Images of Cities, May 1979.

22K. Lynch, ed., *Growing Up in Cities* (Cambridge: MIT Press, 1977); D. Appleyard, *Planning a Pluralist City* (Cambridge: MIT Press, 1976).

23K. Lynch, personal communication, November 1979. See R. Venturi *et al.*, *Learning From Las Vegas* (Cambridge: MIT Press, 1977).

24G. Hack, MIT seminar presentation, April 1979.

25H. Gans, *The Urban Villagers* (New York: The Free Press of Glencoe, 1962); M. Meyerson and E. Banfield, *Politics, Planning and the Public Interest* (New York: The Free Press of Glencoe, 1955); R. Vernon, *The Myth and Reality of Urban Problems* (Cambridge: Harvard University Press, 1966).

26R. Meier, *Planning for an Urban World* (Cambridge: MIT Press, 1974), pp. 23, 487-488; see also I. Sachs, "Environment and Styles of Development," paper delivered at United Nations Symposium on

Population, Resources and Environment, Stockholm, September 1973 (mimeo).

[27] See McGee, *Urbanization Process*, pp. 64–94; B. J. L. Berry, *The Human Consequences of Urbanisation* (London: Macmillan, 1973), pp. 74–114; A. G. Frank, *Latin America: Underdevelopment or Revolution* (New York: Monthly Review Press, 1970), pp. 3–17.

[28] N. V. Sovani, "The Analysis of 'Over-Urbanization'," in *Regional Policy: Readings in Theory and Applications*, ed. J. Friedmann and W. Alonso (Cambridge: MIT Press, 1975), pp. 421–433. For a provocative view of a contrasting image—that of "underurbanization" and of exploitation of adjacent urban villages in countries in southeastern Europe, see I. Szelenyi, "Urban Sociology and Community Studies in Eastern Europe: Reflections and Comparisons with American Approaches," *Comparative Urban Research* 14 (1977), 14–17.

[29] For another, more sympathetic view, see L. Sawyers, "Cities and Countryside in the Soviet Union and China," in *Marxism and the Metropolis*, ed. W. K. Tabb and L. Sawyers (New York: Oxford University Press, 1978), pp. 338–364. See also I. Szelenyi, "Class Analysis and Beyond: Further Dilemmas for the New Urban Sociology," *Comparative Urban Research* 14 (1977), 86–94. There is also a Marxist image of the urban issues in the capitalist city in the more-developed countries. In substance, it generally interprets the policy differences on how to cope with housing, transportation, urban renewal, and public services as simply further evidence of internal quarrels among the ruling classes as to the most effective ways of minimizing costs, maximizing profits, and organizing the environment to serve the interests of the dominant groups.

[30] R. Oppenheimer, "The Growth of Science and the Structure of Culture," *Daedalus*, 1 (1958), 76.

[31] Ibid.

[32] National Resources Committee, *Our Cities* (Washington, D.C.: U.S. Government Printing Office, 1937), p. 53.

CHAPTER SIX

[1] H. W. Richardson, "Basic Economic Activities in the Metropolis," *The Mature Metropolis*, ed. C. L. Leven (Lexington, Mass. and Toronto: Lexington Books, D.C. Heath, 1978), p. 260. For more detail, see Chapter 13; also G. Sternlieb and J. W. Hughes, *Post-Industrial America: Metropolitan Decline and Interregional Job Shifts* (New Brunswick, N.J.: Center for Urban Policy Research, 1975), Section I.

[2] P. Hall, "Statement," in *Successes Abroad: What Foreign Cities Can*

Teach American Cities, Hearings Before the Subcommittee on the City of the Committee on Banking, Finance and Urban Affairs, House of Representatives, 95th Congress, First Session (Washington, D.C.: U.S. Government Printing Office, 1977), p. 4.

[3]Ibid., p. 11.

[4]Ibid., pp. 5–11.

[5]Richardson, "Basic Economic Activities," p. 260, Table 13-5; p. 268.

[6]K. Mera, "The Changing Pattern of Population Distribution in Japan and Its Implications for Developing Countries," in *Growth Pole Strategy and Regional Development Planning in Asia*, Proceedings of the Seminar on Industrialization Strategies and the Growth Pole Approach to Regional Planning and Development: The Asian Experience, Nagoya, Japan, November 1975 (Nagoya: United Nations Centre for Regional Development, 1976), pp. 247–277.

[7]D. R. Vining and T. Kontuly, *Population Dispersal from Major Metropolitan Regions: An International Comparison*, RSRI Discussion Paper Series, no. 100 (Philadelphia: Regional Science Research Institute, 1977), p. 8.

[8]Ibid., pp. 14–24.

[9]W. Alonso, "The Current Halt in the Metropolitan Phenomenon," in Leven, *Mature Metropolis*, p.26.

[10]Vining and Kontuly, *Population Dispersal*, p. 66. "In the first seven of these eleven countries, this reduction or reversal first became evident in the 1970's; in the last four, its onset was recorded in the 1960's. Six countries (Hungary, Finland, Spain, Poland, Taiwan and South Korea) have yet to show an attenuation in the movement of persons into their core regions. Some possibly unreliable British data likewise fail to reveal a slackening in the growth of the regions surrounding London."

[11]Ibid., p. 21.

[12]Alonso, *Current Halt*, pp. 27–28.

[13]Ibid.

[14]M. Tachi, cited in D. R. Vining and T. Kontuly, *Population Dispersal*, p. 78 (Footnote 2).

[15]For a summary volume interpreting the results of these studies, see R. Vernon, *Metropolis, 1985* (Cambridge: Harvard University Press, 1960), especially Chapter 9.

[16]Hall, "Statement," p. 7.

[17]H. S. Perloff, "The Central City in the Post-Industrial Age," in Leven, *Mature Metropolis*.

[18]Richardson, "Basic Economic Activities," p. 270.

[19]J. G. Williamson, "Regional Inequality and The Process of National Development," *Economic Development and Cultural Change 13* (1965); H. Oshima, "The International Comparison of Size Distribu-

tion of Family Incomes with Specific Reference to Asia," *Review of Economics and Statistics 44* (1962), 439–445. For some evidence questioning whether Williamson's hypotheses applied to less-developed countries, see A. G. Gilbert and O. E. Goodman, "Regional Income Disparities and Economic Development: A Critique," in *Development Planning and Spatial Structure*, ed. A. G. Gilbert (New York: Wiley, 1976). For some provocative views on "positional disadvantages," see F. Hirsch, *Social Limits to Growth* (Cambridge: Harvard University Press, 1926), Chapters 1 and 3.

[20]L. Rodwin, *Nations and Cities: A Comparison of Strategies for Urban Growth* (Boston: Houghton Mifflin, 1970), Chapters 5 and 6; Tokyo Metropolitan Government Municipal Library, *An Administrative Perspective of Tokyo* (Tokyo, 1978) Chapters 4–6; CSRT Project Team, *The Coming Society and the Role of Telecommunications* (Tokyo: Research Institute of Telecommunications and Economics, 1975), pp. 25–46; H. Zimmerman, "Statement," in *Success Abroad*, Hearings Before the Subcommittee on the City, pp. 17–23.

[21]Rodwin, *Nations and Cities*, Chapter 7; J. S. Coleman, "Social Processes and Social Policy in the Stable Metropolis," in Leven, *Mature Metropolis*, Chapter 3; R. Netzer, "Public Sector Investment Strategies in the Mature Metropolis," in Leven, *Mature Metropolis*, Chapter 12; T. Muller, "The Declining and Growing Metropolis—A Fiscal Comparison," in Sternlieb, *Post-Industrial America*, pp. 197–220.

[22]Advisory Commission on Intergovernmental Relations, *A Look to the North: Canadian Regional Experience; Substate Regionalism and the Federal System* (Washington, D.C.: U.S. Government Printing Office, 1974), p. 2.

[23]Ibid.

[24]A. K. Campbell, "Metropolitan Governance and the Mature Metropolis," in Leven, *Mature Metropolis*, pp. 203–204.

[25]A. Rose, "Two Decades of Metropolitan Government in Toronto: 1953–1973," in Advisory Commission, *A Look to the North*, Chapter 3.

[26]Ibid., pp. 41–47.

[27]S. Lipset, *Revolution and Counterrevolution: Change and Persistence in Social Structure* (New York: Basic Books, 1968), p. 32.

[28]Rodwin, *Nations and Cities*, Chapter 7.

[29]See, for example, M. Castells, *The Urban Question* (Cambridge: MIT Press, 1977), Chapter 4; T. N. Clark, "The Structure of Community Influence," in *People and Politics in Urban Society*, ed. H. Hahn (Beverly Hills, California: Sage Publications, 1972) Chapter 11.

[30]R. Vernon, *The Myth and Reality of Our Urban Problems* (Cambridge: Harvard University Press, 1962).

CHAPTER SEVEN

[1]This does not include typical suburban-tract developments, recreational or leisure communities, or large-scale urban-renewal projects.

[2]New York State Urban Development Corporation and the New York State Office of Planning Coordination, *New Communities for New York,* December 1970.

[3]In the most recent hearings before the Senate Subcommittee on Housing and Urban Affairs, United States population projections for the year 2000 included an estimated 75 million additional people. A somewhat lower projection has been offered by Anthony Downs, who believes that the population increase in the next 30 years will be only 55 million. ("Alternative Forms of Future Urban Growth in the United States," *Journal of the American Institute of Planners* 36 (1970), 3–11.)

[4]When we speak of the current program we are referring to Title VII of the Housing and Urban Development Act of 1970.

[5]A precedent for state override would be the "anti–snob zoning" bill passed several years ago in Massachusetts. Chapter 774 of the Act of 1969 (H5581) provides for the construction of low- and moderate-income housing in cities and towns in which local resistance hampers such construction. Should a local zoning board of appeals deny a permit to build subsidized low- or moderate-income housing when such housing does not exist in the community in a minimum quantity set by the General Court, then, after a hearing into the facts and a review of the local decision, the State Housing Appeals Committee can issue a permit. For a complete summary of the regulations, see Department of Community Affairs memo, Summary of Chapter 774, September 1969.

[6]The program originated with Title X of the National Housing Act of 1965, which offered loan guarantees for land acquisition and development of large, suburban-type developments. In 1966, Title X was amended to make the development of new communities eligible for these mortgages. As a further expansion of the original idea, the 1968 New Communities Act (Title IV) provided for federal guarantee of bonds sold by private developers to finance new-community development. Title VII of the Housing and Urban Development Act of 1970 is the most recent addition in this legislative history. Not only does it enlarge the New Communities Program to make public developers eligible for guarantees, but it also offers several new types of direct financial assistance in addition to the guarantees.

[7]A variety of experiments, possible innovations, and monitoring strategies are described in L. Susskind and G. Hack, "New Com-

munities and National Urban Growth Policies," *Technology Review* 74 (1972).

[8]L. Rodwin, *Nations and Cities: A Comparison of Strategies for Urban Growth* (Boston: Houghton Mifflin, 1970), especially Chapter 7.

CHAPTER EIGHT

[1]W. Nicoson, "The United States: The Battle for Title VII," in *New Perspectives on Community Development,* ed. M. Apgar (London: McGraw-Hill, 1976), p. 56.

[2]For some criticisms of the new-towns policies, see L. Rodwin, *The British New Towns Policy* (Cambridge: Harvard University Press, 1956); M. Kaplan and E. Eichler, *The Community Builders* (Berkeley: University of California Press, 1965); W. Alonso, "The Mirage of New Towns," *The Public Interest* 19 (1970).

[3]Supplementary grants for public facilities included: water, sewers, parks, and open space under Title IV (1968); and under Title VII (1970) highways, mass transit, airports, hospitals, libraries, neighborhood facilities, and public works in areas of high unemployment.

[4]Under the 1968 legislation only four projects were offered assistance: Jonathan, St. Charles, Park Forest South, and Flower Mound. Developers of the latter two later opted for assistance under Title VII. A project at San Antonio, Texas was also offered assistance under Title VII, but because of a lawsuit has never advanced further.

[5]Government-initiated reviews and evaluations of the New Communities Program include: U.S. Congress, House Committee on Banking and Currency, Subcommittee on Housing, *Oversight Hearings on HUD New Communities Program,* May 30, 31, 1973; Comptroller General of the U.S., *Getting the New Communities Program Started: Progress and Problems,* U.S. General Accounting Office, November 1974 (B-170971); U.S. Congress, House Committee on Banking and Currency, Subcommittee on Housing and Community Development, *Oversight Hearings on the New Communites Program,* September 23, 29, 30, 1975; U.S. Congress, House Committee on Appropriations, *Independent Agencies Appropriations Hearing,* Part V:HUD, 1976; U.S., HUD, New Communities Administration, *New Communities: Problems and Potentials,* December 1976 (report and four appendices). See also R. Burby and S. Weiss, *New Communities USA* (Lexington, Mass.: Lexington Books, 1976), particularly Chapter 7; M. Howland, *Approaches toward Implementation, Intervention and Impact Analysis in Energy Conservation Case Studies,* (University of California, Berkeley: Institute of Transportation Studies, 1977) Chapter 10; Nicoson, *Battle for Title VII.*

⁶There were, of course, other possibilities for less controversial forms of profit taking at the later stage of above-ground construction of housing, industrial buildings, and commercial areas—especially the latter, if the land could be sold high and repurchased low after improvements.

⁷The New Community Development Corporation (NCDC) was set up under Section 729 of Title VII to administer guarantees and loans authorized by the 1970 Act. Subsequently the NCDC has assumed responsibilities for the overall administration of the program, previously the function of the New Communities Administration, which is now abolished.

⁸U.S., HUD, New Communities Administration, *New Communities*, Appendix C, p. III-5.

⁹Ibid.

¹⁰Ibid., p. III-49. At the outset HUD aimed for a Title VII debt-to-equity ratio of 4:1. In practice it was more often 5, 6, 7 or more to 1, in which the developers' contributions took diverse forms. For example, at Maumelle, Arkansas, with a Title VII guarantee of $14 million, the developer's share comprised a letter of credit for $600,000 plus land valued at $1.4 million. At Cedar-Riverside, Minnesota, where Title VII-guaranteed debentures amounted to $24 million, the developer was expected to contribute $7.5 million of cash equity; initially only $100,000 was forthcoming, followed later by $1 million, specifically to pay off liabilities to an affiliate.

¹¹Ibid., p. III-4.

¹²Ibid., p. III-24-25. In one case it was assumed that a new community would capture at best 3% of its metropolitan residential market, a rate achieved in practice by few. In a second case the developers' own revenue projections were accepted, but, to simulate downturns in the business cycle, were reduced by 50% for two years in every period of five years.

¹³Ibid., p. III-4.

¹⁴This warning was issued just at the start of the New Communities Program in an article presented to the AIA Conference in 1971. The article was subsequently placed in the *Congressional Record* by Senator Humphrey. See L. Rodwin and L. Susskind, "New Communities and Urban Growth Strategies," *Congressional Record* (Senate), July 21, 1972, p. S11462.

¹⁵Ibid., p. S11463.

¹⁶However, in face of widespread defaults in the payment of debt-service charges, HUD was obliged to make good its guarantee to loan institutions through borrowings from the U.S. Treasury.

¹⁷In place of 75% planning grants authorized under Section 735 of Title VII, two-thirds planning grants were made under Section 701 of the Housing Act of 1954.

[18]To a certain extent the New Community Development Corporation has been able to make good the lack of funding for some of these programs after the passage of Title I of the Housing and Community Development Act of 1974, with $15–20 million of block grants for community development. Block grants, unlike categorical grants which are subject to tight restrictions, may be used for a wide variety of purposes to be determined at the discretion of recipient authorities.

[19]See, for example a report by the League of New Community Developers, *The Status of the New Communities Program* (Washington, D.C., 1974).

[20]Title VII, Urban Growth and New Community Development Act of 1970, Section 710(f).

[21]Ibid., Section 712(a)7.

[22]Ibid., Section 710(f).

[23]U.S., HUD, New Communities Administration, *New Communities*, Appendix D, p. 39.

[24]U.S., HUD, New Communities Administration, *Regulations*, Section 720.14 (c), 1971.

[25]U.S., HUD, New Communities Administration, *New Communities*, p. 84.

[26]Comptroller General, "Getting the New Communities Program Started: Progress and Problems" (Washington, D.C., 1974).

CHAPTER NINE

[1]I have been unable to identify a first-rate conservative critique of regional planning as such, but there are a great many general critiques of planning, with justifications for reliance on the market economy. For a few of these views, see M. Friedman, *Capitalism and Freedom* (Chicago: University of Chicago Press, 1962) and A. O. Hirschman, *The Passions and the Interests: Political Arguments for Capitalism before Its Triumph* (Princeton: Princeton University Press, 1977).

[2]For one of the most comprehensive reviews of the experience and literature, see W. Stöhr and F. Tödtling, "An Evaluation of Regional Policies: Experiences in Market and Mixed Economies" in *Human Settlement Systems: International Perspectives on Structure and Public Policy*, ed. Niles Hansen (Cambridge, Mass.: Ballinger, 1978), See also L. Coraggio, "Polarization, Development and Integration" in *Regional Development Planning: International Perspectives*, ed. A. Kuklinski (Leiden, The Netherlands: Sijthoff, 1975); J. Friedmann and C. Weaver, *Territory and Function: The Evolution of Regional Planning* (Berkeley: University of California Press, 1979); D. Barkin, "A Case Study of the Beneficiaries of Regional Development," *International Social De-*

velopment Review 4 (1972), 84–94; S. Holland, *Capital versus the Regions* (London: Macmillan, 1976).

[3]J. Weeks, "The Informal Sector and Marginal Groups," *Bulletin of the Institute of Development Studies* 5 (1973), 2–3; J. Weeks, "Policies for Expanding Employment in the Informal Sector of Developing Countries," *International Labor Review* 3 (1974), 1–14; R. Jolly *et al.*, eds., *Third World Employment* (London: Penguin Books, 1973).

[4]There is a growing literature on this subject. For a few examples, see A.G. Frank, *Latin America: Underdevelopment or Revolution* (New York: Monthly Review Press, 1970); O. Sunkel, "Big Business and 'Dependencia': A Latin American View," *Foreign Affairs* 50 (1972), 517–531; D. Slater, *Underdevelopment or Revolution* (New York: Monthly Review Press, 1975); S. Amin, *Unequal Development* (New York: Monthly Review Press, 1976).

[5]T. G. McGee, The *Urbanization Process in the Third World* (London: G. Bell, 1971).

[6]For the most recent systematic and comprehensive articulation of these views, see R. L. Meier, *Planning for an Urban World: The Design of Resource Conserving Cities* (Cambridge: MIT Press, 1974).

[7]G. Fromm, *Tax Incentives and Capital Spending* (Washington, D.C.: Brookings Institution, 1971), p. 243.

[8]*World Development Report* (Washington, D.C.: International Bank, 1978).

[9]J. G. Williamson, "Regional Inequality and the Process of National Development," *Economic Development and Cultural Change* 13 (1965), 44.

[10]S. Kuznets, "Economic Growth and Income Inequality," *American Economic Review* 45 (1955), 1–28.

[11]H. Oshima, "The International Comparison of Size Distribution of Family Incomes with Specific Reference to Asia," *Review of Economics and Statistics* 44 (1962), 439–445.

[12]A. G. Gilbert and O. E. Goodman, "Regional Income Disparities and Economic Development: A Critique," in *Development Planning and Spatial Structure*, ed. A. G. Gilbert (New York: Wiley, 1976).

[13]A. O. Hirschman, *The Strategy of Economic Development* (New Haven: Yale University Press, 1958).

[14]G. Myrdal, *Economic Theory and Underdeveloped Regions* (London: Gerald Duckworth, 1957).

[15]See Footnote 4, above.

[16]Gilbert and Goodman, "Income Disparities," pp. 114–119. See also T. Reiner, "Welfare Differences within a Nation," *Papers of the Regional Science Association* 32 (1974), 65–82; J. B. Parr, "A Comment on Reiner's Paper," *Papers of the Regional Science Association* 32 (1974), 83–91.

[17]Their income data suffer from the same limitations noted above in Williamson's study. In addition, the data are drawn mainly from Latin American countries and therefore do not necessarily represent the situation in other Third World countries.

[18]I. Adelman and C. T. Morris, *Economic Growth and Equity in Developing Countries* (Palo Alto, Calif.: Stanford University Press, 1973).

[19]Stöhr and Tödtling, "Regional Policies."

[20]Ibid., p. 109.

[21]Ibid., p. 110.

[22]H. Chenery *et al.*, *Redistribution with Growth* (Oxford: Oxford University Press, 1974). Ahluwalia, who handled the data analysis, observes, "In common with Kuznets our excuse for building an elaborate structure on such a shaky foundation is the view that speculation is an effective way of presenting a broad view of the field and as long as it is recognized as a collection of hunches calling for further investigation rather than a set of fully tested conclusions, little harm and much good may result" (p. xiii).

[23]Ibid., p. xiii.

[24]Ibid., p. ix.

[25]Ibid., pp. 253–290.

[26]Hirschman, *The Passions and the Interests.*

[27]For examples of this older approach, see H. W. Odum, *Southern Regions of the United States* (Chapel Hill, North Carolina: University of North Carolina Press, 1936); National Resources Board, *Regional Factors in National Planning* (Washington, D.C.: Government Printing Office, 1935).

CHAPTER TEN

[1]The expression "Third World countries" no longer has a clear meaning. Once it stood for the nonaligned, excolonial world of poor countries, and it has been used pejoratively to identify countries which drew their technology from the First World and their ideology from the Second. But because the countries differed so much from one another, there have been repeated efforts to refine the classification in a variety of ways: for example, size of country or population, resource endowment, type of basic economic activities, stages of industrialization, degree of poverty, socialist or market-oriented economies, administrative or cultural heritage, etc. The need for a common typology for our discussion is pressing. For the present, let me simply note that my observations here are intended to apply on the whole to the poor or middling-poor, nonaligned countries with mixed economies, with or without serious population problems and with or without significant resource endow-

ments; and if my observations apply to other countries as well, I shall make a specific reference to that fact.

[2]T. S. Eliot, "London Letter," *The Dial* 73 (1922), 331.

[3]There is a vast literature on this subject and any items listed are bound to be arbitrary. A few famous illustrative examples, however, are: L. Mumford, *The Culture of Cities* (New York: Harcourt, Brace, 1938); P. Abercrombie, *Greater London Plan* (London: HMSO, 1945); D. E. Lilienthal, *TVA: Democracy on the March* (New York: Harper, 1944); National Resources Board, *Regional Factors in National Policy* (Washington, D.C.: U.S. Government Printing Office, 1935). For other interpretations of these and subsequent experiences, see J. Friedmann and C. Weaver, *Territory and Function: The Evolution of Regional Planning* (London: E. Arnold, 1978); J. Friedmann, "Regional Development Planning: The Experience of a Decade," *Regional Policy: Readings in Theory and Applications* ed. J. Friedman and W. Alonso (Cambridge: MIT Press, 1975), Chapter 37; R. P. Misra, *Regional Planning: Concepts, Techniques, Policies, Case Studies* (Prasaronga: University of Mysore, 1969), Chapter 1.

[4]This is the current label for low status, casual labor, petty service employment, and small-family enterprises. (For more detail see the section, later in this chapter, on the informal sector.)

[5]Again there is a vast literature. For a few examples, see D. Seers, "The Meaning of Development," *International Development Review*, 11 (1969), 2-6; C. Furtado, *Development and Underdevelopment* (Berkeley: University of California Press, 1964); S. Boisier, *La Planificacion de Desarrollo Regional Latinoamericano* (Santiago, Chile: Instituto Latinoamericano de Planifacacion Economica y Social, 1979); International Labor Office, *Employment, Growth and Basic Needs* (Geneva: ILO, 1976), Part I; International Labor Office and UNDP, *Employment, Incomes and Equality: A Strategy for Increasing Productive Employment* (Geneva: ILO, 1972); H. Chenery *et al.*, *Redistribution with Growth* (Oxford: Oxford University Press, 1974); M. Lipton, *Why Poor People Stay Poor* (Cambridge: Harvard University Press, 1977); D. A. Kay and E. B. Skolnikoff, *World Eco-Crisis* (Madison: University of Wisconsin Press, 1972).

[6]See for example, B. Higgins and G. Abonyi, *Basic Needs and the Unified Approach: Making them Operational* (Nagoya, Japan: UNCRD, 1978).

[7]I make no distinction, for this discussion, between growth centers and development poles.

[8]B. Higgins, "Development Poles: Do They Exist?" in *Growth Pole Strategy and Regional Development Policy*, ed. F. C. Lo and K. Salih, (New York: Pergamon Press, 1978), pp. 229-242; F. C. Lo and K. Salih, "Growth Poles and Regional Policy in Open Dualistic Economies:

Western Theory and Asian Reality," in Lo and Salih, *Growth Pole Strategy*, Chapter 11, pp. 243–269.

[9]L. Rodwin, *Nations and Cities* (Boston: Houghton Mifflin, 1970), Chapter 1.

[10]H. W. Richardson, "Growth Centers, Rural Development and National Urban Policy," *International Regional Science Review* 3 (1978), 133–152.

[11]A. Strout, untitled manuscript on Indonesia, Chapter 10, pp. 61, 62, 67. I should add that these projections also assume a one-third increase in the number of cities of about 20,000 in size and a doubling of cities of 100,000 or more.

[12]See, for example, D. A. Rondinelli and K. Ruddle, "Integrating Spatial Development," *Ekistics* 43 (1977), 193; W. B. Stöhr, "Some Hypotheses on the Role of Secondary Growth Centers as Agents for the Spatial Transmission of Development in Newly Developing Countries: The Case of Latin America," *Spatial Aspects of the Development Process: Proceedings of the Commission on Regional Aspects of Development*, vol. 2, ed. F. Helleiner and W. Stöhr (London: International Geographical Union, 1974) pp. 75–112; R. P. Misra, "Growth Foci as New Channels for the Transmission of Development Impulses in Space," in Helleiner and Stöhr, *Spatial Aspects*, pp. 135–184.

[13]A. T. Mosher, *Creating a Progressive Rural Structure* (New York: Agricultural Development Council, 1969); A. T. Mosher, *Thinking About Rural Development* (New York: Agricultural Development Council, 1976). See also F. M. Lappe and J. Collins, *Food First* (Boston: Houghton Mifflin, 1977); J. Mellor, *The New Economics of Growth* (Ithaca: Cornell University Press, 1976); Lipton, *Poor People*, Chapter 14.

[14]J. Friedmann, *The Active Community: Towards a Political-Territorial Framework for Rural Development in Asia*, (Nagoya, Japan: UNCRD, 1979).

[15]D. A. Rondinelli and K. Ruddle, *Urbanization and Rural Development* (New York: Praeger, 1978), Chapter 10.

[16]This is an adaptation of a phrase used by Charles Abrams to characterize the small-scale character of the typical building firm in the United States.

[17]T. G. McGee, *The Urbanization Process in the Third World* (London: G. Bell & Sons, 1971), Chapter 3; see also two of his working papers for UNCRD: McGee, "Doubts About Dualism: Implications for Development Planning," UNCRD Working Paper WP 78-03, (Nagoya, Japan, UNCRD 1978); and McGee, "Labour Mobility in Fragmented Markets, Rural-Urban Linkages and Regional Development in Asia," UNCRD WP 79-05, (Nagoya, Japan UNCRD 1979).

[18]L. Peattie, "Anthropological Perspectives on the Contents of Dualism, the Informal Sector and Marginality in Developing Urban Economies," *International Regional Science Review*, 5:1(80).

[19]W. Cornelius, "Urbanization and Political Demand Making: Political Participation Among the Migrant Poor in Latin American Cities," *American Political Science Review* 68 (1974), 1125–1146.

[20]Ibid.

[21]Ibid.

[22]C. L. G. Bell and J. H. Duloy, in Chenery *et al.*, *Redistribution with Growth*, p. 127.

[23]Peattie, "Concepts of Dualism."

[24]L. Peattie, "Conflicting Views of the Project: Caracas versus the Site," in L. Rodwin *et al.*, *Planning Urban Growth and Regional Development* (Cambridge: MIT Press, 1969), p. 455.

[25]J. F. C. Turner, "The Re-education of a Professional" in *Freedom to Build*, ed. J. F. C. Turner and R. Fichter (New York: Macmillan 1972), pp. 132–33.

[26]For an example of the frustrating discrepancy between the plans, at least of expatriate consultants, to help the poor and the actual reality, see L. Rodwin *et al.*, *Planning Urban Growth*, Chapters 1 and 12; J. S. MacDonald, *Planning Implementation and Social Policy* (London: Pergamon Press, 1979), Chapter 10.

[27]L. Peattie, L. Rodwin, and A. Strout, "An Appraisal of the Evaluation Plans and Methodology of the Bangladish Rural Finance Experimental Project," unpublished memorandum, January 1979, p. 1.

[28]Ibid., "Notes and Memoranda: Notes on Some Possible Biases in the Assumptions and Procedures of the Rural Finance Experimental Project" (no page indications).

[29]E. F. Banfield, *Political Influence* (New York: Free Press of Glencoe, 1961), p. 333.

[30]Cornelius, "Urbanization," p. 1146.

[31]L. Peattie, *The View from the Barrio* (Ann Arbor: University of Michigan Press, 1970), p. 53.

[32]A. O. Hirschman, *Exit, Voice and Loyalty* (Cambridge: Harvard University Press, 1970), p. 53.

CHAPTER ELEVEN

[1]There are now 70 graduate schools of planning recognized by the American Planning Association (APA). The American Collegiate Schools of Planning (ACSP) have a membership of almost 100 schools, but these include Canadian programs and degree programs in related fields. APA tallies 2,300 students currently enrolled in its recognized

programs. Enrollment in ACSP schools is probably closer to 4,000. APA says there are 403 faculty members in the schools it recognizes. ACSP lists almost 800 faculty, but many are part-time or cross-listed from related fields. I am indebted to Lawrence Susskind for this information. See also L. L. Corby and F. S. So, "Annual ASPO School Survey," *Planning* (January 1974), 20–25.

[2]The figures in this paragraph were provided by Professor David Boyce in a telephone communication on March 10, 1980.

[3]Sometimes, of course, propinquity and a common department may repel rather than attract, but this holds for people within the same field as well.

[4]The following are a few of the first round of books published by the Joint Center: K. Lynch, *The Image of the City* (Cambridge: MIT Press & Harvard University Press, 1961); J. E. Burchard and O. Handlin, eds., *The Historian and The City* (Cambridge: MIT Press and Harvard University Press, 1963); B. J. Frieden, *The Future of Old Neighborhoods* (Cambridge: MIT Press, 1964); N. Glazer and D. P. Moynihan, *Beyond the Melting Pot* (Cambridge: MIT Press and Harvard University Press, 1963); E. C. Banfield and J. Q. Wilson, *City Politics* (Cambridge: Harvard University Press and MIT Press, 1963); M. White and L. White, *The Intellectual versus the City: From Thomas Jefferson to Frank Lloyd Wright* (Cambridge: Harvard University Press, 1962); S. B. Warner, Jr., *Streetcar Suburbs* (Cambridge: Harvard University Press and MIT Press, 1962); S. Thernstrom, *Poverty and Progress* (Cambridge: Harvard University Press, 1962); R. Vernon, *The Myth and Reality of Our Urban Problems* (Cambridge: Harvard University Press, 1966); M. Anderson, *The Federal Bulldozer: A Critical Analysis of Urban Renewal, 1949–1962* (Cambridge: MIT Press, 1964); D. Appleyard *et al.*, *The View From the Road* (Cambridge: MIT Press, 1964); C. Abrams, *Man's Struggle for Shelter in an Urbanizing World* (Cambridge: MIT Press, 1964); L. Rodwin *et al.*, *Planning Urban Growth and Regional Development* (Cambridge: MIT Press, 1964).

[5]The first grant for a four-year period was for approximately $670,000.

[6]At this time, the Joint Center for Urban Studies of MIT and Harvard University was reorganized. Because of the growth of urban-research centers in Cambridge, the Joint Center's focus was shifted to the problems of housing and it obtained modest financial support not only from MIT and Harvard but increasingly from private firms associated with the field of housing. More recently, it has also initiated research relating to state development programs and population and family studies.

[7]In addition to these educational developments a new research center, the Laboratory of Architecture and Planning, was established within the School of Architecture and Planning. Its aim was to foster research

which would contribute to the understanding, education, and practice of architecture and planning and closely related fields.

CHAPTER TWELVE

[1]For a typical example, see L. R. Vagale, *Proposals for an Integrated Programme of Education and Training in Urban and Regional Planning in Nigeria* (New York: United Nations Office of Technical Cooperation, 1972).

[2]See, for example, the following publications of the regional research program of the United Nations Research Institute for Social Development, directed by A. R. Kuklinski: A. R. Kuklinski, ed., *Regional Policies in Nigeria, India and Brazil* (The Hague: Mouton, 1978); L. Lefeber, *Regional Development Experiences and Prospects in South and Southeast Asia* (The Hague: Mouton, 1971); W. Stöhr, *Regional Development: Experiences and Prospects in Latin America* (The Hague: Mouton, 1975); P. O. Pedersen, *Urban-Regional Development in South America: A Process of Diffusion and Integration* (The Hague: Mouton, 1975); K. Mihailovic, *Regional Development: Experiences and Prospects in Eastern Europe* (The Hague: Mouton, 1972). See also the following studies of the Ford Foundation: C. Rosser, *Urbanization in India* (New York: Ford Foundation, 1972); C. Rosser, *Urbanization in Tropical Africa: A Demographic Introduction* (New York: Ford Foundation, 1972); B. Stuckey: *Urbanization Policies in the Developed Countries* (Cambridge: MIT Press, 1972).

[3]The three main sources for this information are: J. G. M. Hilhorst, "A Review of Present-Day Methods in Training of Regional Planners Around the World," Inter-Regional Symposium on Training of Planners for Comprehensive Regional Development, Warsaw, June 1971; Organization for Economic Cooperation and Development, *Catalogue of Social and Economic Development Institute and Programmes* (Paris: OECD, 1970); and G. Celestin, "Survey of the Possibilities of Training Regional Planners for the Third World," Symposium on European Cooperation on Training Regional Planners from Developing Countries, Stockholm, September 1971 (New York, United Nations, European Social Development Programme, 1972). The first deals exclusively with planning for regional development although not solely for the developing countries, while the third deals exclusively with training for these countries, though not solely with regard to regional planning. For a much larger list of over 180 institutions involved in human-settlement training—by region, nation, and institution—but with no further details as to actual focus, see T. Blair, "Training for Human Settlement Development," *Habitat International* 4 (1979), Appendix B, 30–33.

[4]For other background articles or books, see: D. M. Dunham and J. G.
M. Hilhorst, "International Education for Regional Planning in the
Developing Countries," *Development and Change* 2 (1970-71), 45-50;
A. R. Kuklinski, "Education in Regional Planning," in *Issues in Regional Planning*, ed. D. M. Dunham and J. G. M. Hilhorst (The Hague:
Institute of Social Studies, 1971); H. S. Perloff, "Education for Regional
Planning in Less Developed Countries" in Dunham and Hilhorst, *Issues;* J. R. Friedman, "Education for Regional Planning in Developing
Countries," in *Papers of the Proceedings of the Workshop on Regional
Development Planning* (The Hague: Institute of Social Studies, 1967).
[5]It is possible that all three levels of development may be found in
different regions within the same country, especially in a large country
(e.g., Brazil and India). Also, in some countries, the university program
may be weak or negligible but there may be significant planning programs and on-the-job training activities in the field. In any case, these
are some of the principal situations encountered by the writer in different regions of the world. Specific countries are not cited since such a
characterization may now be inaccurate or give offense, partly because
the situation may have changed.

CHAPTER THIRTEEN

[1]See, for example, J. G. M. Hilhorst, "A Review of Present-day Methods
in Training of Regional Planners around the World," paper delivered
at Inter-Regional Symposium on Training for Planners for Comprehensive Regional Development, Warsaw, June 1971; Organization for
Economic Cooperation and Development (OECD), *Catalogue of Social
and Economic Development Institutes and Programmes* (Paris: OECD,
1970); G. Celestin, "Survey of the Possibilities of Training Regional
Planners for the Third World," in *Symposium on European Cooperation on Training Regional Planners from Developing Countries* (held
at Stockholm, September 1971) (New York: United Nations, European
Social Development Programme, 1972). Cf. also footnotes 3 and 4 of
Chapter Twelve.
[2]E. M. Bassett's *The Master Plan* (New York: Russell Sage Foundation,
1938) summed up the basic ideas on the subject. See also I. D. Gallway
and R. G. Mayhni, "Planning Theory in Retrospect: The Process of
Paradigm Change," *Journal of the American Institute of Planners* 43
(1977), 62-71.
[3]For a few examples, see A. O. Hirschman and C. E. Lindblom, "Economic Development, Research and Development and Policy Making:
Some Converging Views," in A. O. Hirschman, *A Bias for Hope*, (New
Haven: Yale University Press, 1971); A. Altschuler, "The Goals of

Comprehensive Planning," *Journal of the American Institute of Planners* 31 (1965); J. G. March and H. A. Simon, *Organizations* (New York: Wiley, 1958) Chapter 6.

[4]L. Rodwin, "Reflections on Collaborative Planning," in L. Rodwin *et al.*, *Planning Urban Growth and Regional Development* (Cambridge: MIT Press, 1969) Chapter 25.

[5]Cf. A. Altschuler, *The City Planning Process* (Ithaca, N.Y.: Cornell University Press, 1965); M. Meyerson and E. C. Banfield, *Politics, Planning and The Public Interest*, (Glencoe, Ill.: The Free Press, 1955), Chapters 9–11; J. Robinson, *Decision-Making in Urban Planning* (Beverly Hills, Calif.: Sage Publications, 1972); M. Camhis, *Planning Theory and Philosophy* (New York: Tavistock, 1979); H. A. Simon, *The Sciences of the Artificial* (Cambridge: MIT Press, 1969), Chapter 3.

[6]H. W. Richardson, "Basic Economic Activities in the Metropolis," in *The Mature Metropolis*, ed. C. L. Leven, (Lexington, Mass.: Lexington Books, D. C. Heath, 1978); G. Sternlieb and J. W. Hughes, *Post-Industrial America: Metropolitan Decline and Interregional Job Shifts* (New Brunswick, N.J.: Center for Policy Research, 1975); D. R. Vining and T. Kontuly, "Population Dispersal from Major Metropolitan Regions: An International Comparison," RSRI Discussion Paper Series, No. 100 (Philadelphia: Regional Science Research Institute, 1977).

[7]F. de Leeuw *et al.*, *The Market Effects of Housing Policies* (Washington, D. C.: Urban Institute, 1974); L. S. Burns and L. Grebler, *The Housing of Nations* (New York: Wiley, 1977), Chapters 4–5. For an opposing view see J. F. Kain, "What Should Housing Policies Be?" *Journal of Finance* 29 (1974). See also B. Frieden, "Housing Allowances: An Experiment that Worked," *Public Interest* 59 (1980), 15–35; J. Heilbrun, *Urban Economics and Public Policy* (New York: St. Martins Press, 1974), Chapter 11.

[8]L. R. Peattie, "Social Issues in Housing," in *Shaping an Urban Future*, ed. B. J. Frieden and W. W. Nash, Jr., (Cambridge: MIT Press, 1969), Chapter 1; J. F. C. Turner, *Housing By People* (New York: Pantheon Books, 1976); D. J. Dwyer, *People and Housing in Third World Cities* (New York: Longman, 1975), Chapters 4–7; D. Appleyard, "City Designers and the Pluralistic City," in L. Rodwin *et al.*, *Growth and Development*, Chapter 23.

[9]See, for example, C. Abrams, *The Future of Housing* (New York: Harper & Bros., 1946).

[10]This point was made to me when I was his guest for lunch.

[11]R. Crossman, *The Diaries of a Cabinet Minister* (London: Trinity Press, 1975). For example, one particularly interesting observation in October 1964 (vol. 1, p. 31) noted that "The whole Department is there to support the Minister. Into his in-tray come hour by hour notes with suggestions as to what he should do. Everthing is done to sustain

him in the line which officials think he should take. But if one is very careful and conscious one is aware that this supporting soft framework of recommendations is the result of a great deal of secret discussion between the civil servants below. There is a constant debate as to how the Minister should be advised or, shall we say, directed and pushed and cajoled into the line required by the Ministry. There is a tremendous esprit de corps in the Ministry and the whole hierarchy is determined to preserve its own policy. Each Ministry has its own departmental policy, and this policy goes on while Ministers come and go. And in this world, though the civil servants have a respect for the Minister, they have a much stronger loyalty to the Ministry. Were the Minister to challenge and direct the Ministry policy there would be no formal tension at first, only quiet resistance—but a great deal of it. I am therefore always on the look-out to see how far my own ideas are getting across, how far they are merely tolerated by the Ministry, and how far the Ministry policies are being imposed on my own mind."

[12]J. Dinkelspiel, "Administrative Style," in L. Rodwin *et al.*, *Growth and Development*, Chapter 16.

[13]H. Simon, *Models of Man* (New York: Wiley, 1957), Part IV; March and Simon, *Organizations*, Chapters 4-7.

[14]P. Selznick, *Leadership in Administration: A Sociological Interpretation* (Evanston, Ill.: Row, Peterson, 1957); A. Downs, *Inside Bureaucracy* (Boston: Little, Brown, 1967), Chapters 8 and 9.

[15]A. O. Hirschman, "The Principle of the Hiding Hand," *Public Interest* 6 (1967), 10-23.

[16]For a few more detailed studies of this subject, see E. C. Banfield, *Political Influence* (Glencoe, Ill.: The Free Press, 1961), Chapters 10-12; K. J. Gergen, "Assessing the Leverage Points in the Process of Policy Formation," in R. A. Bauer and K. J. Gergen, *The Study of Policy Formation* (Glencoe, Ill.: The Free Press, 1968), pp. 181-204.

[17]Cf., for example, A. O. Hirschman, *Journeys toward Progress* (New York: Twentieth Century Fund, 1963), Chapters 4-5.

[18]R. K. Merton, *The Self-Fulfilling Prophecy* (Glencoe, Ill.: The Free Press, 1949), p. 195.

[19]E. Moscovitch, "Employment Effects of the Urban-Rural Investment Choice," in L. Rodwin *et al.*, *Growth and Development*, Chapter 20.

[20]Ibid., p. 388.

[21]J. Weeks, "Policies for Expanding Employment in the Informal Sector of Developing Countries," *International Labor Review* 3 (1975); International Labor Office, "The Development of the Informal Sector," in *Employment, Incomes and Equality: A Strategy for Increasing Productive Employment in Kenya* (Geneva: International Labour Office, 1972); H. Chenery, M. S. Ahluwalia, C. L. G. Bell, J. H. Duloy, and

R. Jolly, *Redistribution with Growth* (London: Oxford University Press, 1974), pp. xiii–xx.

[22]L. Peattie, "The Informal Sector and Marginality: Some Dualistic Concepts in Light of Field Research," unpublished manuscript.

[23]Cf. *Man's Impact on the Global Environment*, Report of the Study of Critical Environmental Problems (Cambridge: MIT Press, 1970); L. K. Caldwell, *Environment: A Challenge to Modern Society* (New York: Doubleday, 1971).

[24]R. Dorfman and N. S. Dorfman, eds., *Economics of the Environment* (New York: W. W. Norton, 1972), Parts III and V.

[25]See, for example, J. A. Aranjo Castro, "Environment and Development: The Case of the Developing Countries" in *World Eco-Crisis*, ed. D. A. Kay and E. B. Skolnikoff (Madison: University of Wisconsin Press, 1972), pp. 237–254.

[26]I. Sachs, "Environment and Styles of Development," paper delivered at United Nations Symposium on Population, Resources and Environment, Stockholm, September–October 1973.

[27]R. Meier, *Planning for an Urban World: The Design of Resource-Conserving Cities* (Cambridge: MIT Press, 1974).

[28]These data and estimates are based on United Nations, *Trends and Prospects in Urban Rural Populations, 1950-2000 as Assessed in 1973-74 and 1974-75*, Dept. of Economic and Social Affairs ESA/P/ WP.54258, Tables 4 and 5. For other projections, see World Bank, *World Development Report* (Washington, D.C: World Bank, 1980); P. M. Hauser and R. W. Gardner, "World Urbanization: Trends and Prospects," paper prepared for United Nations Fund for Population Activities Conference on Population and the Urban Future, Rome, September 1980.

CHAPTER FOURTEEN

[1]N. Glazer, "The Schools of the Minor Professions," *Minerva* 10 (1974), 348. There is substantial literature on the subject. See, for example, A. Etzione, ed., *The Semi-Professions and Their Organizations* (New York: The Free Press, 1969), especially W. Goode, "The Theoretical Limits of Professionalization," Chapter 6; L. D. Mann, "Planning Behavior and Professional Policy Making" in *"Planning Theory in the 1980's,"* ed. R. W. Burchell and G. Sternlieb (New Brunswick, N.J.: Center for Urban Policy Research, 1978), pp. 113–150. Cf. also Footnote 12 below.

[2]Glazer, "Schools of the Minor Professions," p. 348.

[3]Schools of city planning have greatly expanded in the past two decades. For the period from 1958 to 1979 (for which we have some not-

altogether-satisfactory data for the United States), full-time students enrolled for the professional degree (Master of City Planning) increased from 329 to 2,300; Ph.D. enrollment increased from 4 to 286; and, although data are not yet available, the number of faculty probably increased during this period by some roughly equivalent amount. Undergraduate programs in urban studies also mushroomed. It is not clear, however, whether these trends will change for the number of applicants, enrollments in the schools, and even undergraduate programs are down somewhat from the crest reached in 1973. Meanwhile, current pressures on universities for retrenchment and uncertainty about the future have intensified the perennial debate about what city planning is all about.

[4]Ibid.

[5]Ibid., p. 351.

[6]Ibid.

[7]Ibid., p. 354.

[8]N. Glazer, "Conflicts in Schools for the Minor Professions," *Harvard Graduate School of Education Association Bulletin* 18 (1974), 24. (This article is an abbreviated version of the article that appeared later in *Minerva*, cited in Footnote 2.)

[9]Ibid.

[10]Ibid, pp. 21, 24.

[11]Ibid., p. 21

[12]Glazer's basic arguments are influenced by some of the standard references dealing with the professions: for example, A. M. Carr-Sanders and P. A. Wilson, *The Professions* (Oxford: Clarendon Press, 1933); E. C. Hughes, "Professions," *Daedalus* 92 (1963); T. Parsons, "Professions," *International Encyclopedia of the Social Sciences* (New York: Macmillan, 1968); W. E. Moore and G. W. Rosenblum, *The Professions: Roles and Rules* (New York: Russell Sage Foundation, 1970); E. H. Schein, *Professional Education* (New York: McGraw-Hill, 1972); Also influential are C. Jencks and D. Riesman's study, *The Academic Revolution* (Garden City, N.Y.: Doubleday, 1969), particularly Chapter 5 dealing with the professional schools; and possibly L. Veysey, *The Emergence of the American University* (Chicago: University of Chicago Press, 1965). However, Veysey (pp. 267–268) as well as Jencks and Riesman (pp. xiv–xvi) warn the reader that because of the scope of their studies, they were often led by the the limited resources and the absence of adequate records to reason backward from the evidence of how the academic system functioned toward the causes for its appearance—"a practice full of pitfalls," reflecting, on occasion, "commitments, prejudices and blindspots."

[13]"How to do it" courses in city planning focus on teaching ways of

handling implementation problems, for example, site planning and layout, zoning and subdivision regulations, neighborhood-rehabilitation problems, housing or transportation policies and programs, area-development strategies, cost benefit studies, as well as various modeling, statistical, survey, and other graphic, analytical, and design techniques.

14Glazer, "Schools of the Minor Professions," p. 351.

15For more detail see L. Rodwin, "The Promise and Failure of Urban Research," in *Planning 1967* (Chicago: American Society of Planning Officials, 1967), pp. 153-170.

16No doubt as larger and more influential schools such as MIT, the University of Pennsylvania, and the University of California at Berkeley added to their staff and brought in specialists in land economics, urban sociology and law, research methodologies, and so on, the competitive positions and prestige of other schools depended on whether they could muster equivalent resources to provide effective training. The question was not whether the social scientists were superior in status to the professional practitioner, but how the additional resources enhanced range, versatility, general capabilities, and therefore prestige and recruitment possibilities for faculty and students.

17For a few examples of these critiques, see H. J. Gans, *The Urban Villagers* (New York: The Free Press of Glencoe, 1962); L. Rodwin, *The British New Towns Policy* (Cambridge: Harvard University Press, 1956); M. Meyerson and E. C. Banfield, *Politics, Planning and the Public Interest* (New York: The Free Press of Glencoe, 1955); A. Altschuler, *The City Planning Process* (Ithaca: Cornell University Press, 1965).

18Indeed, the paradigm was dominant for almost a half-century if one traces it back to the period before the professional schools were established. For example, E. M. Bassett's book *The Master Plan* (New York: Russell Sage Foundation) summed up the standard ideas on this subject in 1938; and the idea of the master plan was already in vogue in the 1920s. See also M. Scott, *American City Planning since 1890* (Berkeley: University of California Press, 1969).

19A. N. Whitehead, *Introduction to Mathematics* (London: Williams & Norgate, 1906), p. 223.

20Erik H. Erikson, *Identity: Youth and Crisis* (New York, W. W. Norton, 1968), pp. 84-85.

21Ibid., p. 87.

22Ibid.

23For a few examples of these views, see R. S. Bolan, "Mapping the Planning Theory Terrain," in *Planning in America: Learning from Turbulence*, ed. D. R. Godschalk (Washington, D.C.: *The American*

Institute of Planners, 1974); P. Davidoff, "Advocacy and Pluralism in Planning," *Journal of the American Institute of Planners* 31 (1965), 331–338; A. Altschuler, "Decision Making and the Trend Toward Pluralistic Planning," in *Urban Planning in Transition,* ed. E. Erber (New York: Grossman, 1970); L. Susskind, "The Future of Planning Education," in Godschalk, *Planning in America;* J. Habermas, *Legitimation Crisis* (Boston: Beacon Press, 1973); F. F. Piven, "Planning and Class Interests," *Journal of the American Institute of Planners* 41 (1975), 308–310; N. E. Long, "Another View of Responsible Planning," *Journal of the American Institute of Planners* 41 (1975), 311–316; M. M. Webber, "The Prospects for Policies Planning," in *The Urban Condition,* ed. L. J. Duhl (Basic Books, 1963); Burchell and Sternlieb, *Planning Theory.*

[24] *The Role of University Based Urban Centers* (Cambridge: Joint Center for Urban Studies of MIT and Harvard University, 1971), pp. 6, 108–109.

[25] For example, foundation staffs, university administrations, and young professionals in the field.

[26] For a review of some of the issues, see W. Alonso, "Beyond the Interdisciplinary Approach to Planning," *Journal of the American Institute of Planners* 37 (1971), 171–172.

[27] Kuhn used the term "paradigm" in several ways in his book and this provoked controversy. He tried to clarify the definition in the second edition of his publication. The two meanings he now ascribes to the term "paradigm" are "the entire constellation of beliefs, values and techniques and so on shared by the members of a given community; on the other hand it denotes one sort of element in that constellation, the concrete puzzle solutions which, employed as models or examples, can replace explicit rules as a basis for the solution of the remaining puzzles of normal science." T. Kuhn, *The Structure of Scientific Revolutions,* 2nd ed. (Chicago: University of Chicago Press, 1970), p. 175. Holton uses the notion of "themata" or "theme" to refer to the "dimension of fundamental presuppositions, notions, terms, methodological judgments and decisions. . . which are themselves neither directly evolved from nor resolvable into objective observation on the one hand, or logical, mathematical, and other formal analytical ratiocination on the other hand." G. Holton, *Thematic Origins of Scientific Thought: Kepler to Einstein* (Cambridge: Harvard University Press 1974), pp. 28, 57; cf. also I. Lakatos and A. Musgrave, eds., *Criticism and the Growth of Knowledge* (Cambridge: Cambridge University Press, 1970); in particular M. Masterman, "The Nature of a Paradigm," pp. 59–90. I am using "paradigm" in the revised sense suggested by Kuhn and as a synonym for Holton's "thematic position," that is, "a guiding

theme in the pursuit of scientific work," Holton, *Thematic Origins*, p. 28.

[28]T. Kuhn, *Structure of Scientific Revolutions*, pp. 82–83.

[29]G. Holton, *Thematic Origins*, p. 60. This is not to suggest that a great many other factors do not contribute to the resistance to new ideas. See, for example, Chapter 11 in Holton.

[30]T. Kuhn, *Structure of Scientific Revolutions*, pp. 83–87. Kuhn has provided three telling instances from the field of physics. Thus, commenting on the state of astronomical studies, Copernicus once observed: "It is as though an artist were to gather the hands, feet, head and other members for his images from diverse models, each part excellently drawn, but not related to a single body, and since they in no way match each other, the result would be a monster rather than man." And Wolfgang Pauli, in the months before Heisenberg's paper on matrix mechanics pointed the way to a new quantum theory, wrote to a friend: "At the moment physics is again terribly confused. In any case, it is too difficult for me and I wish I had been a movie comedian or something of the sort and had never heard of physics." Einstein even wrote: "It was as if the ground has been pulled out from under one, with no firm foundation to be seen anywhere, upon which one could have built."

[31]One way of distinguishing Glazer's views from those presented here is that he is suggesting that the problems in the minor professions, including city planning, are currently unsolvable, whereas the position of this paper is that the profession is attacking all of its problems afresh in a different framework.

[32]I. D. Galloway and R. G. Mayhni, "Planning Theory in Retrospect: The Process of Paradigm Change," *Journal of the American Institute of Planners* 43 (1977) 62–71.

[33]These courses dealt with ways of: (a) making an inventory of the physical characteristics of the city as well as the characteristics of the population and households and major activities in the city (industrial, commercial, civic, residential, recreational, etc.); (b) projecting the likely changes and trends; (c) analyzing theories and problems involved in the location of these activities and in preparing area, neighborhood, urban, and regional land-use plans to accommodate these activities, taking account of alternative goals and policies for such development; and (d) learning how to use subdivision, zoning, and other relevant land-use-control techniques and policies to achieve these ends. For a leading text in the field, see F. S. Chapin, Jr., *Urban Land Use Planning*, 3rd ed. (Urbana: University of Illinois Press, 1979).

[34]C. M. Haar, "The Master Plan: An Impermanent Constitution," *Law and Contemporary Problems* 20 (1953), pp 353–418.

[35] For three of the more trenchant expressions of these views, see A. Altschuler, "The Goals of Comprehensive Planning," *Journal of the American Institute of Planners* 31 (1965), 186–195; C. E. Lindblom, "The Science of Muddling Through," *Public Administration Review* 19 (1959), 79–88; E. C. Banfield and J. Q. Wilson, *City Politics* (Cambridge: Harvard University Press and MIT Press, 1963), Chapter 14.

[36] MIT's lack of success in sustaining the Urban Systems Laboratory (established mainly to involve engineering, management, and other departments in urban problems) pointed up the same lesson—that urban and regional questions had only a minor bearing on the central concerns of these other programs.

[37] The Ford Foundation, somewhat disappointed by the results of its efforts and skeptical as to future possibilities, withdrew from the field—perhaps a little prematurely. See W. Pendleton, *Urban Studies and the University: The Ford Foundation Experience* (New York: The Ford Foundation, 1974).

[38] L. Rodwin, "Innovations for Urban Studies," *Planning* 38 (1972), 182–186.

[39] Whitehead, *Introduction to Mathematics*, p. 223.

[40] Alonso, "Beyond the Interdisciplinary Approach," pp. 171–172.

Index